THE
WAFFEN-SS

THE
WAFFEN-⚡⚡

THE THIRD REICH'S MOST INFAMOUS MILITARY ORGANIZATION

NIGEL CAWTHORNE

PICTURE CREDITS

Alamy: 17, 19, 35, 54, 164, 177
Bridgeman Images: 121
Getty Images: 12, 30, 48, 52, 58, 60, 76, 80, 93, 138, 143, 152, 160
Wikimedia Commons: 95, 204

ARCTURUS

ISBN: 978-1-3988-9183-8
AD008864UK

Printed in the UK

2 4 6 8 10 9 7 5 3 1

Contents

Introduction

The *Waffen-SS* was the private army of Adolf Hitler, who had become the brutal dictator of Germany in 1934. It started out as part of his personal Protection Squad, the *Schutzstaffel*, or SS, which defended him from political opponents. Once Hitler took power, it was armed and were organized along the lines of the German armed forces, the *Wehrmacht*.

When Germany went to war, the *Waffen-SS* found itself in the forefront of the fighting in Poland, the Low Countries, France and Russia. Hitler depended on it because of its members' personal loyalty to him. He had always distrusted the army. The commitment to Nazi ideology of the *Waffen-SS* made its members formidable fighters. They were told that they were the spearhead of a master race that could not fail. Even their enemies among the Allies recognized – even admired – their fighting abilities.

Their belief in Nazism led *Waffen-SS* men to commit numerous atrocities. To them, Jews were subhumans who needed to be exterminated, while Slavs were fit only to be robbed and enslaved. Neither pity nor empathy would stand in their way. Communism was an alien creed fostered in the East. It was the duty of the *Waffen-SS* to defend European civilization from it. However, that was not the way the rest of the world saw it.

In the end, fanatical belief in a cause was not enough. Though better equipped, the *Waffen-SS* was relatively small compared to the German army – which itself was outmanned by the numbers the Russians could muster in the East and the Anglo-Americans could deploy in the West.

Inevitably, the Nazi fanatics were culled by casualties and *Waffen-SS* units were diluted by those not quite so committed to what proved to be a losing cause. But even when Germany's defeat seemed certain, the *Waffen-SS* fought on. And its fidelity to Nazism did not end with the war. Following Germany's defeat and Hitler's suicide in 1945, attempts were made to set up '*Werwolf*' sleeper cells. These failed. At the war crimes trials held in Nuremberg, the *Waffen-SS* was declared a criminal organization, along with the SS itself. Many of its leaders were tried as war criminals. Others committed suicide or escaped, largely to South America.

In the 1950s, the Mutual Aid Association of Former *Waffen-SS* Members, or HIAG, sought to rehabilitate the reputation of the *Waffen-SS*, maintaining that its members were merely soldiers like any other. They weren't. The *Waffen-SS* men were the spear carriers of one of the most evil regimes in history. They may have been valiant on the battlefield, but they were committed Nazis, blindly loyal to Hitler and his murderous ideology. Thankfully, the *Waffen-SS* has been expunged from history, but its story should chill the blood of anyone who enjoys the twin luxuries of peace and freedom.

CHAPTER ONE

SS

The Formation of the Armed SS

When Adolf Hitler took the oath of office as Chancellor, administered by the President of the German Republic Field Marshal Paul von Hindenburg on 30 January 1933, his position was far from secure. Despite a torchlit march through Berlin by thousands of Nazis, he was surrounded by enemies. While the Nazi Party was the largest party in Germany, it only had three members in the coalition cabinet formed with the German National People's Party and the nationalists still had an independent paramilitary force – the *Stahlhelm* or Steel Helmet. Hitler was going to change that. He was just 44 years old at the time.

Born in Austria in 1889, Hitler had aspired to be an artist before becoming a down and out in Vienna. Avoiding conscription into the Austrian Army, he moved to Germany in 1913, but joined the German Army at the outbreak of World War I the following year, only rising to the rank of corporal. Following Germany's defeat in 1918, many ex-servicemen blamed Berlin's capitulation on the duplicity of the civilian population, particularly Communists and Jews.

They also blamed the ensuing economic chaos on the peace treaty drawn up in Versailles, ending the war. This demanded unpayable reparations that caused rampant inflation in Germany. On top of that came the Wall Street Crash, which threw the whole world into economic depression. The Versailles Treaty also stripped Germany of territory as the map of Europe was redrawn by the victors. The industrial Rhineland was occupied and strict limits were put on the size and strength of Germany's armed forces. The result was political as well as economic chaos.

Many on the left sought to emulate the Bolshevik Revolution that had taken place in Russia in 1917. German ex-servicemen formed *Freikorps* ('Free Corps') to fight the Communists. These paramilitary units received considerable support from the German government, which also feared a Communist uprising. The *Freikorps* and the Communists fought it out on the streets. However, they fell out with the government after a failed putsch in 1920.

Myriad small political parties sprang up. One of them was the German Workers' Party or DAP. Hitler joined. A gifted orator, he quickly took over, renaming it the National Socialist German Workers' Party (in German *Nationalsozialistische Deutsche Arbeiterpartei*, or NSDAP). It was more commonly known as the Nazi Party. Needing protection from political rivals, the Nazi Party formed the paramilitary *Sturmabteilung* (SA), whose members were known as Stormtroopers or brown-shirts. An inner corps was formed as Hitler's personal bodyguard. This became Hitler's personal Protection Squad, the *Schutzstaffel* or SS, who would soon become easily identifiable by their sinister black uniforms. It was established in 1925, after the SA was temporarily banned following Hitler's failed Beer Hall Putsch, an attempted coup d'etat in Munich in 1923. The leader of the SS was a puny chicken farmer named Heinrich Himmler who went on to become the architect of the Holocaust. Along the way, Hitler became a German citizen and ran for office.

With its paramilitary organization, the Nazi Party became a considerable political force. In the election of July 1932, it won 37 per cent of the vote. But Hitler refused to join a coalition and the government fell. In an election that November, the Nazi Party lost 34 seats in the Reichstag, or German parliament, while the Communists gained 11, taking them to 89 seats, while the Socialists had 133.

With Nazi popularity seemingly on the wane, Hitler this time agreed to join a coalition as Chancellor. The other party leaders were happy with this arrangement as they thought they would be able to control a man they considered a political novice. They were wrong. After another election, Hitler made himself dictator. When von Hindenburg died on 2 August 1934, Hitler combined the offices of Chancellor and President, making himself the undisputed *Führer*, or leader.

Meanwhile, Hitler's rival in the National Socialist German Workers' Party, Ernst Röhm, head of the brown-shirted *Sturmabteilung* (SA), or Storm Battalion, was seeking a 'second revolution' which sought to overthrow capitalism and take over the *Reichswehr*, Germany's small defence force permitted under the Versailles Treaty. The *Reichswehr* itself was also hungry for political power.

ARMED PROTECTION

Hitler needed protection – armed protection – from his enemies, particularly the two million members of the SA, which had 20 times the manpower of the *Reichswehr*. However, within the SA, there were ultra-loyal black-uniformed *Schutzstaffel* (SS) men who were dedicated only to Hitler. On 17 March 1933, the 120-strong Berlin *SS-Stabswache*, under Josef 'Sepp' Dietrich, an artillery sergeant who had served in a newly formed tank unit at the end of World War I, replaced the

Reichswehr as guards inside the Reich Chancellery at the Palais Schulenburg at Wilhelmstrasse 77, after Hitler moved there from his headquarters in the Hotel Kaiserhof. The Army was not overly worried about this move. It dismissed the *Stabswache* as 'asphalt soldiers', good for nothing but ceremonial duties.

Adolf Hitler inspects the Leibstandarte *during the Nuremberg Rally in 1935.*

In September 1933, the *Stabswache* was redesignated as *Leibstandarte SS 'Adolf Hitler'* – Hitler's bodyguard. On 9 November, the men of *Leibstandarte* swore an unconditional personal oath to Hitler alone. They no longer owed an allegiance to the SS or the Nazi Party, or even to Germany. Although Hitler was not yet president or dictator, he had illegally created an independent military corps outside the army and police force. It would go on to become the *Waffen-SS* – the Armed or Weapons SS – though that name would not be used until the outbreak of World War II. They were to be Hitler's private army.

They were joined by the armed guards of the growing number of concentration camps under the command of Theodore Eicke, *SS-*

Standartenführer, or colonel, of the *SS-Totenkopfverbände* – the *SS-TV*, or Death's Head unit. While the *Totenkopf*, or skull, was the universal cap badge of the SS, the *SS-TV* also wore it on the insignia on the right collar tab to distinguish itself from other SS formations. At the outbreak of World War II in Europe, the *SS-Division Totenkopf* was formed from *SS-TV* personnel, comprising 6,500 men and three regiments by 1940. Members of the unarmed *Allgemeine SS* ('General SS') who were over 45 would become guards at the concentration camps, freeing younger and fitter men to reinforce the *SS-TV* and maintain its 'ideological and political spirit'. Eventually all members of the *SS-TV* would join field units of the *Waffen-SS*.

NIGHT OF THE LONG KNIVES

In June 1934, the strength of the armed SS was less than that of a regular infantry regiment. It was equipped only with small arms and was ill-trained. The threat to Hitler's power from within his own ranks at that time was from the disgruntled Storm Troopers of the SA, who then numbered some three million men. To see off Röhm, Hitler decided that he had better side with the Army. Consequently, he eliminated Röhm and other leaders of the SA in a bloody purge known as the Night of the Long Knives that began on 30 June. This was the first outing for the armed SS, which manned firing squads executing death warrants issued by the creator of the ruthless Gestapo secret police Hermann Göring, the head of the SS Heinrich Himmler and his notorious security chief Reinhard Heydrich, who had taken over as head of the Gestapo. The SS was armed with weapons supplied by the Army, on Hitler's orders. At least 85 men were murdered in these extrajudicial killings. Thousands more were arrested. In this one move, the armed SS had made Hitler the undisputed power in Germany.

In the purge of his own followers, the armed SS exhibited the very characteristics demanded by Hitler – unshakeable loyalty and blind obedience. Himmler said: 'We did not hesitate on 30 June 1934 to do the duty we were bidden, and stand comrades who had lapsed up against the wall and shoot them... We have never discussed it among ourselves... It appalled everyone, and yet everyone was certain that if it is necessary and such orders are issued he will do it again.'

Hitler was quick to show his gratitude. In the official Nazi newspaper, the *Völkischer Beobachter*, he wrote: 'In consideration of the very meritorious service of the SS, especially in connection to the events of 30 June 1934, I elevate it to the standing of an independent organization within the NSDAP.'

Until then the SS had been nominally part of the SA. Now it was able to conduct what were clearly more than police actions while the Army stood by. On 2 August 1934, Hindenburg died. Thereafter, the office of President was combined with that of Chancellor, making Hitler *Führer*. Now nobody could legally remove him from office. He was also commander-in-chief of the armed forces, whose members now had to take a personal oath of loyalty to him.

SS-VERFÜGUNGSTRUPPE

On 16 March 1935, Hitler re-introduced conscription with the aim of building an army of 36 divisions, in violation of the Versailles Treaty. At the same time, he announced the formation of the *SS-Verfügungstruppe* – SS-VT, or SS Dispositional Troops. This was a fully militarized formation that comprised the *Leibstandarte*, SS Special Detachments (*SS-Sonderkommandos*) and other SS Headquarters Guard (*SS-Stabswache*) units. Though not yet designated a division, the SS-VT was to be made up of three regiments – the *Leibstandarte*, the *Deutschland*, raised in Munich, and the *Germania* from Hamburg – each with three battalions, a motorcycle company, a mortar company, a combat engineering company and a communications section. As such, it was a challenge to the *Reichswehr*, which became the burgeoning *Wehrmacht* (defence force) in 1935. In March 1936, the men of *Leibstandarte SS 'Adolf Hitler'* were the first troops into Saarbrücken during the march into the Rhineland, which had been demilitarized under the Versailles Treaty.

On 1 April 1936, having formerly been party formations, the *SS-VT* and the *SS-TV* became organizations in the service of the state, but to prevent conflict with the Army their funding was put on the police budget of the Ministry of the Interior. Hitler maintained they were neither part of the Army nor the police, but were exclusively at his own disposal. Their job was to protect the *Führer* and 'guarantee the security of the Reich from the interior'. As the Nazis blamed the collapse of civilian morale in 1918 for Germany's defeat in World War I, Hitler ordered that, in the event of any dissent, they were to shoot civilian leaders – including those of the Catholic Party – along with everyone in the concentration camps, already filling with Jews, Bolsheviks and trades unionists.

To be an effective fighting force, the *SS-VT* needed field training, so on 1 October 1936 the Inspectorate of *Verfügungstruppen* was set up under career army officer Paul Hausser. He was given the rank of *SS-Brigadeführer*, or brigadier general. Under him, the *SS-Junkerschulen* – Leadership, or Junker Schools – at Bad Tölz and Braunschweig pumped out well indoctrinated cohorts.

Unlike in military academies, in the *SS-Junkerschulen* all class barriers were removed. Former army officers had to serve in the ranks and the title 'sir' was dropped when addressing a superior officer. Military ranks were used instead. This created a stronger bond between officers and men.

Although numbers were restricted by the Army, quotas were secretly exceeded and numbers outstripped those produced by the Army's own cadet programme. With the stress on physical and political training, SS alumni generally had a lower standard of education, but graduates of the *SS-Junkerschulen* were more aggressive, leading to higher losses among them when war came.

'ARYAN' ANCESTRY

Recruits to the SS-VT had to be over 1.78 m (5 ft 10 in), or 1.80 m (5 ft 11 in) for the *Leibstandarte*. They had to be of 'Aryan' ancestry. Enlisted men had to provide birth and marriage records that went back to 1 January 1800, officers back to 1 January 1750, showing they had no Jewish blood. Until 1936, men with even one filled tooth were not accepted. Despite this there was little trouble recruiting men, particularly from the Hitler Youth set up by the Nazi Party for male youths from the ages of 14 to 18.

While members of the armed SS retained the black SS dress uniform, they adopted the Army's field-grey service uniform, adding the lightning bolt SS insignia. Also emulating the Army, they adopted coloured piping denoting their particular branch of the service.

SS infantry men were trained as assault troops to the standards of US Army Rangers and the later British Commandos. Athletic pursuits scheduled daily meant they were extremely fit and an esprit de corps was encouraged to a level unknown in the Army. Ideological indoctrination – at first the province of the *SS-Schulungsamt*, or Office of Education, whose instructors acted as Soviet-style political commissars – was handed over to line officers in order to maintain a unified structure of command.

PREPARED FOR WAR

By 1938, the SS-VT was 'prepared for war', in the words of Himmler. He then got permission to conduct live-fire exercises on Army grounds without the usual safeguards. Though men were lost in manoeuvres, Himmler said 'every drop of blood spilt in peacetime saved streams of blood' in battle. Nevertheless, the casualty rate of the *Waffen-SS* in wartime remained determinedly high. But it was only by its willingness to shed its blood on the battlefield that the *Verfügungstruppe* would retain 'the moral right to shoot malingerers and cowards on the home front', Himmler maintained.

To maintain its prestige, the SS had to make war. This was vital as the armed SS was the army of National Socialism, while the officer corps of the *Wehrmacht* was largely opposed to Nazi ideology. But Hitler still needed the support of the Army and there was no time to replace experienced officers who were not sympathetic to the cause.

The problem was easily solved. Heydrich trumped up charges that the Commander-in-Chief of the Army General Werner von Fritsch was a homosexual and that his boss, the Minister of War Field Marshal Werner von Blomberg, had married a prostitute, though Hitler himself had attended his wedding a few weeks earlier. They were sacked and Hitler took personal command of the *Oberkommando de Wehrmacht* (the OKW, or High Command of the Armed Forces).

When German troops marched into Hitler's native Austria on 11 March 1938 in the so-called *Anschluss* ('annexation'), among the leading elements was a motorized battalion of *Leibstandarte SS 'Adolf Hitler'* under the command of *SS-Obergruppenführer* (lieutenant-general)

Field Insignia of the Standard of the Leibstandarte SS Adolf Hitler.

Sepp Dietrich. The *SS-VT* was then reinforced with a new regiment, 'Der Führer', raised in Austria after the *Anschluss*. A new unit of the *SS-Totenkopfverbände* was also formed.

On 17 August 1938, Hitler issued orders clarifying the delineation between the armed SS and the Army. While the unarmed *Allgemeine SS* would remain a political organization, the *SS-VT*, *SS-TV* and the *SS-Junkerschulen* would be armed and trained as military formations under *Reichsführer SS* and Chief of Police Heinrich Himmler. Their equipment would be supplied by the *Wehrmacht*, though no other connection between them should exist.

The armed SS would remain part of the Nazi Party and Hitler would retain personal command. Membership was voluntary and would supersede conscription into the Army among those who had completed their compulsory labour service. The Ministry of the Interior would still pick up the tab, but as a sop to the Army the OKW could check its budget and inspect its units.

PROCUREMENT

There was still the matter of arming the *Waffen-SS*. In the field, *Waffen-SS* units were tactically part of the Army, so it had no choice but to equip them. But it dragged its feet when it came to the *Totenkopf* regiments. The chief of the SS Procurement Office, *SS-Oberführer* Gärtner, suggested securing the stock of the Skoda arms factory in Czechoslovakia. Short of artillery itself, the Army objected. But in March Hitler ordered the formation of a new motorized heavy artillery regiment for the *Waffen-SS* – with one battalion for each of the three field divisions – along with a light artillery battalion for *Leibstandarte SS 'Adolf Hitler'*. The *Wehrmacht* conceded a dozen 150 mm howitzers for the first line units, but the rest would have to wait until the Army was fully equipped, it said.

Hitler's elite *Leibstandarte* was equipped within a week. Others had to wait, though the equipment was in plain sight in Army field depots and motor pools, while the *Polizeidivision* – not at that time considered a first-line unit – was give old horse-drawn artillery. Gärtner sought to solve the problem by setting up an independent procurement programme for the SS which, he told the newly created Reich Ministry for Arms and Munitions, would not interfere with the *Wehrmacht*'s programme. He presented its head, *Reichsminister* Fritz Todt, with an order for 20,000 rifles, 50,000 bayonets, 10,000 pistols and 10,000 submachine guns, along with thousands of machine guns, antitank guns, hundreds of artillery pieces, millions of rounds of ammunition and 250 field kitchens. In return, Todt asked for 20,000 Polish workers for his munitions factories.

Meanwhile, Gärtner put in his own order for 30,000 smoke grenades with a private firm. The *Wehrmacht* objected and took over the order. The *Waffen-SS* continued to be supplied by the Army until Todt

Totenkopf Division in 1939 on training exercise.

died in 1942 and Albert Speer took over as Minister of Armaments and Munitions. He was sympathetic to the argument that its control of the *Waffen-SS*'s procurement gave the Army an insight to the structure, strength and purpose of SS formations. Speer required the SS concentration camp inmates to work as forced labour in his munitions factories. In exchange, he would give the *Waffen-SS* a percentage of their output.

While the *Leibstandarte* was well provided for, the rest of the *Waffen-SS* had to go into battle with a shortage of heavy weapons and inadequate transport because of the Army's attitude; the *Totenkopf* and *Polizeidivision* were armed almost entirely with captured Czech weapons. Although these were just as good as those made by German manufacturers, they created training and supply problems.

SUDETENLAND

Hitler demanded the annexation of the Sudetenland, a largely German-speaking province of Czechoslovakia. This was conceded by the British and French governments at a meeting in Munich on 29 September 1938. In October 1938 all three regiments of the SS-VT were deployed, along with two battalions of the SS-TV 'Oberbayern' regiment. They had supported cross-border operations of the home-grown *Sudetendeutsches Freikorps* (Sudeten German Free Corps), which was then incorporated into the SS.

The SS-VT was then reorganized as a mobile assault force and joined the Army armour and *panzer* ('tank') divisions in the takeover of the rest of Czechoslovakia in March 1939. That summer, Hitler and Himmler visited the *Verfügungstruppe* to watch a live-fire manoeuvre by the SS regiment *Deutschland*, supported by an artillery barrage by the Army. He was impressed and issued orders to turn the SS-TV into the *SS-Verfügungsdivision* with the Army supplying the equipment to form an artillery regiment, the *SS-Standarte-Artillerie*, in Munsterlager.

POLAND

On 1 September 1939, Hitler addressed the Reichstag, then housed in the Kroll Opera House, announcing that Germany had declared war on Poland.

'From now on,' he said, 'I am just the first soldier of the German Reich. I have once more put on that coat that was the most sacred and dear to me. I will not take it off again until victory is secured, or I will not survive the outcome.'

He had discarded the brown blouse of the Party and was already wearing a field-grey jacket like that worn by the *Waffen-SS*. As a result of the invasion of western Poland, Britain and France declared war on Germany, while under a secret accord the Soviet Union (Communist Russia and its satellites in Eastern Europe – principally Belorussia and Ukraine – along with the occupied nations of Central Asia) took over eastern Poland. World War II was underway. It was what the *Waffen-SS* had been waiting for.

CHAPTER TWO

⚡⚡

First Blood

A t the outbreak of the war, the *Waffen-SS* was only 25,000 strong. Within a year, it expanded six-fold to 150,000 men, becoming the fourth branch of the *Wehrmacht*, along with the *Heer* (Army), *Kriegsmarine* (Navy) and the *Luftwaffe* (Air Force).

In the summer of 1939, the *SS-VT* had been moved up into East Prussia, a German province on the Polish border separated from the main body of Germany during World War I, in preparation for *Fall Weiss* – 'Case White', the invasion of Poland. However, it was not to fight as one formation. The *SS-Standarte Deutschland* under *SS-Standartenführer* (Colonel) Felix Steiner, a motorized infantry unit, was attached to the Army's 4. *Panzer-Brigade* under Major-General Werner Kempf, along with the *SS-Standarte-Artillerie* and the reconnaissance battalion *SS-Aufklärungsabteilung*, which consisted of two motorcycle companies, an anti-tank platoon, an armoured car platoon and a signal platoon under *SS-Sturmbannführer* (Major) Brandt.

SS-Standarte 'Deutschland' was to lead Kempf's division on Polish defence lines at Mlava in a frontal assault supported by *panzers*. These were bogged down by the Polish anti-tank defences and support by *Luftwaffe* dive bombers failed to turn up, leaving the infantry at the mercy of the enemy's heavy artillery. But they got to within 100 m (328 ft) of the Polish bunkers before being ordered to withdraw.

The next day, they were rushed to Chorzele, where the Germans had broken through. Advancing to Rozan on the River Narew, they met stiff opposition and a counterattack by the Polish cavalry. But the Poles were soon in full retreat to Warsaw and the SS crossed the River Bug to cut them off. Although the Poles put up stout resistance, Warsaw was soon encircled.

Battlegroups from the *Deutschland* then joined the attack on the major fortifications at Modlin and Zacrozym. With Steiner in the lead, they took Zacrozym in 90 minutes. The rest of the fortifications fell that afternoon.

DEFENDING THE FLANKS

The *Leibstandarte*, supported by the combat engineering battalion *SS-Pionieresturmbann* raised in Dresden under *SS-Sturmbannführer* Blumberg, saw considerable fighting as a reconnaissance role defending the flanks of 17th Infantry Division with General Walter von Reichenau's 10th Army as it advanced from Silesia, then a partition between the German Reich and Poland. The *Leibstandarte* was then transferred to 4. *Panzer-Division*, which took Lodz on its way to Warsaw. It was then withdrawn to take part in the encirclement of Polish forces on the River Bzura.

The *SS-Standarte 'Germania'* under *SS-Standartenführer* Carl-Maria Demelhuber took part in the push through the industrial areas of Polish Upper Silesia. But its reconnaissance platoon was then attached to 5. *Panzer-Division*. It was then stripped of its reinforced motorcycle units, which were deployed to other formations. The rest was attached to *XXII Armee Korps* to secure the flanks of 2. *Panzer-Division* and 4. *Leichte-Division* ('Light Division').

The 15th Company under *SS-Hauptsturmführer* Johannes Muhlen took 500 prisoners when it surprised a retreating Polish battalion on 13 September. But it was badly mauled when a larger Polish force counterattacked. Four days later, the regiment was attached to the *XVII Korps* to protect its flank. After the Polish were overrun, the regiment was reunited in Beraun near Prague.

SS-Totenkopf Sturmbann 'Götze' was formed to perform SS police duties in Danzig, now Gdansk. Formerly part of Prussia, it had been declared a 'free city' by the Versailles Treaty, under the auspices of the League of Nations, at the Baltic end of the Polish Corridor giving Poland access to the sea. As a reinforced infantry battalion, it joined *SS-Heimwehr Danzig* (Danzig Home Defence) which, under Army command, took the city. They committed a number of atrocities, massacring civilians – largely Jews. The formation went on to become *3. SS-Totenkopfdivision*.

CASUALTIES AND ATROCITIES

The Army High Command was not impressed by the performance of the SS troops. They had suffered proportionally heavier casualties and the Army attributed this to poor officer training. The SS leadership countered this, arguing that their formations had been broken up and had been sent to serve under Army officers. They had been switched from one sector to another and used as 'fire brigades' where the fighting was heaviest, often with inadequate support.

When it came to the atrocities, including the murder of Jews, Himmler refused to allow his men to be tried in regular military courts. The Army made sure that reports of these atrocities reached Hitler, but he had already warned the generals that things would happen in the conquered areas that would not be to their taste and told them that they should restrict themselves to their military duties. Nevertheless, a member of the SS Artillery Regiment was court-martialled alongside an Army military policeman for shooting 50 Jews who had been conscripted for forced labour. The prosecuting officer demanded the death penalty, but the murderers were given only short prison sentences for manslaughter. Even these were dropped due to pressure from Himmler. He also got Hitler to amend his earlier decree that had placed the armed SS under Army jurisdiction in wartime. In future, members of the SS would only be tried in special SS courts, whose members would be appointed by Hitler from a list prepared by the *Reichsführer SS*.

Criticism of SS behaviour in the occupied areas by the Army continued. This led to a conference between the commander-in-chief, General (later Field Marshal) Walter von Brauchitsch, and Himmler who admitted that mistakes had been made in carrying out the regime's 'ethnic policies'. In future, he said, they would be carried out 'in as considerate a manner as possible and with the minimum of bloodshed'. It was an empty promise.

SS DIVISIONS

Hitler had ordered the creation of three SS divisions. After the ceasefire in Poland, *Leibstandarte* was brought up to strength as a reinforced motorized regiment and the three regiments of the *SS-Verfügungstruppen* were brought together as the *SS-Verfügungsdivision*. However, recruiting for the other two divisions would bring the SS into conflict with the Army, which was also competing for recruits. Himmler had a simple solution. A decree was already in place that allowed him, as *Reichsführer SS* and Chief of Police, to transfer enough men from the *Totenkopf* and Police Force to form two divisions. In October 1939, the *SS-Totenkopfdivision* was formed with 6,500 members of the *Totenkopfverbände*, *Verfügungstruppe* veterans, police and SS reservists. The *Polizeidivision* was then formed with thousands of *Ordnungspolizei* who, as Himmler admitted, were 'neither National Socialist nor SS men'.

Another decree then allowed Himmler to bring the *Totenkopf* strength up to the 40,000 to 50,000 required as 'police reinforcements' in wartime. A nationwide recruitment network was set up under *SS-Brigadeführer* Gottlob Berger. It got around Army objections by recruiting men below the conscription age. This was done with the help of Dr Robert Ley, Chief of the German Labour Front, who released volunteers from compulsory labour service. Those who volunteered for 12 years would be given the status of civil servants and freed from ordinary military service. Ley committed suicide while awaiting trial for war crimes and crimes against humanity at Nuremberg in 1945.

Older men came from the SA, who were told that it was an honour to serve in the National Socialist corps, and Germany was flooded with posters, leaflets and circulars that said: 'The *SS-Totenkopfstandarten*, set up for the solution of special tasks, will immediately begin accepting volunteers.' Recruits were between 28 and 39 who could prove their Aryan ancestry and were over 171 cm (5 ft 7 in) tall. The military authorities objected to the *Totenkopf* wearing their field-grey uniform as they were not soldiers. The SS replied that they were entitled to do so as they had been 'committed by the *Führer* for special military duties'.

Another source of recruits was the *Volksdeutsche*, ethnic Germans from the occupied territories who were not eligible for conscription into the Army, so there could be no objections. These would eventually outnumber native Germans.

To absorb this flood of recruits, *Ersatz* ('replacement') regiments were set up for each field division, with smaller *Ersatz* units for specialized troops such as artillery, combat engineers and tank destroyers. On 23 January 1940, Himmler was given complete control over them no matter where they were. The commander-in-chief of the Army only retained the right to inspect them and advise on military training. The liquidation of the Warsaw ghetto in 1943 and the murder of the last 60,000 Jews there was carried out by *Ersatz* units.

FOURTH BRANCH

The armed SS was now becoming so big that some settlement had to be made with the Army, which officially recognized the *Waffen-SS* as the fourth branch of the *Wehrmacht* on 2 March 1940. It comprised the *Leibstandarte SS 'Adolf Hitler'*, the *SS-Verfügungsdivision*, the *SS-Totenkopfdivision*, the *Polizeidivision* and the *SS-Junkerschulen* in Bad Tölz and Braunschweig, along with all their training and replacement units. Service in them was recognized as military service – except in the *SS-Totenkopfverbände*, whose status had yet to be decided. On 1 April seven ancillary organizations were set up to handle administration, recruitment, supply, legal matters, weapons development, medical service and welfare. These were staffed by personnel drawn from active *Waffen-SS* units, making the *Waffen-SS* an autonomous force.

Arguments over the status of the reserve continued as Hitler believed that the war would be a short one and envisioned a return of the *Waffen-SS* to a peacetime role. As it was, apart from some older men and skilled workers demobilized after the fall of France, all *Waffen-SS* personnel served until their deaths or the end of the war, whatever their original terms of enlistment. Meanwhile the *Wehrmacht* grew wary of the *Waffen-SS* in case there was a clash between the Army and the National Socialists after the war.

THE INVASION OF WESTERN EUROPE

Plans were soon underway for operation *Fall Gelb* ('Case Yellow'), the invasion of Western Europe. The *Blitzkrieg* was to be spearheaded by ten *panzer* divisions, four of them newly created. However, the Army still had only the four motorized infantry divisions used in the Polish campaign. These were to be supplemented by the *SS-Verfügungsdivision*, the *SS-Totenkopfdivision* and the reinforced regiment *Leibstandarte SS 'Adolf Hitler'*.

With the non-motorized *Polizeidivision*, reinforcements in training and the *SS-Totenkopf* regiments, the *Waffen-SS* had over 125,000 men in uniform when the attack began. The SS field formations were attached to various Army corps along Germany's western frontier. They were to adopt Army ranks, rather than use their SS or former police rank. However, they were permitted to use the Nazi salute and were excused church parade.

The older SS regiments, those who had fought in Poland and were commanded by veterans such as Sepp Dietrich, Paul Hausser and Felix Steiner, commanded respect from the Army, while the newer divisions had yet to prove themselves. The Army was sceptical. The *Polizeidivision*, armed with Czech weapons and old horse-drawn artillery, comprised former policemen and was commanded by Police General Karl von Pfeffer-Wildenbruch. And the *SS-Totenkopfdivision* was made up of former concentration camp guards under the command of *SS-Gruppenführer* (Major General) Theodor Eicke, Himmler's camp supervisor.

The *Polizeidivision* was assigned a static role opposite the Maginot Line, the French fortifications along its borders with Italy, Switzerland, Germany and Luxembourg. Himmler did not mind this slight as its members were not SS men. However, he wanted the Death's Head units of the *SS-Totenkopfdivision* to earn their spurs in the first-wave attack. However, the Chief of the Army General Staff Colonel General Franz Halder overruled him and it was assigned to the 2nd Army reserve that was to follow the lead divisions into Belgium and Luxembourg.

In command of the 2nd Army was General Maximilian Freiherr von Weichs, an aristocrat and devout Catholic. He had little time for the SS and did not mind showing it. When he visited the *SS-Totenkopfdivision* on 4 April, Eicke described his manner as 'cold and hostile'. However, his attitude changed when he discovered that it was a modern motorized infantry division – at a time when the entire German Army had just seven – and was to have a heavy artillery section. He was impressed with the men's discipline and physical fitness. Like other ranking Army officers, he was surprised to discover that they

Sepp Dietrich.

were not the Nazi street brawlers they had encountered in the SA, though he was critical of their leadership. Later, Field Marshal Erich von Manstein, author of the invasion plan, said the *SS-Totenkopfdivision* 'was probably the best *Waffen-SS* division'.

CHAPTER THREE

SS

The Spearhead

I n *Fall Gelb* the *Waffen-SS* was to prove itself as a fighting force. This time, it was to fight in divisional formations under the command of its own officers. By the time the invasion of Denmark and Norway began on 9 April, it were up to strength, but still short of artillery and transport.

Leibstandarte SS 'Adolf Hitler' and the *Der Führer* regiment, detached from the *SS-Verfügungsdivision*, were on the Dutch border, ready to overrun The Netherlands and deny the RAF use of the airfields there. The *SS-Totenkopfdivision* was held in reserve near Kassel, ready to follow the lead units into Holland, while the *Polizeidivision* was in reserve at Tübingen, behind the upper Rhine front.

At 5.30 am on 10 May 1940, *Leibstandarte* crossed the Dutch border. By midday, it had advanced 113 km (70 miles) and captured the provincial capital of Zwolle. The two nearby bridges across the Yssel had already been blown by the Dutch Army, but *Leibstandarte*'s 3rd Battalion forced a crossing to the south, capturing the town of Hoven and 200 of its defenders. A reinforced platoon of SS troops pushed on another 72 km (45 miles), capturing a further 127 prisoners. In this action, *SS-Obersturmführer* (Captain) Hugo Kraas became the first SS officer to win the Iron Cross First Class during the campaign. *Leibstandarte* then moved south to join the 9. *Panzer* and the *SS-Verfügungsdivision* in the main drive towards Rotterdam.

The 3rd SS Regiment *'Der Führer'* spearheaded the advance of the 207th Infantry Division, crossing the Yssel near Arnhem, going on to attack the fortifications along the Grebbe Line and losing a third of its strength in heavy fighting before moving on towards Utrecht.

9. *Panzer-Division* and the *SS-Verfügungsdivision* crossed the Maas on a railway bridge at Gennep which had been left intact. As they headed on towards the Moerdijk bridges, which were in the hands of German paratroopers, they ran into a French column which, with the help of air support, was driven back to Breda. A second French column was caught by Ju 87 Stuka dive bombers. The *SS-Verfügungsdivision* was then sent to Zeeland to mop up French and Dutch stragglers there.

The *Leibstandarte* caught up with 9. *Panzer-Division* outside Rotterdam, while an air raid reduced much of the city to rubble. The Dutch defenders surrendered. General Kurt Student, commander of the airborne troops, and Lieutenant Colonel Dietrich von Choltitz took over the Dutch military headquarters. Outside, Dutch troops were surrendering their weapons.

Suddenly, the *Leibstandarte* under Sepp Dietrich stormed into the square. Dietrich was unaware of the surrender and, seeing armed Dutch troops, the *Leibstandarte* opened fire with machine guns. Student and Choltitz rushed to the window to see what was happening. A stray bullet clipped the side of Student's head and he fell against Choltitz, badly wounded. The *Leibstandarte* then went careering on through Rotterdam to face heavy fighting on the road to Delft. That day, the regiment took 3,536 prisoners. It reached The Hague the next day when the Dutch Army capitulated.

Waffen SS troops in Holland, 1940.

Student survived to win the Knight's Cross of the Iron Cross in Crete, where he was responsible for a number of massacres, taking reprisals against civilians. However, after he was captured by the Allies in 1945, he faced eight charges of maltreatment and murder of prisoners of war. Convicted on three of the charges, he was sentenced to five years imprisonment, but was released in 1948.

REACHING THE COAST

The *Leibstandarte* then moved on to Amsterdam before heading south to join the campaign in France. Supported by the *Luftwaffe*, the 3rd SS Regiment 'Der Führer' smashed through to the coast, capturing the port of Vlissingen while French destroyers evacuated the survivors. The *SS-Verfügungsdivision* was then ordered into France.

With fighting in The Netherlands over and the Belgian defences breached, the *SS-Totenkopfdivision* was released from the reserves and sent across roads choked with military vehicles and refugees to give infantry support to *XV Panzer Korps*, which had halted at Cambrai. The *Totenkopf* went into battle to consolidate the Germans' hold on Cambrai and Cateau, and suffered its first casualties – 16 dead and 53 wounded on 19–20 May. While the *Totenkopf* was held up, four other German armoured divisions reached the Channel, cutting off 40 British, French and Belgian divisions – nearly one million men – from the main body of the French Army to the south.

The following day more than 130 British and French tanks, along with two battalions of infantry, counterattacked. The *Waffen-SS* troops were shocked to find that their small 37 mm antitank guns had little effect on the heavily armoured Allied tanks. Instead, they had to use heavy artillery. Eventually they were saved by the arrival of Stukas, but not before some *Totenkopf* men had fled in panic. Nineteen were killed, 27 wounded and two went missing.

STIFF RESISTANCE

On 22 May, French forces trapped in the east tried to break out, but the *Leibstandarte SS 'Adolf Hitler'* arrived to hold the line, beating off a number of weak French attacks. By 24 May, the Allies were contained in a triangular area based on the Channel. The British Expeditionary Force (BEF) had established a defensive line in the south along a series of canals. The *Leibstandarte* approached after a forced night march from Valenciennes, while to the southeast the *Totenkopf* and the rest of the *SS-Verfügungsdivision* fought their way to the canal against stiff British resistance.

When the *SS-Verfügungsdivision* reached the canal, it sent in a reconnaissance patrol comprising 32 men in armoured cars. Eight kilometres (5 miles) beyond the canal at Merville, it was cut off by enemy tanks. Reporting by radio that only eight men remained uninjured, they were told to destroy their equipment and return on foot. None of them made it.

Further south, other elements of the *SS-Verfügungsdivision* were mopping up British troops northeast of Arras, which was still in British hands, though surrounded by German divisions. On the night of the 23 May, most of the garrison pulled back behind the canal line. The tanks covering the withdrawal engaged *Waffen-SS* troops, who lost three of their field guns and their crews; the British lost most of their tanks in the action.

As the reconnaissance patrol had got as far as Merville without opposition, it was apparent that the defence line along the canal was not fully manned. Indeed, a French unit had been withdrawn before the British turned up to take over. The *SS-Verfügungsdivision* seized the opportunity and crossed the canal unopposed.

HALT ORDER

On 24 May, the controversial 'halt order' came from Hitler, telling the troops not to cross the canal. It was too late. The *SS-Verfügungsdivision* was already across and the *Leibstandarte* was preparing to cross at Watten. The regiment was under heavy artillery fire, so Sepp Dietrich ignored the halt order. In heavy fighting, the *Leibstandarte* crossed the canal and took the heights near Watten.

The British used the halt to prepare for the evacuation of the BEF from Dunkirk. German forces used it to consolidate their position and repair their vehicles. But the *SS-Verfügungsdivision* and the *Leibstandarte* were across the canal and had bridgeheads to defend. The *SS-Verfügungsdivision* had also taken St Venant, which lay on one of the British exfiltration routes. The British sent a brigade to take the town back and rebuild the bridge there. This was the first time the *Waffen-SS* had been forced to give up territory. The British held St Venant for just two days.

The halt order was rescinded on the night of 26 May and the *Germania* and *Der Führer* regiments of the *SS-Verfügungsdivision* attacked through the Nieppe forest, suffering heavy casualties. The third infantry regiment, *Deutschland*, led 3. *Panzer-Division* in an attack on the British units on the Lys Canal near Merville. Steiner's 3rd Battalion launched the attack, supported by two batteries of SS artillery. They overwhelmed the British infantry and machine gun posts. By the following afternoon, they were holding a bridgehead across the canal. The *SS-Totenkopfdivision*, which was supposed to advance on the left, was still miles to the rear while 3. *Panzer-Division* was bogged down to the south.

HEROIC ACTS

Combat engineers were constructing crossings when some 20 British tanks counterattacked. With no heavy weapons, the *Deutschland* had to fight back with small arms. Steiner wrote: 'Even though it is not customary, in this battle certain individual heroic acts must be mentioned.'

One young SS officer attacked a British tank with grenades at close range and was crushed. An SS private leapt onto the rear deck of a tank to throw a grenade into the observation slot and was shot off by the tank following behind. *Waffen-SS* troops refused to fall back in the face of overwhelming odds, still firing at the tanks with small arms from a range of under 5 m (15 ft).

'The regiment is unfortunately unable to recommend these men for an award since they were killed in the process,' wrote Steiner. However, three company commanders were recommended for the Iron Cross First Class. This was the first recorded example of the *Waffen-SS*'s fanatical will to fight, whatever the odds.

The *Deutschland* was saved when a *Totenkopf* anti-tank platoon turned up. But British tanks out of range of the *Totenkopf* continued to rain down shells on the Germans, destroying five of their antitank guns and holding them back long enough for the bulk of the British forces to withdraw. Himmler was so proud of the *Deutschland*'s valour that he gave Steiner's report to Hitler who said: '*Sehr schön*' ('Very nice').

MASSACRE AT LE PARADIS

By then the main body of the *SS-Totenkopfdivision* had crossed the canal at Bethune, against ferocious opposition and sustaining heavy casualties. At Le Paradis, the men of the Royal Norfolk Regiment held off 4. *Kompanie* of *Infanterie-Regiment 2*, which lost 17 killed and 52 wounded. In retaliation, *SS-Obersturmführer* Fritz Knöchlien ordered the machine-gunning of 99 British soldiers after they had surrendered. Survivors were shot or bayoneted. Two injured men crawled out from under the bodies after the SS troops had left. They were picked up by another German unit and taken to hospital, surviving the war to tell the tale.

Other *Waffen-SS* officers condemned this, challenging Knöchlien to a duel and threatening to resign. Men refused to serve under him. But Eicke blocked any investigation. *SS-Gruppenführer* Karl Wolff, chief of Himmler's personal staff, visited the scene shortly after, but merely complained that a large number of SS dead in the area had not been buried.

Himmler succeeded in covering up the incident. Knöchlien was promoted to *SS-Obersturmbannführer* and awarded the Knight's Cross of the Iron Cross. In 1948, Knöchlien was tried as a war criminal, convicted and hanged.

Meanwhile, other elements of the *SS-Totenkopfdivision* continued their pursuit of the British. On 28 May, while the *Leibstandarte* was advancing towards Dunkirk, Sepp Dietrich's car came within 45 m (150 ft) of a British position and was hit. Dietrich and his driver leapt out as it burst into flames. Taking cover in a roadside ditch, they smeared themselves with a thick layer of wet mud to protect themselves from the burning petrol from the car that threatened to engulf them. They stayed in the ditch for five hours.

MASSACRE AT WORMHOUDT

Angered by the apparent loss of their commander, 12 men of the *Leibstandarte*'s 2nd Battalion under the command of *SS-Hauptsturm-führer* Wilhelm Mohnke herded 100 British prisoners into a barn near Wormhoudt, 16 km (10 miles) from Dunkirk, and threw in grenades. Two British NCOs, Sergeant Stanley Moore and CSM Augustus Jennings, hurled themselves on top of the grenades to protect the others. Two groups of five prisoners were ordered to come out and were shot in the back. The SS troops then opened fire into the barn. Eighty men perished, with nine more dying of their wounds shortly after. Survivors were picked up by a regular Army unit. Their wounds were tended before they were sent to prisoner of war camps.

Mohnke never faced trial for the killings and strenuously denied giving the order. The case was re-examined in 1988 and 1993, but the German prosecutor decided that there was insufficient evidence to bring charges. Mohnke died in 2001, aged 90.

When it was discovered what had happened to Dietrich, two companies of SS troops were sent to rescue him, but they were driven back with heavy losses. An Army *panzer* company was then sent, losing its commander and four tanks before withdrawing. It took the entire 3rd Battalion of the *Leibstandarte* with a platoon of armoured cars and five heavy tanks to rescue Dietrich and his driver from the ditch.

The 2nd Battalion Royal Warwickshire Regiment had been given orders to hold Wormhoudt until nightfall before retiring to Dunkirk. It managed to hold off the German attack until the *Leibstandarte* arrived. In house-to-house fighting the SS took 11 officers and 320 men prisoner. That night, the surviving British soldiers tried to withdraw, but the *Leibstandarte* pursued them, taking a further six officers and 430 men prisoner.

With the BEF bottled up behind the Dunkirk perimeter, the *Leibstandarte* withdrew to Cambrai to refit, where it was joined by the rest of the *SS-Verfügungsdivision*. The *SS-Totenkopfdivision* moved up to Boulogne while the BEF and some French and Belgian troops were evacuated from Dunkirk. Then it was moved into central France.

FALL ROT

Fall Rot ('Case Red') was the operation to annihilate what remained of the French Army. It began on 4 June. To bring the *Waffen-SS* up to strength replacements were sent from Germany – 270 men to the *Leibstandarte*, 2,020 to the *Verfügungsdivision* and 1,140 to the *SS-Totenkopfdivision*. The *Polizeidivision* was as yet unblooded. As in Poland, the heaviest casualties had been among officers and cadets were sent from *SS-Junkerschulen* as replacements.

The two SS divisions in France finally received their heavy artillery battalions and, on 4 June, the *Verfügungsdivision* began an artillery duel with the French forces south of the Somme, suffering two killed and 17 wounded. The following day, the *Leibstandarte* and the *Verfügungsdivision* joined *Panzergruppe 'Kleist'* in its drive on Paris, while the *Totenkopf* was moved up to St Pol in case it was needed.

The *Verfügungsdivision* crossed the Somme and sped south, but as it approached the Avre River on 7 June its lead elements were pinned down by heavy fire from the south bank. With artillery support, the 3rd SS Regiment *'Der Führer'* crossed the river and established a bridgehead. But *Panzergruppe 'Kleist'* had run into stiff resistance north of Paris, losing 30 per cent of its tanks. Hitler decided to reinsert it to the east where the infantry had already made a breakthrough, so the *Verfügungsdivision* was pulled back across the Somme, having lost 24 killed and 113 wounded for no gain in three days of battle.

The *Leibstandarte SS 'Adolf Hitler'* was also pulled back across the Somme, but it was then put under the *XLIV Armee Korps* and crossed the Somme again to follow up the corps' rapid advance to the Marne. On the way it met with only sporadic resistance from French stragglers, who quickly surrendered. Crossing the Marne, the *Leibstandarte* joined up with *Panzergruppe 'Kleist'* again. The *SS-Totenkopfdivision* then joined them.

SHARP PURSUIT

On 10 June, the French government left Paris. Three days later German troops entered the city. Hitler ordered a 'sharp pursuit' of the French to prevent them establishing a new front to the south. The *Leibstandarte*, *Verfügungsdivision* and *Totenkopfdivision* headed for Dijon with *Panzergruppen 'Kleist'*. With Dietrich acting on his own authority, the *Leibstandarte* raced ahead with the SS divisions following the *panzers*.

By 15 June, the *Totenkopfdivision* was with *XIV Armee Korps* when it was told to follow *10. Panzer-Division*, which had made contact with the retreating French forces. As it advanced on Clamecy, the *Totenkopf* saw no fighting but took 400 prisoners in two days. However, two were killed and three wounded when they were attacked by a French aircraft, which was then shot down.

Meanwhile, the *Verfügungsdivision* secured the left flank of *XIV* and *XVI Korps*. French forces fleeing the German attack on the Maginot Line tried to break through, but were thrown back with heavy losses. Many were taken prisoner. Continuing south, the *Verfügungsdivision* met with desperate resistance from the retreating French. By 17 June, it had taken over 30,000 prisoners at a loss of three officers and 30 men killed, and three officers and 91 men wounded.

The *Leibstandarte* got so far ahead that, for three days, no one knew where it was. On 18 June, General Paul Ludwig von Kleist caught up with it 24 km (15 miles) south of Nevers while out on a routine inspection trip and ordered it to establish a bridgehead across the Allier southwest of Moulin. It raced ahead again, but no sooner had the first German soldier set foot on the bridge at Moulin than the French blew it up. However, the *Leibstandarte* did manage to cross the Allier over a burning railway bridge.

It made another wild advance towards Vichy, smashing barricades with its armoured cars and firing automatic weapons from its vehicles, while the following infantry dealt with the towns still occupied by the French. The *Leibstandarte* linked up with other German troops at Vichy, capturing nearly a thousand French troops in a day. It headed on south towards Clermont-Ferrand, taking an airfield along with 242 aircraft, eight tanks, numerous other vehicles, 4,075 soldiers and 287 officers, including one general. Heading on, it took Saint-Étienne and its garrison on 24 June, the deepest penetration into French territory of the campaign.

MOPPING UP

Meanwhile the *SS-Verfügungsdivision* and *SS-Totenkopfdivision* were guarding the flanks. There was little to do but mopping up. But, on 19 June, the *Totenkopfdivision*, which had seen little action up to this point, joined the forward elements of *Panzergruppe 'Kleist'* advancing on Tarare 145 km (90 miles) to the south and reconnoitring Lyon. The *Totenkopfdivision*'s reconnaissance squadron caught up with some French colonial troops at Tarare and took 6,000 prisoners for light losses. The former concentration camp guards showed little compunction, shooting French colonial prisoners who they considered 'racially inferior'.

While the motorized units of the *Waffen-SS* raced through France, the horse-drawn *Polizeidivision* plodded along behind. It saw some action in a bitterly contested assault across the Aisne River and the Ardennes Canal. On 10 June it took the wooded heights near Vonq, but finding its antitank guns powerless against French medium tanks, it was driven back. That night it took Vonq, only to find the French had withdrawn from the area. In the Argonne Forest, it overcame a French rearguard action in ferocious hand-to-hand fighting and went on to take the town of Les Islettes.

ARMSTICE

By then, negotiations for an armistice were underway. Under its terms, the Germans would occupy the entire French coast from Belgium to Spain. The *SS-Verfügungsdivision* and *SS-Totenkopfdivision* headed for Bordeaux to occupy the coast south to the Spanish border. The *Polizeidivision* joined the reserve in the upper Maas near Rondilly, while the *Leibstandarte* headed back to Paris for the victory parade.

Once again, the performance of the *Waffen-SS* drew mixed opinions. The Army still considered them political soldiers and condemned their lack of self-control at Le Paradis and Wormhoudt. But Hitler was delighted. On 19 July 1940, in a victory speech where he raised 12 generals to the rank of field marshal, he told the Reichstag that 'the valiant divisions and regiments of the *Waffen-SS*... have a share in this honour'.

They were, Hitler said, 'inspired by a fierce will, troops with an unbeatable turnout – the sense of superiority personified'. Special praise was reserved for 'Party Comrade Himmler, who organized the entire security system of our Reich as well as the units of the *Waffen-SS*'.

He awarded the Knight's Cross of the Iron Cross, Germany's highest award for gallantry, to six soldiers of the *Waffen-SS* – Sepp Dietrich, *SS-Oberführer* Felix Steiner of the *Deutschland* SS regiment, *SS-Oberführer* Georg Keppler and *SS-Sturmbannführer* Fritz Witt of *3. SS-Regiment 'Der Führer'*, *SS-Obersturmführer* Fritz Vogt of *SS-Aufklärungsableilung*'s 2nd company and *SS-Hauptscharführer* Ludwig Kepplinger of the 11th company of *3. SS-Regiment 'Der Führer'*.

From then on, the *Waffen-SS* would have no problem securing the best equipment.

CHAPTER FOUR

ᛋᛋ

Turning East

After the fall of France, the *Waffen-SS* was set to expand again. This was not Hitler's intention. After the war, he said he wanted the SS to be 'a militarized state police capable of representing and imposing the authority of the Reich within the country in any situation'. To have the authority to do that, it had to be organized along military lines and have proved itself on the battlefield alongside the *Wehrmacht*.

In its ranks there had to be 'men of the best German blood and that identifies unreservedly with the ideology on which the Greater German Reich is based'. To maintain those standards, the *Waffen-SS* had to be small, not exceeding 5 to 10 per cent of the peacetime strength of the Army. Hitler had set the peacetime strength of the Army at 64 divisions. Consequently, the *Waffen-SS* should have six divisions.

Already, older men in the reserves were due to be demobilized, along with those who were farmers or who worked in vital industries – though most would be called up again before the end of the war.

Hermann Göring was also demanding a greater share of the manpower available for the *Luftwaffe*, which he headed.

RECRUITS

Once more, the SS found itself in competition for recruits with the *Wehrmacht*, which complained that recruiting officer Gottlob Berger was exceeding his quotas. Again, he turned to non-Germans of 'Nordic blood'. Himmler was not opposed to this. At the end of 1938, there were 20 non-German volunteers in the SS. By May 1940, there were 100, including three from Sweden, five from the United States and 44 from Switzerland. That month, a further thousand *Volksdeutsche* were recruited in Romania and were sent for SS training in Prague.

The conquest of Denmark, Norway, Belgium and the Netherlands presented fresh recruiting opportunities. Volunteers from Denmark and Norway were formed into the SS regiment *Nordland*, and those from Belgium and the Netherlands in the SS regiment *Westland*. With

Waffen SS 'Nordland' swearing-in ceremony, Spring 1941.

the *Germania* regiment from the *SS-Verfügungsdivision* and *SS-Artillerie-Regiment 5*, they were formed into a division initially called *Germania* but, to prevent confusion, its name was changed to *Wiking*. The *SS-Verfügungsdivision* was reorganized and strengthened with another *Totenkopf* regiment and renamed 'Reich' (becoming 'Das Reich' after 1942).

The *Leibstandarte* was brought up to brigade strength, while men from the various *Totenkopf* regiments were formed into the *Kampfgruppe* ('Battle Group') *Nord* and posted to northern Norway.

On the battlefield *Waffen-SS* formations came under the command of the Army, but Himmler retained a personal army of his own. Five *SS-Totenkopfstandarten* were formed into a motorized SS military reserve. This comprised the 1st and 2nd SS Infantry Brigades, the 1st and 2nd SS Cavalry Regiments, and SS Infantry Regiment 5, along with a squadron of bicycle troops and a battery of horse-drawn artillery. The Army insisted that those not under Army command did not have the right to wear military badges of rank or the field-grey uniform.

With the number of concentration camps expanding, more guards were needed. They wore *Waffen-SS* uniforms and carried *Waffen-SS* pay books. Wounded *Waffen-SS* men were sent to guard the camps while able-bodied men were sent to frontline units as replacements. Himmler also created three *Höheren SS- und Polizeiführer* ('Higher SS and Police Leaders') units and assigned to each a *Polizei* regiment, comprising two armoured-car platoons, two antitank platoons and three Police battalions. This Police 'army' was under the *Kommandostab Reichsführer-SS* ('Command Staff *Reichsführer-SS*'), which was itself under the personal control of Himmler. They were to carry out the 'special tasks' the *SS-Totenkopf* units had originally been created to undertake – that is, the 'ethnic cleansing' of Jews and the murder of political opponents.

Some of these SS Police units were thrown into the front line in moments of crisis. Himmler also created battalions of auxiliary policemen from what he called *wilde Völker* ('wild people') – Latvians, Lithuanians, Estonians, Poles and Ukranians who also murdered Jews in the occupied areas.

While these changes were being made, the *Leibstandarte*, *Reich*, *Totenkopf* and *Polizei* divisions were in training in France for Operation Sea Lion – the invasion of Britain. Even before this operation was put on indefinite hold in 1940, Hitler had begun his plans to attack the Soviet Union.

THE BALKANS

Operation Barbarossa – the invasion of the Soviet Union – was planned to begin on 15 May 1941 and the *Waffen-SS* was to play a significant role in it. But before its units were moved up to Poland, they found themselves sent into the Balkans.

Jealous of Hitler's military successes, the previous October his ally the Italian dictator Benito Mussolini had, without warning, attacked Greece from occupied Albania. However, the Greeks were no pushover and the Italian Army lost battle after battle against their hardened mountain troops. Hitler could not risk advancing into Russia with an uncertain military situation on his southern flank.

Sixteen German divisions were moved into southern Romania, a German ally at the time. In February 1941, the *Leibstandarte* was sent to join them. The situation worsened in March when a British Expeditionary Force landed in Greece.

The Germans negotiated a pact with Yugoslavia, a country created after the collapse of the Austrian Empire in World War I and lay between Austria and Greece. This should have opened the way to the Greek border. However, the day after the pact was signed there was a military coup in the Yugoslav capital Belgrade which installed an anti-German government.

Hitler was enraged and postponed Barbarossa for 'up to four weeks [to] destroy Yugoslavia militarily and as a nation', he said.

More German divisions were sent to crush Yugoslavia 'with merciless brutality... in a lightning operation'.

CLASHES WITH THE ARMY

On 28 March the SS division *Das Reich* was sent by road from Vesoul in eastern France to Romania. Along the way, there were clashes with the Army that brought Himmler formal complaints from the Commander-in-Chief Field Marshal von Brauchitsch. The problem was that vehicles broke down. Others ran out of fuel and the SS columns proceeded as a snail's pace. They were overtaken by better-organized Army columns.

When SS Infantry Regiment 11 found itself overtaken by a fast-moving Army convoy, the SS company halted it. When the convoy's commander protested, the SS officer put two Teller mines under the front wheels of the Army column's lead vehicle and ordered an SS man to stand guard with a fixed bayonet.

The next day another SS officer stopped a passing Army convoy, telling its commander: 'If you drive on without my permission, I will order my men to fire on your column.'

THE RACE TO BELGRADE

The *Leibstandarte* and *Das Reich* were attached to General Georg-Hans Reinhardt's *XLI Panzer Korps*. When the operation began on 6 April, *Das Reich* raced ahead towards Belgrade. It was assumed that resistance would end once the capital had fallen. However, the division got bogged down in a marshy area, but a motorcycle reconnaissance unit under *SS-Hauptsturmführer* Fritz Klingenberg discovered it could make headway down railway tracks.

While *Das Reich* was halted at the banks of the Danube, Klingenberg reached the river just opposite Belgrade. He commandeered a small boat and took a group of ten volunteers across the river. Finding the city badly bomb damaged and lightly defended, he took over the

Waffen-SS *motorcycle unit in the Balkans campaign, 6 April 1941.*

German embassy. From there, he phoned the mayor of Belgrade, saying that he was ahead of a large formation. If the mayor did not surrender the city he would order a massive air raid. The mayor complied and Klingenberg was award the Knight's Cross of the Iron Cross.

Later, Klingenberg was promoted *SS-Standartenführer* and given command of the SS division *Götz von Berlichingen*. He was killed by an American tank shell in Saarland in March 1945.

While Klingenberg was taking the surrender of Belgrade, the *Leibstandarte SS 'Adolf Hitler'* was moving into southern Yugoslavia through Bulgaria in the other prong of the attack. With *9. Panzer-Division*, it advanced though Skoplje, taking the stronghold of Monastir near the border with Greece. By then it had suffered just five casualties, all wounded.

PASSES INTO GREECE

On 10 April, it was ordered to open the Klidi Pass into Greece. It was held with veteran Australian and New Zealand troops with the BEF. It took the *Leibstandarte* two days to flush them from their positions at a cost of 53 dead, 153 wounded and three missing.

Next, it moved on to the Klisura Pass, which was held by Greek infantry. As it moved up the narrow roads and tracks, it was harassed by Greek troops. An attempt was made to get behind them, but the SS troops were dispersed as night fell. In the morning though, supported by the Germans' dreaded 88mm guns, it rushed the defenders.

Two companies of the *Leibstandarte*'s *Aufklärungsabteilung* tried scaling the cliffs while a small advance group under *SS-Sturmbannführer* Kurt Meyer moved along the road through the pass. Suddenly, there was a huge explosion. The Greeks had detonated demolition charges, sending the roadway crashing into the valley below.

Meyer's men were then pinned down by machine-gun fire. Taking cover behind rocks, the attack was halted, but Meyer was determined to get it going again and pulled out a hand grenade.

'I shouted at the group,' he said in a post-war memoir. 'Everyone looks thunderstruck at me as I brandish the hand grenade, pull the pin, and roll it precisely behind the last man. Never again did I witness such a concerted leap forward as at that second. As if bitten by tarantulas, we dive around the rock spur and into a fresh crater. The spell was broken. The hand grenade has cured our lameness. We grin at each other, and head forward towards the next cover.'

More than a thousand prisoners were taken at the cost of six killed and nine wounded. The following day, the *Leibstandarte* took the heights around Kastoria and the town itself, along with 11,000 prisoners. It went on to take the Metzovon Pass on 20 April, cutting off the Greek armies west of the Pindus mountains.

The Greeks realized that the position was hopeless and sued for peace. Dietrich himself took the surrender of 16 divisions, which were treated with honour as a gallant foe. Mussolini was infuriated that the Greeks had surrendered to the Germans, not to the Italians, and complained to Hitler, who passed on his displeasure to Dietrich.

However, he was secretly delighted by the courage of the unit bearing his name.

The *Leibstandarte* then set off in pursuit of the British forces. The terrain was rugged and Meyer commandeered local fishing boats to transport his men across the Gulf of Patras. The *Leibstandarte* continued down the west coast of the Peloponnese to reach Pirus, where it captured elements of the Royal Tank Regiment. Meanwhile, troops from the *Aufklärungsabteilung* under *SS-Hauptsturmführer* Hugo Kraas advanced along the coast to make contact with German paratroops who had been dropped at the Corinth Canal. But it was too late. The bulk of the British had been evacuated from Corinth.

Athens was taken on 27 April. The *Leibstandarte* then took part in another victory parade there, before being sent to Czechoslovakia to prepare for Operation Barbarossa. Altogether, 223,000 Greeks and

Soldiers of the Leibstandarte in Greece, 1941.

21,000 other prisoners had been taken. British prisoners later testified that they were well treated by their *Waffen-SS* captors.

Kurt Meyer and *SS-Hauptsturmführer* Gerd Pleiss, commander of 1. *Kompanie* of the *Leibstandarte*, were awarded the Knight's Cross for their gallantry at the Klidi and Klisura Passes.

CHAPTER FIVE

⚡⚡

Barbarossa

The campaign in the Balkans delayed the start of Operation Barbarossa until 22 June 1941. The *Leibstandarte SS 'Adolf Hitler'* and *Wiking* divisions were with Army Group South under Field Marshal Gerd von Rundstedt. This would drive southeastwards into Ukraine. The SS division *Das Reich*, which was with Army Group Centre under Field Marshal Fedor von Bock, would attack through Belorussia (Belarus today) and head for Moscow. *SS-Totenkopfdivision*, with *Polizeidivision* initially in reserve, was with the Army Group North under Field Marshal Wilhelm von Leeb, which would sweep through the Baltic States towards Leningrad – the city formerly and now once again known as St Petersburg. *SS-Kampfgruppe* (later SS Division) *Nord* was assigned to the Finnish Front under General Nikolaus von Falkenhorst. Finland was on the side of the Germans at the time, after the Soviet Union had tried to invade in the Winter War of 1939–40.

The strict enforcement of Nazi ideology led to numerous atrocities being committed by the *Waffen-SS* on the Eastern Front. The SS had a fanatical hatred of Jews. Many were massacred. Some 33,771 Ukrainian

Jews were murdered at Babi Yar, a large ravine to the north of Kiev on 29–30 September 1941. Bolshevik Communism was the ideological enemy of Nazism, so SS *Einsatzgruppen* – 'deployment groups' or death squads – summarily executed Soviet Commissars.

In return, the Soviet state police hated the SS. At the GPU headquarters in Taganrog in Russia, six members of the *Leibstandarte SS 'Adolf Hitler'* were beaten and hacked to death with axes, shovels and bayonets. In response, Sepp Dietrich had all prisoners taken in the next three days shot – 4,000 of them in all. Throughout the campaign in the east, both sides shot and killed prisoners of war and enemy wounded. Many *Waffen-SS* men also obeyed the *Führer*'s order and shot themselves rather than be captured.

German tanks of Waffen-SS deployed in Operation Barbarossa, 1941.

LIVING SPACE

Hitler intended to expand his empire to the east as far as the River Volga to give the German people *Lebensraum*, or 'living space'. The

Slavs who lived there were considered to be *Untermenschen*, or subhumans, who were to be killed, dispossessed or enslaved.

Himmler constantly reiterated the theme of racial struggle in his speeches to *Waffen-SS* officers, telling them they were a 'National Socialist Military Order of Nordic men, a fighting force... bound by ideological oaths, whose fighters are selected from the best Aryan stock'.

He reinforced Nazi indoctrination, telling them: 'Obedience must be unconditional. It corresponds to the conviction that National Socialist ideology must reign supreme... Every SS man is therefore prepared to carry out blindly every order issued by the *Führer* or given by his superiors, regardless of the sacrifice involved.'

The stated aim of the Nazis was to eliminate the 'Jewish-Bolshevik revolution of subhumans'. This had largely been achieved in the Reich. Now it was time to destroy it in its breeding ground, the Soviet Union. After the war, many former *Waffen-SS* men said that fighting men dismissed the rantings of Himmler and considered him a comical figure. This may have been true later in the war when the SS had to resort to conscription. But, in 1941, there can be little doubt that the well indoctrinated members of the *Waffen-SS* – particularly the officers and NCOs – were true believers. They were a brotherhood who regarded war with the Soviet Union as a crusade to defend Western civilization from the onslaught of 'Asiatic Bolshevism'.

WAR CRIMES

At the war crimes trial held in Nuremberg after the war, *SS-Obergruppenführer* Erich von dem Bach-Zelewski, who oversaw the murder of Jews in Riga and Minsk, was asked whether he thought that Himmler's demand that 30 million Slavs were to be exterminated was in line with Nazi ideology. He replied: 'When, for years, for decades, the doctrine is preached that the Slav is a member of an inferior race and that the Jew is not even human, then such an explosion is inevitable.'

One of his small *Einsatzgruppen* alone killed 90,000 Jews. Bach-Zelewski did not stand trial at Nuremberg. Rather he appeared as a witness for the prosecution. Later, in a West German court he was convicted for ordering the murder of a fellow SS officer *SS-Obersturmbannführer* Anton Freiherr von Hohberg und Buchwald, who he had a personal feud with, during the Night of the Long Knives and other political opponents in the 1930s. He spent 21 years in jail, dying there in 1972. But he did not spend a day in prison for his activities in the Soviet Union, his participation in the Holocaust or other war crimes. In Poland he was responsible for the mass resettlement of 18–20,000 Poles and established the camp at Auschwitz, initially for Polish political prisoners after Hitler ordered the destruction of the Polish leadership and intelligentsia. He also led the brutal suppression of the Warsaw Uprising in 1944 where some 200,000 civilians died.

At Nuremberg, he distanced himself from the Nazis' anti-Semitic policies, saying: 'Contrary to the opinion of the National Socialists,

Waffen-SS troops entering a burning village during Operation Barbarossa, October 1941.

that the Jews were a highly organized group, the appalling fact was that they had no organization whatsoever. The mass of the Jewish people were taken completely by surprise. They did not know at all what to do; they had no directives or slogans as to how they should act.

'This is the greatest lie of anti-Semitism because it gives the lie to that old slogan that the Jews are conspiring to dominate the world and that they are so highly organized. In reality, they had no organization of their own at all, not even an information service. If they had had some sort of organization, these people could have been saved by the millions, but instead, they were taken completely by surprise. Never before has a people gone as unsuspectingly to its disaster. Nothing was prepared. Absolutely nothing.

'It was not so, as the anti-Semites say, that they were friendly to the Soviets. That is the most appalling misconception of all. The Jews in the old Poland, who were never communistic in their sympathies, were, throughout the area of the Bug eastward, more afraid of Bolshevism than of the Nazis. This was insanity. They could have been saved.... After the first anti-Jewish actions of the Germans, they thought now the wave was over and so they walked back to their undoing.'

In 1961, he testified at the trial of *SS-Obersturmbannführer* Adolf Eichmann, the chief architect of the Holocaust, captured by Mossad in Argentina in 1960 and sentenced to death in Israel the following year.

INTO ACTION

On the night of 24 June, the *Totenkopf* went into action to cover the right flank of General Erich von Manstein's *LVI Panzer Korps*, which had advanced 160 km (100 miles) from its starting point in just two days. By 30 June, the *Totenkopf* had reached Dvinsk – now Daugavpils – in southeastern Latvia, spending six days mopping up the remnants of the Soviet Red Army units smashed in the initial assault.

Then, on 2 July, it ran into the Red Army's 42nd Rifle Division, where its lead battalion under *SS-Oberführer* Max Simon was halted with the loss of ten killed and 100 wounded. The Soviets then pushed the *Totenkopf* back. The retreat was only halted by the intervention of Stuka dive-bombers. By 11 July, the *Totenkopf* had taken Opochka inside Russia itself. Along the way, it had lost 82 officers and 1,620 NCOs and men killed or wounded, almost ten per cent of its strength. One of the injured was Theodore Eicke, who was temporarily replaced by *SS-Oberführer* Matthias Kleinheisterkamp, then *SS-Brigadeführer* Georg Keppler, before Eicke resumed command in September 1941.

Kleinheisterkamp went on to take a number of commands in the *Waffen-SS* and won a Knight's Cross of the Iron Cross. It is thought that he committed suicide in Soviet captivity in 1945. Keppler also took a number of commands in the *Waffen-SS*. He surrendered to the Americans on 2 May 1945 and was interned until 1948.

Between the middle of July and the end of August 1941, the *Totenkopf* was involved in heavy fighting in the heavily wooded and marshy terrain before Leningrad. By 8 September the city was surrounded and a siege that lasted over two years had started. The Red Army tried to break the siege, launching a counterattack which the *Totenkopf* helped repulse at the cost of 6,500 casualties. The *Waffen-SS* then dug in between Lakes Ilmen and Seliger, waiting for the expected Soviet winter offensive.

While criticizing its methods, von Manstein wrote: 'In no circumstances must we forget, however, that the *Waffen-SS*, like the good comrades they were, fought shoulder to shoulder with the Army at the front and always showed themselves courageous and reliable.'

WAFFEN-SS DEFEAT

On 2 July, *SS-Kampfgruppe 'Nord'* with a Finnish and a German Army division, launched an attack on the Russian stronghold of Salla in Lapland. The SS battalions were repelled twice with heavy losses. On their third attempt, the Soviets drove them back beyond their starting point.

According to eyewitnesses, SS men threw away their weapons and fled, shouting: 'Russian tanks are coming.' They ran right through the German artillery lines. Meanwhile, the Finnish and German Army divisions took their objectives, forcing the Soviets back and preventing the SS being completely overrun. Nevertheless, the *Nord* lost 13 officers and 60 men killed, 13 officers and 219 men wounded, and 147 missing.

Himmler was most concerned that most of the missing had been taken prisoner, despite Hitler's order that they should kill themselves rather than be captured. The *Waffen-SS* men were supposed to fight to the death. General von Falkenhorst had so little faith in the survivors that he divided the *Nord*'s battalions among his Finnish and German Army formations.

It appeared that ideological conviction was not enough. The two former *Totenkopfstandarten* brought together to make up *Kampfgruppe* '*Nord*' were Nazis by conviction. But its men were trained as policemen rather than as soldiers and its officers' experience of command had been limited to the direction of concentration guards in the murder of defenceless civilians. Others were reservists. They were no match for the Soviets, who had been fighting the Finns since 1939. The Army was disgusted by their cowardly behaviour. They were withdrawn for reorganization and retraining as mountain troops, then upgraded to divisional status as 6. *SS-Gebirgs-Division* before returning to the line.

The *Polizeidivision* also served in the actions around Leningrad. Although it was never accepted as a proper *Waffen-SS* division, it had the prefix SS- added to its divisional title in 1942. Until then members wore police insignia on their collar patches and helmets. In June 1943, the *SS-Polizeidivision* was upgraded to a *panzer-grenadier* division. It never reached the combat proficiency of the other units, though it developed an unpleasant reputation for its brutal actions against partisans.

The defeat of the *Waffen-SS* in Finland was kept from the German public. New *Waffen-SS* men were to be sent as replacements. On 13

July, Himmler travelled to Stettin – now Szczecin, Poland – to address them. In a speech classified as 'Secret', he said:

> To you SS men I need not say much. For years – over a decade – we old National Socialists have struggled in Germany with Bolshevism, with Communism. One thing we can be certain of today: what we predicted in our political battle was not exaggerated by one single word and sentence. On the contrary, it was too mild and too weak because we did not, at that time, yet have the insight we have today. It is a great heavenly blessing that, for the first time in a thousand years, fate has given us this *Führer*. It is a stroke of fate that the *Führer*, in his turn, decided, at the right moment, to upset Russia's plans, and thus prevent a Russian attack.
>
> This is an ideological battle and a struggle of races. Here in this struggle stands National Socialism: an ideology based on the value of our German, Nordic blood. Here stands a world as we have conceived it: beautiful, decent, socially equal, that perhaps, in a few instances, is still burdened by shortcomings, but as a whole, a happy, beautiful world full of culture; this is what Germany is like. On the other side stands a population of 180 million, a mixture of races, whose very names are unpronounceable, and whose physique is such that one can shoot them down without pity and compassion. These animals that torture and ill-treat every prisoner from our side, every wounded man that they come across and do not treat them the way decent soldiers would, you will see for yourself. These people have been welded by the Jews into one religion, one ideology that is called Bolshevism, with the task: now we have Russia, half of Asia, a part of Europe, now we will overwhelm Germany and the whole world.

When you, my men, fight over there in the East, you are carrying on the same struggle, against the same subhumanity, the same inferior races, that at one time appeared under the name of Huns, another time – a thousand years ago at the time of King Henry and Otto I – under the name Magyars, another time under the name of Tartars, and still another time under the name of Genghis Khan and the Mongols. Today they appear as Russians under the political banner of Bolshevism.

Despite the setback on the Finnish front Himmler told Propaganda Minister Joseph Goebbels that the ideological commitment of the *Waffen-SS* troops enabled them 'to hold on in an instant that [they] would normally break down', and in 'the hour of need permits [them] to transcend themselves'.

CENTRAL SECTOR

Things were going better in the central sector. The *Das Reich* SS division had reached Berezino in Belorussia by 2 July, where the *Aufklärungsabteilung* succeeded in holding a bridgehead on the other side of the Berezina River. This allowed 2. *Panzergruppe* under General Heinz Guderian, architect of *blitzkrieg* warfare, to cross and advance towards the Dnieper with *Das Reich* guarding his flank. The *Das Reich* division crossed the river on 14 July, passing Smolensk and reaching the Yelnya River, which it held while the main thrust of the attack turned south towards Comel. It held off attacks of up to 11 divisions with heavy losses. Near breaking point, it was pulled out of the line on 8 August.

On 4 September, Guderian visited the division and ordered SS-*Obergruppenführer* Hausser to attack Sosnitsa. By then the autumn rains had come, turning the roads into seas of mud. Even so, the *Das Reich* division got through and took Sosnitsa after only one day. It continued fighting over the waterlogged terrain until the fall of Kiev on 26 September.

OPERATION TYPHOON

Four days later, Operation Typhoon began. This was the advance on Moscow. *Das Reich* was to be part of Guderian's spearhead. Its first task was to cut the main Smolensk-Moscow highway. The strategic town of Gzhatsk was captured after fierce fighting in the surrounding woods. When the division's *Deutschland* regiment entered it found the bodies of many civilians butchered by the Soviet state police force, the NKVD.

Fighting continued for several days while the Red Army tried to build up forces to retake the town. This was thwarted by determined attacks by the division's *Der Führer* regiment. After that, *Das Reich* continued to advance on Moscow. The closer it got, the more intense the Russians' resistance became. And the weather got worse.

BORODINO

Near the main highway to Moscow, 96 km (60 miles) west of the city, lay the battlefield of Borodino, where the Russians gave Napoleon's *Grande Armée* a bloody nose in 1812. This was such a significant event in Russian history that Stalin decreed that the Germans should suffer a similar fate and he sent his most battle-hardened troops to confront them there. They fell on the *Waffen-SS* with savage fury. German anti-tank guns were found to be useless against the Soviet T-34 tanks, so SS troops resorted to attaching satchel charges to the tracks or to the tanks themselves.

The *Der Führer* regiment took Borodino on 15 October. Next, *Das Reich* was to capture the vital road junction at Mozhaisk. It took it on 18 October after fierce fighting. Then the *Deutschland* regiment ran into two battalions of Mongolian troops near the village of Otyakova, who fought with unparalleled ferocity. Ignoring loses, they charged again and again, only to be cut down by machine-gun fire. The *Waffen-SS* troops held, with heavy loses. By then *Das Reich* had posted nearly 7,000 men killed from a strength of 19,000 at the beginning of Barbarossa.

With the ground now frozen, the division advanced again, but was halted 18 km (11 miles) west of Moscow when 18 divisions of fresh Soviet troops staged a counterattack. The German supply lines had stretched to breaking point. Ammunition was running out fast and, like the *Wehrmacht* troops around them, the *Waffen-SS* men were still dressed in their thin summer uniforms. In what turned out to be the coldest winter of the twentieth century, some froze to death, but their esprit de corps remained undimmed.

TO THE SOUTH

The *Leibstandarte* and the *Wiking* had been drawn up with *XIV Korps* of 1. *Panzergruppe* around Lublin in Poland. They began their advance on 27 June as the *Panzergruppe*'s reserve. The *Leibstandarte* crossed the Vistula River, formerly the Soviet border, on 1 July. Then it held off the Red Army's attempts to sever the main highway at Dubno and Otyka in a battle that lasted several days. Next, it took Moszkov and held the Rovno-Luck line, fending off Soviet attacks.

By this time the *panzers* were advancing so fast that it was difficult for the supporting infantry to keep pace on foot, leaving the German flanks vulnerable. As the *Leibstandarte* was fully motorized, it was used to fill the gaps. It smashed through Soviet defences at Miropol and advanced quickly towards Zhitomir.

The spearhead of the advance was held up by a large Red Army formation, outnumbered until the rest of the division arrived. Kurt Meyer's *Aufklärungsabteilung* moved on quickly to take the key road junction at Kudnov on 8 July. The Red Army counterattacked en masse. There was vicious hand-to-hand fighting, with some German units sustaining more casualties than they had lost in all their previous campaigns.

But the momentum of the German advance was too great to be halted. The *Leibstandarte* went on to take Shepovka and Zhitomir, west of Kiev. Von Rundstedt had planned to take the Ukrainian capital, but

Hitler ordered him to send the 6th Army southeastwards, towards Uman, to cut off Soviet forces engaging the 11th and 17th Armies. Again, the *Leibstandarte* was used to protect the column's flank, fighting off divisions from the Soviet 5th Army. It also helped rescue the beleaguered *16. Panzer-Division* when it was attacked by three Soviet armoured divisions. Uman was captured in late July, along with 100,000 Soviet soldiers.

The *Wiking* division, which had set off on 29 June, advanced through Lemberg and Tarnopol to join up with the main force at Zhitomir. Reaching Byela Tserkovusin at the end of July, it also took part in the encirclement of Soviet forces at Uman on 3 August.

The *Leibstandarte* captured Bubry on 9 August, then took the road junction at Sasselje. The *Aufklärungsabteilung* and field artillery units fought off several ferocious Soviet counterattacks. The division then moved on to the industrial city of Cherson, taking it on 20 August after three days of house-to-house fighting. Dietrich and his men were then sent back to the reserve to rest. Meanwhile, *Wiking* crossed the Dnieper and saw off heavy resistance at Dniepropetrovsk.

The division rejoined the advance in early September as it headed towards the Black Sea. It met stubborn rearguard resistance from Red Army units pulled back into the Crimea. The *Leibstandarte* broke off and turned eastwards towards Rostov-on-Don. On the way, it took Romanovka, Berdyansk and Maripol along the northern coast of the Sea of Azov, in the face of fierce fighting. Moving on into Russia, it took Taganrog on 17 October. Besides killing prisoners of war there, *Einsatzgruppe D* and collaborators rounded up Jews, driving them to a gully at nearby Petrushino where some 1,500 were shot. Other citizens were sent to Germany as forced labour and children were used as forced blood donors.

In the deteriorating weather, the pace slowed. The *Leibstandarte* did not reach Rostov until mid-November. On 17 November, amid heavy snow and plummeting temperatures, the division began an attack with III *Panzer Korps*. Commanding 3. *Kompanie, SS-Hauptsturmführer* Heinrich Springer took the main railway bridge across the Don intact and held it against determined Soviet attacks to recapture it. This earned him a Knight's Cross. Although wounded, he survived the war and died in 2007, aged 92.

With this vital crossing in German hands, the city fell on 20 November. But, again, German supply lines were overstretched. Running short of ammunition, the *Leibstandarte* pulled out of Rostov to shorten the front and consolidate for winter. It were joined in the line by *Wiking*. Behind them came the *Einsatzgruppen*, murdering Jews and other civilians.

THE WINTER OFFENSIVE

The Red Army's Winter Offensive began on 5 December. A million men pushed the Germans back. Hitler refused permission for any strategic withdrawal and ordered his soldiers to defend every inch of the frozen ground, 'digging trenches with howitzer shells if needs be'. When Guderian pointed out that losses from the cold weather outnumbered combat losses he was dismissed, along with von Bock and von Brauchitsch, who were sacked for failing to take Moscow.

During defensive operations from January 1942 to March, when it was withdrawn to France, the *Das Reich* division suffered 4,000 casualties. However, two mixed battalions from the *Deutschland* and *Der Führer* regiments remained behind as a battle group under *SS-Obersturmbannführer* Werner Ostendorff. This too was withdrawn in June. Ostendorff was wounded commanding *Das Reich* in Hungary and died in May 1945.

On 1 June the *SS-Infanterie Standarte Langemarck* joined the division. The Flemish regiment's I *Bataillon* was formed around the division's *Kradschützenbataillon* ('motorcycle battalion'), while II *Bataillon* and its staff came from 4. *SS-Infanterie Standarte*. *Langemarck* took part in the abortive operation to prevent the scuttling of the

French fleet at Toulon on 27 November 1942. While in France, *Das Reich* was refitted as a *panzer-grenadier* division, returning to the Eastern Front in January 1943.

TO THE NORTH

In the north, the Soviet 1st, 11th and 34th Shock Armies smashed through the German lines between Lakes Ilmen and Seliga on 7 January 1942. They also penetrated German positions south of Lake Seliga in an attempt to encircle the whole of the German 16th Army.

The *Totenkopfdivision*'s reconnaissance and pioneer battalions and part of its artillery regiment were rushed to Staraya Russa, south of Lake Ilmen, to hold the road and railway junction there, arriving on 9 January. A few days later two more battalions were sent to Demyansk to bolster the vulnerable southern flank.

Field Marshal von Leeb asked Hitler for permission to make a tactical withdrawal behind the River Lovat. Hitler refused. Von Leeb resigned and General Georg von Küchler replaced him. But there was little he could do. The 16th Army was cut off, along with II and X *Armee Korps*, squeezed into a pocket at Demyansk, where they had to be supplied by air.

The *Totenkopf* units at Staraya Russa held off the Red Army, which then turned south. But on 8 February the 1st Shock Army and the 11th Army closed the encirclement, trapping the *Totenkopfdivision* and five Army divisions – 100,000 men in all. *Totenkopf* split itself into two battle groups, boosting the defences in hard-pressed points. They held out until 22 April, when the siege was lifted and the *Totenkopf* managed to break out.

Totenkopf remained in the front until October, when it was relieved. By then 12,600 of its 17,000 men had been killed or wounded, half of them in the Demyansk pocket. The survivors were sent back to Germany, then to France for rest and refitting. During its battles that winter, 11 officers and men were awarded the Knight's Cross of the Iron Cross. No other *Waffen-SS* division was awarded so many in such a short period.

The first Iron Cross of the campaign was awarded to *SS-Gruppenführer* Paul Hausser for his leadership of *Das Reich*. Like other SS officers, he led from the front, losing an eye during the battle for Yelnya, giving him his distinctive eye patch.

The second was awarded posthumously to *SS-Unterscharführer* Erich Rossner of *SS-Panzerjäger-Abteilung 2*. He singlehandedly knocked out 13 Soviet tanks before being fatally wounded. He died on 30 July 1941.

SS-Sturmmann (Lance Corporal) Fritz Christen of the *Totenkopf-division* was with an anti-tank unit that came under concerted attack. The guns were knocked out one by one and the crews killed. He fought on alone, loading, aiming and firing himself. By the time reinforcements arrived, he had knocked out over 12 guns and more than one hundred infantrymen. He got his Knight's Cross on 24 September 1941. After the war, he spent ten years in a Soviet labour camp, before being returned to Germany where he died in 1995, aged 74.

The Red Army launched an offensive in the south in January 1942. As part of *III Panzer Korps*, the *Leibstandarte* helped halt Soviet incursions near Dniepropetrovsk. The Soviets attacked again in mid-May, pre-empting a German summer offensive, but within a week the Germans had sealed off the Russian salient near Kharkov. The *Leibstandarte* was then withdrawn to Stalino (now Donetsk) in Ukraine for a refit, but when it was feared that the Allies were planning landings in Western Europe it was rushed to France, where it remained for the rest of the year.

In operations on the Eastern Front, the disparagement of the *Waffen-SS* abated. The commander of *III Panzer Korps*, General Eberhard von Mackensen wrote to Himmler, saying:

It will perhaps be of some value to you to hear, from the mouth of that commanding general under whom the *Leibstandarte* has served during this long and difficult campaign and one who is a member of the Army and not the SS, what he and the other divisions think about this unit.

Herr *Reichsführer*, I can assure you that the *Leibstandarte* enjoys an outstanding reputation not only with its superiors, but also among its Army comrades. Every division wishes it had the *Leibstandarte* as its neighbour, as much during the attack as in defence. Its inner discipline, its cool daredevilry, its cheerful enterprise, its unshakable firmness in a crisis (even when things become difficult or serious) – all these are outstanding and cannot be surpassed. In spite of this, the officer corps maintains a pleasant degree of modesty. A genuine elite formation that I am happy and proud to have under my command and, furthermore, one that I sincerely and hopefully wish to retain! This unrestrained recognition was gained by the *Leibstandarte* entirely on the strength of its own achievements and moreover on the basis of its military ability against an enemy whose courage, toughness, numbers and armaments should not be slighted. The aura which naturally surrounds the *Führer*'s Guard would not have sufficed, here at the front, to allow this recognition to fall into its lap.

By mid-November 1942, the *Waffen-SS* had lost 407 officers and 7,930 men killed in action, 816 officers and 26,299 men wounded, 13 officers and 923 men missing, and four officers and 125 men killed in accidents. Despite the high rate of casualties, both Himmler and Hitler were delighted by its performance on the Eastern Front. Between June 1941 and the end of December 1942, three Knight's Crosses had been awarded to *Leibstandarte* personnel, eight to *Das Reich*, eight to *Wiking*, nine to the *Polizeidivision* and two to the SS cavalry brigade.

NEW BRIGADES

Early success in the East caused problems. The Germans had captured huge numbers of Soviet soldiers. If they were not contained in camps, they would take to the forests as partisans, harassing German frontline troops from the rear and disrupting supply lines. However, the *Wehrmacht* could not spare soldiers for guard duty as they were needed for the continued fighting to the east.

Police regiments were sent to Russia to free up soldiers. As Himmler was Chief of Police as well as *Reichsführer-SS*, this was something he organized. Under his auspices, these police regiments also became responsible for security and anti-partisan action, as well as murdering Jews.

Consequently, two new *Waffen-SS* divisions were formed. 7. *SS-Freiwilligen-Gebirgs-Division 'Prinz Eugen'* was initially raised from German-speakers in northern Serbia in 1942. It spent the rest of the year in training and saw no combat. It was named for Prince Eugene of Savoy, a successful general in the army of the Holy Roman Empire at the turn of the eighteenth century. The rest of its name, *'Freiwilligen-Gebirgs-Division'* means 'volunteer mountain division',

8. *SS-Kavallerie-Division 'Florian Geyer'* was centred around the SS cavalry brigade formed in 1941 from the two pre-war *SS-Totenkopf Reiterregiments* ('Rider Regiments'). Florian Geyer was a nobleman who fought on the side of the peasants in the German Peasant War that broke out in 1524. New recruits were *Volksdeutsche* from Romania and Serbia. The brigade was used primarily for *Bandenbekämpfung* – 'bandit-fighting' or anti-partisan actions – and gained a bloodthirsty reputation under *SS-Standartenführer* Herman Fegelein, murdering

13,788 Jews in August 1941 alone, along with another 3,500 civilians.

It was upgraded to divisional status in the autumn of 1942. Command was given to *SS-Gruppenführer* Wilhelm Bittrich after Fegelein was wounded by a sniper. In 1943, command was returned to Fegelein, who became an *SS-Gruppenführer* and married the sister of Hitler's mistress, Eva Braun. Wounded again in October 1943, he was sent to Hitler's headquarters as a liaison officer for Himmler. Two days before Hitler's own death, he ordered the execution of Fegelein for treason when it was discovered that Himmler had tried to make peace overtures to the Allies and Fegelein was caught trying to escape Berlin with large amounts of cash and forged passports.

Escaping prosecution for war crimes in the East, Bittrich was extradited to France, where he served five years for having ordered the execution of 17 members of the French Resistance in Nîmes. He went on to become chairman of HIAG, dying in 1972, aged 92.

CHAPTER SIX

⚡⚡

Foreign Legions

By 1945, there were half a million foreign soldiers in the *Waffen-SS*. They were portrayed as gallant volunteers, idealists bent on defending Western Civilization from the onslaught of Asiatic Bolshevism. However, most were conscripted or coerced into joining.

The largest contingent of non-German SS men were Eastern Europeans. Along with the *Volksdeutsche*, ethnic Germans who had found themselves in other countries when the borders were redrawn at the Versailles Peace Conference, there were Latvians, Estonians, Lithuanians, Ukrainians, Bosnians, Croats, Serbs, Albanian, Hungarians, Romanians, Bulgarians and even some Russians. Those who did volunteer usually did so for narrow nationalistic reasons. The Baltic peoples and the Ukrainians, for example, sought to free their countries from occupation by the Soviet Union. This was ironic, because the Baltic states had been delivered into Soviet hands by a secret protocol to the non-aggression pact signed by Hitler and Stalin in 1939 which had also divided Poland.

Levy of the SS-Freiwilligen-Legion' in Riga, Latvia, 1943.

Some 125,000 foreigners served in the *Waffen-SS*. Around half joined before the war turned irrevocably against Germany, although 60,000 also joined in the last years of the war. Some were Frenchmen and Walloons, who became SS men by default when their units were transferred from the *Wehrmacht* into the *Waffen-SS* in 1943. Others were collaborators who had fled their countries when the Allies arrived. Then there were youths who had been brought to Germany as forced labour and were later persuaded to swap being slaves and become SS soldiers in the hope of improved conditions.

NAZI SYMPATHIZERS

Recruits from Western Europe tended to be Nazi sympathizers, though some pressure was exerted by the Germans on Fascist groups in occupied countries. There were Nazi parties in The Netherlands, Norway and Denmark, along with two parties in Belgium who modelled themselves on the Fascists but were separated along language lines.

In the eyes of the SS, the peoples of Denmark, Norway, The Netherlands and Flanders were seen to be 'Germanic'. Volunteers were offered German citizenship at the end of their service. Himmler said: 'We must attract all the Nordic blood in the world to us, so that never again will Nordic or Germanic blood fight against us.'

However, while the Dutch-speaking inhabitants of Belgium were considered Nordic, the French-speaking Walloons were not, initially, and were passed on to the Army. This was to change after Barbarossa and the high rate of casualties in the *Waffen-SS* which meant it needed all the men it could get.

Some 50,000 Dutch joined the *Waffen-SS*, along with 40,000 Belgians, 20,000 French, 6,000 each from Denmark and Norway and 1,200 from other countries, mainly Switzerland, Sweden and Luxembourg. There were also 1,000 Finns from 1941–3, when Finland and Germany were allies. Early recruits do not seem to have been out to save Europe, or even their home countries, from Bolshevism. Indeed, they signed up when the German-Soviet non-aggression pact was still in force. Most acquired their anti-Communism convictions after witnessing fighting on the Eastern Front, while the Finns and Ukrainians were not fighting Bolshevism, but rather age-old Russian imperialism. However, recruitment did pick up after the invasion of the Soviet Union got underway in June 1941, with volunteers answering Hitler's call for a 'Crusade again Bolshevism' at a time when it looked as though the Red Army was going to be a pushover.

Western recruits were often shunned by their families, even their wives. A study after the war concluded that volunteers sought adventure, better food, money and status, or to escape boredom, prosecution for minor crimes or compulsory labour – or even just to wear the glamorous SS uniform. Few signed up for ideological reasons. Recruiter Gottlob Berger noted that many recruits had criminal records. But despite their lack of moral integrity they made outstanding soldiers.

'We will never be able to prevent men from joining the legions and the *Waffen-SS* who are neither National Socialists nor idealists, and instead take this step for more materialistic reasons,' he wrote. 'That is the way it is everywhere in the world and it was no different in Germany during the *Kampfzeit*' – the 'time of struggle' that brought the Nazis to power in 1933.

Many young people had had their prospects blighted by the Great Depression following the stock market crash of 1929. They saw hope in the miraculous economic revival of Germany under the Nazis, though much of it was based on corruption and kleptocracy; many were also impressed – or possibly scared – by Germany's military might, which at the start of the war had routed the great French Army, the largest in Europe at the time, in a matter of weeks.

Himmler also sought to fulfil his racial fantasies by recruiting exemplary 'Aryan' specimens with offers of land and political prefer-ment in their native countries at the end of the war. This failed. When the *Wiking* SS division went into action in the summer of 1941, less than one third of its men were foreigners from Western Europe.

RACIAL IDEOLOGY

Initially, the recruitment of foreigners required no alteration in Himmler's racial ideology. A camp was set up at Sennheim in Alsace where foreign recruits were given physical and ideological training. Those who wanted to join the *Waffen-SS* took the SS oath which said: 'I swear to you, Adolf Hitler, as *Führer* and Chancellor of the German Reich, that I will be loyal and brave. I pledge obedience unto death to you and those you appoint to lead. So help me God.' After 30 January 1941, foreign-born recruits, with the exception of the *Volksdeutsche*, dropped the 'and Chancellor of the German Reich', leaving only

'Hitler as *Führer*'. After that, they were sent on to their active units for further training.

Recruits were in for a shock when they reached their Spartan barracks in Germany. Discipline was rigid and recruits were bullied by NCOs who abused them over their national origins. Himmler stamped down on this as he was a keen advocate of the recruitment of foreigners and ordered that recruits be handled sympathetically by officers and NCOs of their own nationality.

After 1943, the growing number of non-Germanic recruits forced the SS to tailor its ideological training. Ukrainians were spared lectures on the inferiority of the Slav race, while Muslim Bosnians heard no criticism of organized religion.

As the war went on, there was less time for ideological training. The doctrine was also modified. Foreign recruits were no longer told of the need for a Greater German Reich. Instead, there would be a union of self-governing states where the *Waffen-SS* would be the core of a new European army comprising national contingents from each country, united in their opposition to Bolshevism.

POLITICAL GROUPS

It soon became clear that sizeable numbers of recruits could not be raised in Denmark, Holland, Belgium and Norway without the co-operation of sympathetic local political groups. But as these were, by their very nature, nationalistic, they insisted that their countrymen serve in their own national formations. Initially Hitler was against this, but manpower was needed and he relented.

To bolster the *Wiking* SS division, Gottlob Berger looked to Finland, which had recently fought off an invasion by the Soviet Union in the Winter War from November 1939 to March 1940. Himmler gave Berger permission to start recruiting in February 1940. Negotiations between the German Foreign Office and the Finnish Government allowed him to establish a Finnish Volunteer Battalion. On May 16 Finnish combat veterans arrived in Germany. By the beginning of Barbarossa in June, 400 Finns were serving in the *Waffen-SS*. Further recruiting that year raised the number to 1,000.

As their numbers grew, Finnish volunteers were allowed to serve in their own battalion under Finnish officers. This set a precedent, and in April 1941 Hitler authorized the formation of *SS-Freiwilligen-Standarte 'Nordwest'*, which recruited some 2,500 men from Flanders and The Netherlands. While recruits did not have to meet the SS racial criteria, and so would not be considered SS men, they would be serving with the SS with all its privileges and obligations.

The establishment of a Dutch-Flemish regiment appealed to Anton Mussert, leader of The Netherlands' *Nationaal Socialistische Beweging* (National Socialist Movement), and Staf de Clerq, leader of Belgium's *Vlaamsch Nationaal Verbond*, or VNV (Flemish National Union). They assisted with recruitment. Both favoured an autonomous

Dutch ('Germanic') volunteers from the SS-Standarte 'Nordwest' in training, Spring 1941.

Dutch-Flemish union within a Greater Germanic Reich. The VNV further advocated the break-up of Belgium, with Flanders joining a new 'Greater Netherlands'.

As the *Das Reich* division rolled into Yugoslavia in 1941, SS-*Gruppenführer* Paul Hausser began recruiting there. However, Himmler was not ready to drop his philosophy of the Übermensch – that is that Aryan SS men were Supermen, or 'Overmen'. When Berger suggested forming a Ukrainian volunteer unit with '64 racially suitable and 615 racially unsuitable Ukrainians', Himmler refused. It would be two more years and hundreds of thousands of casualties before a Slav would be able to wear an SS uniform.

While Operation Barbarossa was in the planning, Himmler ordered the recruitment of another 20,000 men. Hitler got the OKW to drop its quotas on SS recruitment and, for the month of May, enlistment would be unlimited. However, the *Wehrmacht* added the proviso that recruits must sign up for 12 years, thinking it would put recruits off. It didn't, as this was considered a mere formality. It was still thought that the war was going to be short. After a quick victory, SS recruiters said they would be stood down. By 9 June, Berger had 22,361 fresh recruits in *Waffen-SS* barracks.

To do this, Berger had taken youths under call-up age, along with men from *Allgemeine SS* – that is, the General SS who were more involved in politics than fighting. But foreign recruitment proved disappointing. On top of the 400 Finns sent to *Wiking*, Berger only managed to muster around 2,000 men from Western Europe.

NATIONAL LEGIONS

After Barbarossa began, Hitler approved the formation of national legions in the occupied territories and from ideologically sympathetic states such as Italy, Spain and Croatia. At a high-level conference in July it was decided that legions of Norwegians, Netherlanders, Swedes, Danes and Flemings would be set up within the *Waffen-SS*, while units of French, Spaniards and Croats would fall under the *Wehrmacht*. This proved popular and hundreds enlisted in the first week.

Before the *SS-Freiwilligen-Verband 'Dänemark'* was even established on 12 July 1941, 500 Danes – almost half from the armed forces – volunteered, despite the opposition of the Danish government, which branded deserting servicemen as traitors and stripped them of their pension rights. Himmler was furious and ordered that their pensions would be paid by the SS. The bill would then be sent to the Danish government which, being under the administration of a German 'protectorate', would have no choice but to pay. As a result, 1,000 recruits volunteered for the *Waffen-SS*.

While recruitment was going on in the Low Countries, Flemings and Netherlanders were transferred from *SS-Freiwilligen-Standarte 'Nordwest'* to form the cores of volunteer legions *Flandern* and *Niederlande*. Norwegian volunteers under army Captain Jørgen Bakke arriving at Kiel were formed into the *Norwegen* legion. In four weeks, the *Waffen-SS* had started four legions. The first 480 Danes under Danish Army Colonel Christian Peder Krhyssing were under training in Germany. The 600 men of *Flandern* were sent for training in Poland, where they were joined by 1,000 volunteers from *Niederlande* under the command of Dutch Army Colonel Gerhard Stroink, though the nominal head was General Hendrik Seyffardt, formerly Chief of the Dutch General Staff.

With such a distinguished figure at its head, the legion attracted so many volunteers that it was thought that a full division could be formed. However, the Germans rejected many officers and NCOs who had no combat experience and replaced them with Germans. Colonel Stroink and 23 of the Dutch officers promptly resigned.

The Flemings fared even worse at the hands of their German trainers, having no Flemish commander to intercede for them. Staf de Clerq sent a list of complaints to Himmler. Recruits had been verbally abused, called 'filthy people', a 'nation of idiots' and a 'race of Gypsies'.

They had also been beaten and threatened with pistols. The promise to Belgian Army officers and NCOs that they would maintain their former rank and status was not honoured. Himmler had to step in again to rectify matters.

Discouraged, the legion had just 875 recruits by the beginning of 1942. Most had been tricked into joining. Five hundred men who had been working in northern France were promised higher wages if they volunteered for labour in Poland. When they arrived, they were told they had actually volunteered for service in the *Waffen-SS*.

Formed around some 400 Flemings that had volunteered for *SS-Freiwilligen-Standarte 'Nordwest'*, the first commander of *SS-Freiwilligen-Standarte 'Flandern'* was *SS-Sturmbannführer* Michael Lippert, a veteran Nazi party member who had been adjutant to Theodor Eicke when he was commandant of Dachau concentration camp. On the Night of the Long Knives, he assisted Sepp Dietrich's *Leibstandarte SS 'Adolf Hitler'* in the arrest and imprisonment of SA commanders and was complicit in the murder of Ernst Röhm – a crime for which he and Dietrich were arrested in 1956 and sentenced to 18 months the following year. The judge at their trial said that Lippert was 'filled with a dangerous and unrepentant fanaticism'. Lippert died in 1969; Dietrich in 1966, both aged 75.

Having completed their brief training in Poland, the Dutch and Flemish legions were set to join the 2nd SS Infantry Brigade in front of Leningrad. Before they left, Himmler issued a directive concerning the status of the national legions. Legionnaires were placed under German military law and SS regulations. Although they were not granted German citizenship, they swore a personal oath to Hitler and were given SS ranks equivalent to those they had been awarded in their national armies. They were not officially SS men, though. While they wore SS uniforms a national emblem replaced the SS runes. Nevertheless, they received regular SS pay and compensation for their dependents if they were wounded or killed. And while they would normally serve in their national formations under their own officers, they could be seconded into other SS formations.

The *Niederlande* legion was sent to the Eastern Front in January 1942 to hold the area north of Lake Ilmen. After weeks of ferocious fighting, the legion mounted a counterattack, but by March it had been beaten back to its start line with heavy losses. Losing 80 per cent of its strength, it was commended by the *Wehrmacht* for its fighting spirit.

In the autumn of 1941, *Flandern* was sent to the northern sector of the Eastern Front near Leningrad. Early the following year, it held off heavy assaults near Novgorod. In March, it went on the offensive, but suffered crippling losses. Nevertheless, it was kept in the line until joining the reserve in February 1943.

Although the two divisions from the Low Countries were already engaged on the Eastern Front, the Danes and Norwegians were nowhere near combat ready. Himmler ordered *SS-Sturmbannführer* Friedrich-Wilhelm Krüger, who was responsible for mass murder in Poland and atrocities in Yugoslavia, to investigate. He concluded the problem was that Danish Army *Legion-Obersturmbannführer* Krhyssing and his deputy *Sturmbannführer* Thor Jörgensen were anti-Nazis. Krhssying was replaced by *SS-Sturmbannführer* Christian Frederik von Schalburg, a former National Youth Leader of the Danish Nazi Party who had won an Iron Cross serving in the *SS-Panzer Division* 'Wiking'. Krhssying retrained as an artillery officer and served with the *Totenkopf* and *Wiking* divisions. As *SS-Brigadeführer*, Krhyssing became the highest-ranking foreigner in the *Waffen-SS*. After the war, he served two years in prison for his membership of the SS. His two sons were killed fighting for the Germans on the Eastern Front.

Meanwhile, Krüger later took command of the *Nord* SS division, then 5. *SS-Gebirgs Korps*, and committed suicide at the end of the war.

Weeks after von Schalburg took over, the *Dänemark* legion was sent to the Eastern Front as a replacement unit in the *Totenkopf* SS division. Schalburg was killed during its first action in June 1942 and was buried with full military honours. Himmler posthumously promoted him to *Obersturmbannführer*. He was replaced by *SS-Obersturmbannführer* Knud Børge Martinsen, another former Danish army officer and member of the Nazi Party. He was executed by firing squad for two murders in 1949.

By August 1942, *Dänemark* was down to just 22 per cent of its unit strength. It was withdrawn and sent home to Denmark for rest and recuperation. Its home-coming parade was met by jeering crowds.

The Germans also had problems with Jørgen Bakke, the first commander of the *Norwegen* legion, whose 1,200 recruits were divided into two battalions – *Viken* and *Viking*. He was quickly replaced by *Legion-Sturmbannführer* Arthur Qvist. He remained its commander until its disbandment in March 1943 and became the first Norwegian to win the Iron Cross. After the war, Qvist spent eight years in prison. Bakke won an Iron Cross, later serving with the *Wiking* division.

The Norwegians joined the other national legions in the northern sector of the Eastern Front, around Leningrad. By March 1942, *Norwegen* had all but been annihilated. Recruitment in Norway slowed and *Norwegen's* remnants joined those of *Dänemark* in the 1st SS Infantry Brigade, who went on to fight alongside the 2nd SS Infantry Brigade. Badly depleted, it returned to Norway in March 1943, where it was disbanded.

PROMISES NOT KEPT

The national legions were supposed to have been kept separate from the Germanic formations in the *Waffen-SS*. However, recruitment stemmed the manpower available for the *Wiking* division and by mid-1943 the legions and the Germanic SS had been merged.

There was also discontent among the volunteers. Again, foreign officers who had been told that they would retain their rank found themselves serving as enlisted men. Some were discharged and sent home without explanation. Finnish NCOs who were veterans of the Russo-Finnish War were not allowed to progress beyond the rank of private. They found themselves commanded by Germans who had no combat experience and they threatened to shoot their German officers the first time they were sent into action.

Men who had been told that they would serve in formations with their compatriots found themselves in German units. Nine Danes with just four weeks' training were sent to the *Das Reich* division and were killed in action soon after arriving. Danes and Norwegians who had signed up for just one year's service in the *Wiking* division were not released at the end of their enlistment. On leave, some took the opportunity to slip across the border into neutral Sweden. A Dane and a Norwegian serving in the *Nordland* regiment of the *Wiking* SS division defected to the Soviets in March 1942, the first recorded incident of a defection from the *Waffen-SS*.

Foreign recruits were not treated well by their German *Waffen-brüder* ('brothers-in-arms'). No allowance was made for their inability to speak or understand German. The well indoctrinated German SS officers assumed that foreign volunteers were committed Nazis and would therefore suffer any ill treatment out of idealism. But many were nationalists who were more willing to put their trust in Germany than Britain and thought that Germany was going to win. They believed in the superiority of the German system – until they experienced it first-hand. Even committed Norwegian Nazis became disillusioned.

The problem was that recruiting was done by Berger's *SS-Hauptamt*, the SS Main Office. But once the recruits had taken their service oath, they came under the authority of the *SS-Führungshauptamt*, the SS Leadership Main Office under *SS-Obergruppenführer* Hans Jüttner, which dealt with administrative matters. They considered the foreigners as so many bodies that needed to be trained, equipped and sent to the front as quickly as possible. After the war, Jüttner was sentenced to ten years, serving four. He went on to testify in the trial of Adolf Eichmann.

Berger made a number of recommendations to Himmler, who implemented them. Men whose enlistments had expired were released.

Native officers in foreign units were increased and foreign recruits were sent to the SS officer academy at Bad Tölz. German officers sent to command foreign units were given a two-week orientation course conducted by specialists from the *SS-Hauptamt*.

Somewhat placated, the Finnish authorities allowed the 1,180 men on the Finnish Volunteer Battalion to fight with the *Wiking* SS division. But the unceremonious discharge of a Swedish officer had discouraged them from volunteering. Generally, recruitment fell below the level needed to cover the losses sustained in battle. As a result, foreign nationals had to be regrouped into larger formations.

The core of this would be the *Nordland* SS division, which Hitler had authorized at the end of 1942 as the first major expansion of the *Waffen-SS*. The 650 survivors of the *Dänemark* legion became part of *SS-Panzer-Grenadier-Regiment 'Danmark'* – using the native spelling. The 1,700-strong *Niederlande* legion became the nucleus of *SS Panzer-Grenadier-Regiment 'Nederland'* – again using the native spelling. And the *SS-Panzer-Grenadier-Regiment 'Norge'* was formed around the remaining 600 men from the *Norwegen* legion.

The three regiments of *Nordland* were filled out with new recruits from Germanic lands, transfers from the *Wiking* division and native Germans. Meanwhile, *Flandern* was broken up and its men sent to other *Waffen-SS* units. A further expansion of the *Waffen-SS* took place in the last two years of the war as things went badly for Germany. Its numbers were swelled by collaborators who feared not just the Allied invaders but also resistance movements at home.

By the end of 1943, the *Nederland* regiment had been pulled out of the *Nordland* division to form an independent brigade, leaving *Nordland* a German-Scandinavian formation. A reconstituted Flemish formation, the *SS-Freiwilligen-Sturmbrigade 'Langemarck'*, was enlarged with transfers from the French Volunteer Regiment and the Walloon Legion already serving with the *Waffen-SS*.

As the war drew to a close, these were given divisional status – though not the manpower – as 23. *SS-Freiwilligen-Panzer-Grenadier-Division 'Nederland'*, 27. *SS-Freiwilligen-Panzer-Grenadier-Division 'Langemarck'*, 28. *SS-Freiwilligen-Panzer-Grenadier-Division 'Wallonien'* and *Waffen-Grenadier-Division der SS 'Charlemagne'*.

THE *WALLONIEN* DIVISION

When Germany occupied Belgium in 1940, the Flemish half of the population was considered Germanic and was eligible to join the *Waffen-SS*, while the French-speaking Walloons were only considered suitable for the *Wehrmacht*. However, a far-right party – the Rexists – flourished in Wallonia. Both nationalist and Catholic, it supported Germany's attack on the 'Godless' Soviet Union in 1941.

When Germany called for a 'Crusade against Bolshevism', more than a thousand Walloons followed Léon Degrelle, leader of the *Parti Rexiste*, to volunteer. Degrelle was offered a commission in the Walloon volunteer force. He declined as he had no military training and said he was happy to learn the art of warfare in the ranks.

The volunteers were sent for training in Poland in August 1941, joining the German Army's order of battle as *373 Infanterie Bataillon*. They honed their skills in anti-partisan operations before being sent to the front in February 1942. Degrelle quickly won himself the Iron Cross First and Second Class, and was commissioned as a lieutenant in May 1942.

To replace losses in heavy fighting on the Don and in the Caucasus, the lower age limit for volunteers was dropped and the upper limit raised. By May 1943, *373 Infanterie Bataillon*'s strength stood at 1,600. Always eager to expand the *Waffen-SS*, Himmler co-opted them as the *SS-Sturmbrigade 'Wallonien'* in June and they were attached to the *Wiking* division on the southern sector of the front.

In January they were involved in the Battle of Korsun–Cherkassy, where some 60,000 Germans were caught in a pocket by the advancing

Red Army in Ukraine. The breakout was costly, leaving the *Wallonien* with just 632 men. When the brigade's commanding officer was killed, Degrelle took command and was awarded the Knight's Cross of the Iron Cross.

After regrouping, the brigade was sent back in action in Estonia in the Battle of Narva in July 1944, again sustaining heavy losses. The brigade was then upgraded as 28. *SS-Freiwilligen-Panzer-Grenadier-Division 'Wallonien'*, though it was only a division on paper, never gaining full strength.

Degrelle was personally awarded the Oakleaves to his Knight's Cross by Hitler, along with the prestigious Close Combat Clasp given for 75 days of hand-to-hand fighting. He later claimed Hitler told him: 'You are truly unique in history. You are a political leader who fights like a soldier. If I had a son, I would want him to be like you.'

The division returned to the front in Estonia in January 1945, with Degrelle promoted *SS-Obersturmbannführer*. With 700 men left, it was evacuated to Denmark. Degrelle ordered his men to make for the Baltic port of Lübeck to surrender to the British. He headed for Norway, where he commandeered a Heinkel He 111 and flew to Spain. Attempts to extradite him failed and he was sentenced to death *in absentia*. Asked years later if he had any regrets about the war, he said: 'Only that we lost!'

THE *CHARLEMAGNE* DIVISION

With France under German control, a French volunteer force, the *Légion des Volontaires Français*, was raised in 1941. Designated *Infanterie Regiment 638*, it was sent to the Eastern Front with the German 7th Infantry Division during the advance on Moscow. After suffering heavy losses, it was transferred to anti-partisan duties in Belorussia and Ukraine. In July 1944 it was returned to the central sector where it proved its worth, but again sustained heavy casualties. The remnants were attached to 4. *SS-Polizei-Panzer-Grenadier-Division* until it was disbanded.

Meanwhile the *SS-Freiwilligen-Sturmbrigade 'Frankreich'* was formed in 1943. The first 800 volunteers were trained in Alsace, while some 30 French officers were sent to the *SS-Junkerschule* at Bad Tölz in Bavaria and 100 NCOs to the *Unterschulen*. Other French volunteers were temporarily attached to 18. *SS-Freiwilligen-Panzer-Grenadier-Division 'Horst Wessel'*, which had also seen fierce combat against the Red Army.

It was then decided to gather all the French volunteers together as 33. *Waffen-Grenadier-Division der SS 'Charlemagne'*. This also included personnel from the French colonies in Indo-China and one volunteer from Japan. It was also said several French Jews joined to elude detection.

Early in 1945, it was sent to the front in Pomerania where, heavily outnumbered by the Red Army, it was smashed in two. One group tried to make a fighting withdrawal, but was virtually wiped out. Another made it to the Baltic coast and was evacuated to Denmark, then to Neustrelitz in Germany. There, the divisional commander *SS-Brigadeführer* Gustav Krukenberg released the men from their oath of allegiance. Nevertheless, while 700 men stayed in Neustrelitz, 500 volunteered to join Hitler's last stand in Berlin.

Finally reduced to around 30 men, some surrendered to the Red Army while others escaped the encirclement to reach the Allies. Twelve who had been turned over to French authorities by the US Army were shot as traitors. *Haupsturmführer* Henri Joseph Fenet, winner of the Knight's Cross, was returned to France by the Soviets. Convicted as a collaborator, he was sentenced to 20 years' hard labour.

THE *LANDSTORM NEDERLAND*

The Dutch also had a home guard unit, the *Landwacht Nederland*, formed in March 1943 using conscripts. Its control passed to the SS in October 1943 and the *Landwacht* became *Landstorm*. This joined the *Waffen-SS* proper in November 1944, bolstered by fresh recruiting by the SS in The Netherlands and members of the youth movement of the NSB, the Dutch Nazi Party.

In March 1945, this became 33. *Waffen-Grenadier-Division der SS 'Landstorm Nederland'*. It wore an armband with *Landstorm Nederland* on it, a collar patch showing a flaming grenade and a sleeve shield in the Dutch colours of orange with white and blue stripes.

Never reaching the strength of more than a brigade, the division fought a few skirmishes before the German surrender in May. Its morale suffered when it faced the Free-Dutch *Koninklijke Nederlandse Brigade 'Prinses Irene'*. Reluctant to fight their fellow countrymen, some of whom were their own relatives, several troops in the *Landstorm Nederland* deserted.

A plot to assassinate several officers and surrender was leaked, and the responsible men were court-martialled and shot. Other division members were involved in atrocities. After surrendering to the British, *Landstorm Nederland* survivors were imprisoned as collaborators, though several were murdered in acts of revenge.

OTHER RECRUITS

The Fascist government in Spain sent its Blue Division to support Operation Barbarossa. It saw action in the Battle of Krasny Bor outside Leningrad in February 1943. When things began to turn decisively against the Germans, it was ordered home in November. But many of the most vehemently anti-Communist division soldiers refused and joined the *Waffen-SS*. They formed *SS-Freiwillingen-Kompanie (spanische)* 101 and *SS-Freiwillingen-Kompanie (spanische)* 102, and took part in the Battle of Berlin. Those taken by the Red Army were kept prisoner until 1954.

Swedes also fought in the *Waffen-SS*, but not enough of them to form a separate unit. They were concentrated in 3. *Kompanie SS Aufklärungs Abteilung* 11, part of the *Nordland* division. This company became known as the *'Swedenzug'*.

More than 20 Swedes graduated from the *SS-Junkerschule* in Bad Tölz. Some served in the *Wiking* division, others in the *SS-Kriegsberichter 'Kurt Eggers'* as war correspondents.

THE BRITISH FREE CORPS

The British Free Corps was a unit of the *Waffen-SS* comprising British and Dominion prisoners of war recruited by the Nazis. In all there seem to have been around 60 members, though some only served for a few days and its strength never seems to have risen above 27.

The BFC was the brainchild of John Amery, son of Leo Amery, secretary of India in Churchill's cabinet. An admirer of National Socialism, John Amery remained in Vichy France after the armistice. He gave pro-Nazi speeches in French in Paris and found his way to Berlin, where he suggested forming a British anti-Bolshevik legion. Inspired by the collaborationist *Légion des Volontaires Français*, which later formed the core of the *Waffen-Grenadier-Division der SS 'Charlemagne' (französische Nr.1)*, he began recruiting for the 'British Legion of St George' in prisoner of war camps, claiming he could recruit a brigade of 1,500 fighting men. The German authorities did not think this was realistic, but could see the propaganda value of even a small British unit.

In months of recruiting, Amery came up with only four volunteers: an elderly academic named Logio, Maurice Tanner, Oswald Job and Kenneth Berry, a 17-year-old deckhand on the SS *Cymbeline*, which had been sunk. Logio was released, while Job was recruited by German intelligence and trained as a spy. He was caught while trying to get into England and hanged in March 1944. Amery ended up with two recruits and only Berry would actually join what was later called the BFC. Meanwhile, the *Waffen-SS* decided it could do without Amery's services.

The Nazis then began their own recruitment drive by creating two 'holiday camps' near Berlin, where English-speaking guards would

John Amery, creator of the British Free Corps, and his wife.

gather information about likely recruits among their fellow prisoners of war. They put Quartermaster Sergeant John Brown in charge. A former member of the British Union of Fascists, he had been captured at Dunkirk. He seized the opportunity to become a double agent.

Also in the camp was Thomas Haller Cooper, another member of the BUF who called himself Boettcher, the German for 'cooper'. His mother was German and he had been visiting Germany in 1939 when war was declared. He joined the *Waffen-SS*, serving in the *Leibstandarte* and the *Totenkopf* infantry training battalion. Posted to the Eastern Front, he boasted of having committed atrocities against Soviet PoWs, Polish civilians and Jews. Injured while serving with the *SS-Polizeidivision* he received the Wounded Badge in Silver, the only Briton to be awarded a German combat decoration.

Then there was Roy Courlander, who had been captured while serving with the New Zealand Army in Greece. His mother was English and his father a Lithuanian Jew. Nevertheless, he made vehement anti-

Soviet propaganda broadcasts before arriving at the BFC recruiting camp.

When 200 British PoWs turned up at the camp Cooper and Courlander tried to recruit them, while Brown tried to subvert the exercise by performing a double bluff, to see who was really susceptible to Nazi influence. Out of the first batch, they only managed to recruit one man, Vivian Minchin, a merchant seaman from the SS *Empire Ranger* that had been sunk off the coast of Norway. A bombing raid damaged the camp before a second batch of prisoners arrived. Meanwhile, Francis George MacLardy of the Royal Army Medical Corps, who had been captured in Belgium, and Edwin Martin of the Canadian Essex Scottish Regiment, captured at Dieppe in 1942, arrived bringing the strength of the Legion of St George to seven.

A new camp was set up at Luckenwalde, where the Germans had decided to try and recruit freshly captured prisoners who would be disorientated, rather than men who had settled into months or years in captivity. First, they were maltreated, then interviewed by Germans pretending to be Americans, or cajoled by men masquerading as other British PoWs. If that failed, they were threatened with solitary confinement. Blackmail and coercion were also used to ensnare volunteers. This garnered another 14, including Trooper John Wilson of 3 Commando and members of the Argyll and Sutherland Highlanders. However, the recruits were told that they were going to join thousands of their countrymen, only to discover that there were only a handful of Fascists and others who were swinging the lead. Meanwhile, Edward Martin had been causing disruption and, by December 1943, the number of men in the Legion of St George went down to eight.

SS-Hauptsturmführer Walter Roepke, formerly with the *Allgemeine SS* and the *Wiking* division, was put in charge. He felt that the Legion of St George sounded too religious. Himmler suggested the British Legion, but that name had already been taken by the veterans'

Kenneth Berry and Alfred Minchin, two early recruits to the BFC.

organization started after World War I. Eventually Roepke came up with the name British Free Corps, although the name *Britisches Freikorps* was sometimes used in correspondence. His aim was to swell the numbers to 30, so that they could be commissioned as an infantry platoon and go into action. Under pressure from the recruits, he made certain concessions. The BFC would be under British command, when a suitable British officer could be found. They would not have to get the SS blood-group tattoo, which was supposed to give SS men preferential treatment in hospital but, after the war, made them easy to identify, even when they had had the tattoo surgically removed. Nor did they have to swear an oath of loyalty to Hitler, nor would they be subject to German military law and they would not be used in any action against British or Commonwealth forces or used for intelligence gathering. But they would receive pay equal to the German soldiers of their rank. Meanwhile, Roepke put in an order for 800 SS uniforms with BFC insignia to the SS clothing department. They had three lions on the collar patches, a cuff band with 'British Free Corps' on it and a Union Flag arm badge. This caused consternation. The German eagle was on the left sleeve with the Union Flag under it. 'Look, the eagle is shitting on the flag,' said one recruit. Eventually, permission had to be sought from Himmler to switch the Union flag to the right sleeve.

Private Thomas Freeman of 7 Commando and Layforce, a precursor of the SAS, arrived. He joined, hoping to sabotage the unit and, possibly, escape. When ranks were assigned, he was made senior NCO. He set about trying to set members against each other. The men were then sent back to the PoW camps they had originally come from to recruit others, but only managed to recruit six new faces. Two of these were John Leister, the son of a German whose family had Nazi ties, and Eric Pleasants, a former member of the BUF. Both held pacifist views and had been sent as agricultural workers to Jersey. When the islands were occupied by the Germans, they tried to escape with 'triple cross agent' Eddie Chapman. Interned, they had joined the BFC in the hope of getting access to better food, alcohol and women.

Successive recruiting drives got the strength up to 23. Fearing that it might make the crucial 30 and they would be sent into action, Freeman and another man got 14 members to sign a letter requesting they be sent back to their prisoner of war camps. Freeman and the other instigator were charged with mutiny and sent to a penal *stalag*. Freeman escaped, reached Soviet lines and was repatriated in March 1945.

Wilson had lied about his rank when captured and was now made senior NCO, while Cooper tried to instil SS-style discipline. This did not go down well with the lackadaisical Brits. Four more recruits arrived. Three had been coerced into joining. One had made his German girlfriend pregnant, a capital offence at the time. Another's liaison with a German woman had been discovered by the Gestapo. Then there was Lieutenant William Shearer, the only officer to join the BFC. He had been recruited from a mental hospital as a potential commander. Not only did Shearer refuse to put on the BFC uniform, he would not even leave his room. After a few weeks, he was returned to the mental hospital, then repatriated on medical grounds.

Following the success of the D-Day landings, BFC recruits saw the writing on the wall. Eight were sent to SS punishment camps for insubordination and the theft of a pistol. Nevertheless, recruitment was stepped up and *SS-Sturmbannführer* Vivian Stranders joined as second in command of the BFC. Originally British, he had taken German nationality when he joined the Nazi Party in 1932. After war began, he was posted to the *Waffen-SS*, which used him as an expert on British affairs.

MacLardy left the BFC to join the *Waffen-SS* medical unit. Courlander joined the war correspondent unit *SS-Standarte 'Kurt Eggers'*, named for the former editor of the SS magazine *Das Schwarze Korps* killed outside Kharkov in 1943 and manned by volunteers skilled in writing in German and foreign languages. Americans Peter Delaney and Martin Monti were members, along with Swedes Gösta Borg, Sten Eriksson, Hans-Caspar Kreuger, Carl Svensson and Thorkel Tillmann.

Pilot Officer Railton Freeman, who wrote an article for Goebbels' newspaper *Der Angriff* (The Attack) under his own name, and BFC men Walter Purdy, John Leister and Francis Maton also joined. Removing their BFC insignia, Courlander and a companion managed to board a train bound for Brussels with a Flemish *Waffen-SS* unit and hand themselves over to the British. However, two more men joined after having liaisons with German women.

In October 1944, the BFC was sent to the *Waffen-SS* Pioneer School in Dresden to be trained as combat engineers. Members were instructed on clearing minefields, demolition and the use of heavy weapons. Issued with rifles, steel helmets, camouflage uniforms and gas masks, they were trained in the use of machine guns, flamethrowers and explosives, and drilled into physical shape. BFC men were even assigned guard duty. However, all attempts to fashion the BFC into a fighting unit were abandoned when Stranders successfully ousted Roepke, replacing him with *SS-Obersturmführer* Walther Kuhlich, who had been wounded during his service with *Das Reich* and was unfit for frontline duty.

Cooper was accused of anti-Nazi acts by other BFC men. He was returned to *Leibstandarte SS 'Adolf Hitler'* as a military policeman. Wilson was now in charge of recruiting. Although he was more interested in womanizing, he tried to get men who had left the BFC to return as he considered it a softer option. Meanwhile, Pleasants wooed Annelise, Kuhlich's secretary, marrying her in February 1945.

While training for the Eastern Front resumed, morale slumped, with men getting drunk and going AWOL. Five more recruits joined, including two South Africans, taking the number up to 27. Two had wanted to join the *Totenkopf* division until they were swayed by Kuhlich. Then six Maoris volunteered, which would have put the unit numbers over the magic 30, but they were rejected on the grounds that the SS was a 'whites-only' organization.

While Wilson was away, Hugh Cowie, a Gordon Highlander, took over as senior NCO. He had been captured in France in 1940. After attempting to escape, he had been threatened with court martial, but joined the BFC instead. With four other men, he headed east, hoping to make contact with the incoming Soviets. On board the train they removed their insignia, but were betrayed to the Gestapo.

During the bombing of Dresden in February 1945, more members of the BFC tried to escape, but were double-crossed by the girlfriend of one of them. The entire BFC was arrested, but two managed to mingle with PoWs who were being marched westwards and made their escape. The rest were taken to Berlin. As the Allies closed in, a sympathetic officer provided three of them with British uniforms. Another, who had a girlfriend with connections to the SS-Standarte 'Kurt Eggers', managed to get transferred. Pleasants, who had been an amateur boxer before the war, put on exhibition bouts with former heavyweight champion Max Schmeling.

Kuhlich gave the rest of the BFC a choice: fight or be sent to an isolation camp. They were sent to join the III 'Germanic' SS Panzer Korps, taking off their BFC insignia on the way. Billeted outside Stettin, they were shelled. There was only one casualty – a man who came down with a severe case of gonorrhoea and had to be sent to a military hospital. The rest were given a half-track and an amphibious vehicle and assigned to the armoured reconnaissance battalion SS-Panzer-Aufklärungsabteilung 11 of the Nordland division. They spent a month on the front line.

Cooper was then serving with the III 'Germanic' SS Panzer Korps and took SS-Obergruppenführer Felix Steiner in to inspect the BFC. Finding it of dubious combat value, it was pulled from the line – Steiner was also concerned with the post-war legal consequences of using PoWs in action, a clear violation of the Geneva Conventions.

The BFC then returned to Berlin, where its members tried to locate their Red Cross parcels to which they were entitled as they were still, technically, PoWs. But it was at this moment that they discovered they had an officer ready to lead them back into action. This was *SS-Hauptsturmführer* Douglas Berneville-Claye, a.k.a. Lord Charlesworth, a notorious bigamist and conman, resplendent in the uniform of the *SS-Panzer Korps*. Having been drummed out of the RAF, he had talked his way into the SAS. Captured in North Africa, he had been removed from *Oflag 79* for his own safety as a suspected informer. Cooper was not impressed with Berneville-Claye's credentials. When he came under suspicion, Berneville-Claye commandeered a car, taking one of the BFC men as a driver. They then drove west and surrendered to the Allies.

How much action individual BFC men saw is not clear. Wilhelm 'Bob' Rossler went into action with the *Norland* division during the Battle of Berlin. It is thought that Ron Courlander was also there and put a Soviet tank out of action. The rest of the BFC men accompanied Steiner when he headed west to surrender to the British. Meanwhile, Cowie and his fellow would-be escapees seized control of their isolation camp. Heavily armed, they made their way west and surrendered to the US Ninth Army at Schwerin.

Amery, Cooper and Purdy stood trial for high treason alongside the propagandist William Joyce, popularly known as 'Lord Haw-Haw'. Amery and Joyce were hanged. Cooper and Purdy's sentences were commuted to life imprisonment. Cooper was released in 1953; Purdy the following year. The rest were dealt with under military law. MacLardy was sentenced to life, reduced on appeal to 15 years. Cowie was sentenced to 15 years and released after seven. Wilson got ten years, while Berry, the first recruit, served just nine months. Courlander was court-martialled by the New Zealand forces, sentenced to 15 years and served seven. Freeman successfully defended himself on all charges, and was acquitted. Berneville-Claye was acquitted due to lack of evidence and served another year in the army before being discharged for theft.

In mid-1946, MI5 discovered that three former BFC members, who had been demobilized, had escaped punishment. Rather than recalling them to service to face a court-martial, they were summoned to MI5 headquarters and told not to do it again.

As the Red Army closed in, Pleasants and his wife escaped from Berlin though the sewers. He claimed to have killed two Russian soldiers with his bare hands along the way. Pleasants and his wife made their way to her parents in Dresden, in Soviet-occupied East Germany. Pleasants then joined a circus as a strong man, but the couple were arrested in 1946. Although he confessed to being member of the SS, the Cold War was underway and Pleasants was force to admit spying for the UK. He was sentenced to 25 years in a labour camp in Arctic Russia, but was released in 1953, after the death of Stalin. His wife, Annelise, was never heard of again.

INDIAN LEGION

While the British Empire fought as one entity for the Allies, there was some dissent. The movement for Indian independence was already underway when World War II began and the Nazis sought to take advantage of it.

An Indian Legion was first raised by the German Army in April 1943 as the *Infanterie-Regiment 950 (indisches)* and manned by Indian soldiers taken prisoner while serving with the British in North Africa. It was taken over by the SS in November 1944, becoming the *Indische Freiwilligen Legion der Waffen-SS* (the *Waffen-SS* Free India Legion). It was the idea of Indian independence leader Subhas Chandra Bose, who sought the help of Imperial Japan and Nazi Germany to free India from British rule. Bose hoped to recruit 100,000 men, but volunteers never exceeded 3,000. They swore allegiance to Hitler as well as Bose himself.

While it was unlikely that the Free Indian Legion would be strong enough to achieve independence on its own, Bose envisaged an Indo-German invasion of British India across the Northwest Frontier. However, the German defeat at El-Alamein in 1942 and Stalingrad in 1943 made any attack from Persia (now Iran) or through the Caucasus impossible. Bose headed for Japan. With its help, he managed to raise a force of 60,000 men to march on India. Fighting alongside the Japanese, more than half were killed. The rest surrendered, while Bose died in a plane crash in August 1945.

The Free India Legion was posted to The Netherlands and, at the time of the Normandy landings, was stationed at Lacanau near Bordeaux in France to reinforce the Atlantic Wall. The men were not happy with the change of command when they were seconded into the *Waffen-SS*. They saw action against French and Allied forces, as well as the French Resistance when they were pulled back to Germany, suffering several casualties.

The 9th Company of the 2nd Battalion saw action in Italy, facing the British V Corps and the Polish II Corps in spring 1944. This company was later used for anti-partisan operations until surrendering to Allied forces in April 1945.

With the Third Reich on the brink of collapse, the remainder of the Free India Legion sought to escape to Switzerland, but was captured by American and French forces and handed over to the British. The men were shipped back to India, where several stood trial for treason. This proved unpopular in a country on the brink of independence. Some served short prison sentences before being released.

Hitler never took seriously the foreign legions that fought for Germany, accusing them of taking weapons that could be used by Germans. He was particularly dismissive of the Indians.

'The Indian Legion is a joke,' he said. 'There are Indians that can't kill a louse, and would prefer to allow themselves to be devoured. They certainly aren't going to kill any Englishmen... I imagine that if one were to use the Indians to turn prayer wheels or something like that they would be the most indefatigable soldiers in the world. But it would be ridiculous to commit them to a real blood struggle... The whole business is nonsense. If one has a surplus of weapons, one can permit oneself such amusements for propaganda purposes. But if one has no such surplus, it's simply not justifiable.'

CHAPTER SEVEN

𝕊𝕊

Recruitment in the East

I n the autumn of 1941, everything was going well for the Germans. Kiev was in German hands, along with most of Ukraine. Leningrad was under siege. The final push on Moscow was underway and German tanks were entering Rostov, opening the way to the oil-rich Caucasus. Then the winter set in.

Stalin called in the combat-hardened Siberian troops of the Far Eastern Command. They had been fighting the Japanese along the Manchurian border since 1932. However, Richard Sorge, a German double agent based in Japan, reported that Japan's next attack would be to the south, not along the borders with the Soviet Union and its client state Mongolia. This freed up the Siberian troops for the defence of Moscow.

They were trained and equipped for winter warfare and pushed the Germans back in what was to be their first major setback in World War II. Hitler purged his top generals. Dismissing von Brauchitsch, Hitler took over as Commander-in-Chief of the Army himself. While the *Wehrmacht* advised withdrawal to a winter defensive line, the

Waffen-SS followed Hitler's order for 'fanatical resistance' regardless of the cost in lives. This strengthened the position of the *Waffen-SS* in Hitler's eyes, while depleting its manpower.

Although the Soviets had sustained higher casualties, the German Army still lost over a million men – some 35 per cent of its strength. Over 200,000 were dead, almost ten times as many were killed in the Western campaign in 1940. *Waffen-SS* casualties were much higher proportionally. By November 1941, the *Das Reich* SS division had lost 60 per cent of its strength, including 40 per cent of its officers. By 10 February 1942, it had lost 10,690 men, not including officers.

Altogether, the *Waffen-SS* had lost over 43,000 men in the Soviet counteroffensive. All the reserves had been used to keep frontline units up to combat strength. As attempts to recruit Germanic volunteers in Western Europe had run into difficulties, the eyes of the recruiters turned East. There was still the *Volksdeutsche* they could call on. By mid-1944 over 150,000 ethnic Germans were serving in the *Waffen-SS*.

The first push came in Romania, then a somewhat unwilling ally of Germany. Through his son-in-law, the political leader in Transylvania Andreas Schmidt, Berger secured over 1,000 recruits, who were transported to Germany under the guise of industrial and agricultural workers.

With the fall of Yugoslavia, recruiting started there and, on its way back to Germany, the *Das Reich* division picked up another 600 recruits from Romania. With partisan activities increasing, German units, badly needed in Russia, were being held down in the ethnically divided Yugoslavia, so Hitler approved the creation of a new SS division of ethnic Germans, formed around an existing SS-led militia, the *Selbstschultz*, comprising Serbian *Volksdeutsche*. This was to be 7. *SS-Freiwilligen-Gebirgs-Division 'Prinz Eugen'*. However, recruitment was poor, so Berger ordered his recruiting teams to employ stronger methods. This eventually led to straightforward conscription in Serbia in 1942.

There were legal complaints, but Berger shrugged them off. 'Nobody cares what we do down there with our racial Germans... to proclaim compulsory service in Croatia and Serbia is impossible under public law. And it is not at all necessary either, for when a racial group is under a moderately good leadership everybody volunteers all right, and those who do not volunteer get their houses broken into pieces.'

Berger then went on to Hungary, another German ally. He secured permission from the government there to recruit among the ethnic Germans. Between March and May 1942, SS recruiters manage to ship 16,527 men to Germany. In all some 42,000 Hungarian *Volksdeutsche* served in the *Waffen-SS*.

Again, *SS-Gruppenführer* Jüttner at the *SS-Führungshauptamt* complained that he was being saddled with entirely unsuitable replacements. The Hungarian recruits had plainly not been seen by doctors or SS officers, he said, 'because their physical disabilities are so obvious that a soldier could never declare these men fit for military service'. There were men with tuberculosis, epilepsy and other physical disabilities. They were not volunteers, but had been persuaded to join the transports by false pretences or by force. There were complaints about the recruiters' methods by relatives in the *Volksbund*, or People's Union of Hungary. What's more, the recruits weren't all *Volksdeutsche*. Ethnic Hungarians had joined up, seemingly for what they thought was going to be 'short sports training'. Once an elite of German ideologically-motivated volunteers, the *Waffen-SS* was now being diluted with foreigners, non-Nazis and conscripts.

Eventually, agreements were reached with the governments of Romania and Hungary, and the puppet administrations in Croatia and Slovakia, permitting the unrestricted conscription of the *Volksdeutsche*. In Poland and Serbia, ethnic Germans were conscripted into the *Waffen-SS* as they were within the Reich. By 1944, Slovakia contributed 5,390 recruits, Croatia 17,538, Serbia 21,516, Romania 54,000, Hungary 22,125, and North Schleswig (Denmark) 1,292. Eventually, all *Volksdeutsche* of military age in Slovakia and Hungary serving in their armed services were transferred to the *Waffen-SS*.

THE HORST WESSEL DIVISION

As one of the vanquished in World War I, Hungary, like Germany, lost territory in the peace treaties drawn up afterwards. Consequently, in the interwar period, it allied itself with the Nazis in Germany and the Fascists in Italy. Their political pressure and the use of force clawed back this territory, and on 20 November 1940 Hungary signed the Tripartite Pact with Germany, Italy and Japan. Having joined the Axis Powers, Hungary declared war on the Soviet Union on 26 June 1941, four days after the beginning of the German invasion.

The many *Volksdeutsche* who were Hungarian citizens were eligible for conscription, so Himmler prevailed on the Hungarian government to continue allowing the *Waffen-SS* to recruit there. However, the Hungarians insisted on strict conditions. Recruits must be genuine volunteers who had not been coerced in any way. Those under 18 must have parental consent and all recruits must renounce their Hungarian citizenship.

By mid-1942, some 18,000 volunteers had been inducted and were sent to 7. *SS-Freiwilligen-Gebirgs-Division 'Prinz Eugen'* and 8. *SS-Kavallerie-Division 'Florian Geyer'*. With the growing manpower shortage in 1943, Himmler increased the upper age limit for recruits and raised a further 30,000–40,000 troops, who were seconded into the *Nordland* and the *Reichsführer-SS* divisions.

With the annihilation of the Hungarian Army at Stalingrad, Hitler feared that Hungary might sue for a separate peace and invaded. The country's regent Mikós Horthy was placed under house arrest. Himmler then demanded that all Hungarian *Volksdeutsche* complete their military service in the *Waffen-SS*.

At the same time, Hitler was demanding that a new division be named after the Nazi Party's greatest martyr, Horst Wessel. An SA

Sturmführer, or Assault Leader, he had been killed by Communists in 1930, and a march he had written was renamed the *Horst Wessel Song* and became the party anthem. This irked Himmler, as Wessel had been in the SA, not the SS. Worse, recruits to the new division would wear his name on their armbands and the SA runes on their collar patch.

18. *SS Freiwilligen-Panzer-Grenadier-Division 'Horst Wessel'* was formed in 1943 around a cadre from the 1st SS Infantry Brigade. The *Freiwilligen* ('Volunteer') element of their name was a farce, as recruits were given little option but to join. In July 1944, a battle group was sent to bolster the crumbling front in Ukraine. It rejoined the division in December and fought in the retreat through Poland and Slovakia, before being captured by the Red Army outside Prague.

The *Horst Wessel* division won seven Knights Crosses. It first commander was *SS-Brigadeführer* Wilhelm Trabandt, formerly of the *Leibstandarte SS 'Adolf Hitler'*. Then he was posted to the 1st SS Infantry Brigade which murdered Jews in the Soviet Union. He remained in command of the *Horst Wessel* until 3 January 1945 and was imprisoned in the Soviet Union until 1954. The next, *SS-Gruppenführer*, Josef Fitzhum, former Special Representative of the *Reichsführer-SS* in Albania, died in a car accident after a week in office. He was followed by *SS-Standartenführer* Georg Bochmann, who won the Knights Cross and Oak Leaves in Silesia, but was dismissed after refusing to make a suicidal attack. He surrendered to the Americans and died in 1973, aged 59. The *Horst Wessel* division's last commander was *SS-Standartenführer* Heinrich Petersen, who committed suicide rather than go into Soviet captivity at the end of the war.

THE BALTIC LEGIONS

Under the secret protocol of the non-aggression pact signed by Hitler and Stalin in 1939, the Baltic states of Estonia, Latvia and Lithuania were annexed by the Soviet Union in 1940. The following year, as part of Operation Barbarossa, the Soviets were ousted by Germany and the Baltic states, along with western Belorussia, became the province of German-administered Ostland with its capital at Riga in Latvia. Three days after its formation, on 31 July 1941, the first batch of 396 Estonian volunteers was handed over to the *Höheren SS- und Polizeiführer Russland-Nord* for police work.

Soon after, *Schutzmannschaft-Bataillonen*, or security battalions, were formed with Estonian and Latvian volunteers. Also known as *Schuma-Bataillonen*, they were auxiliary police units created to provide security in occupied territories, particularly to combat anti-Nazi resistance. They participated in the Holocaust and murdered countless Jews. The *Wehrmacht* recruited eight more battalions. Himmler tried to get his hands on them, but the Army resisted and four of them were sent into the front line during the Red Army counteroffensive that winter. Poorly trained and ill-equipped, they were slaughtered.

When it looked like the Soviets were going to break through, the German Army sought to mobilize the military formations of Estonia, Latvia and Lithuania, but the SS insisted that it should be in charge to give the Balts 'the proper ideological orientation and National Socialist leadership'. The danger receded before a Baltic SS could be formed. Instead, more Estonians and Latvians were recruited into the police. This was done by both the Army and the SS. They were supposed to be used for anti-partisan operations. Nevertheless, they were often sent to the front line.

Nationalist collaborators warmed to the idea of having an indigenous force to preserve their national identity. Berger approved and submitted a proposal to Himmler in May 1942. He was not keen at first, but growing casualties resulting in a shortage of manpower forced his hand. Estonia was the most pro-German of the Baltic states, so in August 1942 Himmler approved the formation of an Estonian Legion within the *Waffen-SS*.

Many of the recruits were from the Estonian Army who had fled to the forests as partisans when the Soviet Union invaded. They were anti-Communists and formed a number of self-defence units. Enough came forward to raise three full-strength Army battalions, six border guard regiments and a number of police regiments.

Himmler had his reservations about their racial purity, but after inspecting 54 Estonian legionnaires at a *Waffen-SS* academy for non-commissioned officers his doubts were banished.

'Racially they could not be distinguished from Germans,' he said. 'The Estonians really belong to the few races that can, after the segregation of only a few elements, be merged with us without any harm to our people.'

With proper ideological and language training, he believed that the Estonians could be made to see that a country of just 900,000 people was not viable and, as a racially related nation, they belonged in the Reich. Within two months, 700 Estonians and 200 Germans had been recruited for the Legion. Four months later, its strength was 6,500, many formerly members of the Estonian Army. The head of the Nazi administration, *Generalkommissar* Karl-Siegmund Litzmann, had started the recruitment with an announcement made on the anniversary of the 'liberation' of Tallinn by German forces. Later in the war, Litzmann went missing. He died in mysterious circumstances in August 1945 in Schleswig-Holstein, where he was living under a false name.

The puppet regime in Latvia then asked the *Reichskommissar* for Ostland Hinrich Lohse for permission to reform its army (Ostland was the name given to the German-administered province of the Baltic States combined with Belorussia). Berger opposed this, telling Himmler that if the Latvians really did want to fight Bolshevism they should 'create a unit of volunteers who are racially acceptable and put them at the disposal of the *Reichsführer-SS*... as police battalions for combating partisans or, if they are especially suitable, as a Latvian Legion'. The Reich Minister for the Occupied Eastern Territories, Nazi theorist Alfred Rosenberg, approved. Himmler went along with it, leading Hitler to order the formation of a Latvian Legion for the *Waffen-SS*. Fifteen-thousand Latvians signed up. Tried as a war criminal, Lohse was sentenced to ten years for the atrocities that took place in Latvia while he was in office, though he served only three years due to illness. Rosenberg was hanged at Nuremberg for crimes against peace; planning, initiating and waging wars of aggression; war crimes; and crimes against humanity.

The authorities were not prepared for such an influx. There were neither the barracks to house them, nor the weapons to arm them, so by 15 April 1943 only 2,850 Estonians and 2,478 Latvians had been inducted. No Lithuanians were permitted to join as Himmler thought them politically unreliable and racially inferior. The Estonians were formed into the three battalions of *SS-Freiwilligen-Regiment 1*, one of which saw action with the *Wiking* Division.

No sooner had they been trained than they were involved in the reorganization of the *Waffen-SS* into brigades and divisions, and the smaller size of their units was not suitable for the type of warfare being conducted on the Eastern Front. Reinforced by a portion of the 1st SS Infantry Brigade, the Estonian Legion became the *Estnische SS-Freiwilligen Brigade*. The Latvian Legion, along with the survivors from the 2nd SS Infantry Brigade, became the *Lettische SS-Freiwilligen Brigade–Estnische* being German for 'Estonian' and *Lettische* 'Latvian'. As a proportion of their men were German or ethnic German, these brigades were never purely Baltic. They soon saw action on the Eastern Front.

These brigades were then enlarged to divisions while the remaining Latvian *Schutzmannschaft-Bataillonen* became the nucleus of the 3rd Baltic SS division. With three divisions to fill, Himmler introduced conscription for men between 19 and 28. This was extended from 18 to 40 in 1944. Estonian officers up to the age of 60 and NCOs up to 55 were also drafted.

The Germans had problems with conscription in Latvia. This was initially left in the hands of former Latvian War Minister Rudolf

Bangerskis, who was appointed *SS-Gruppenführer* and Inspector General of the Latvian SS, but the collaborators that he used as recruiters were so inefficient that many of those who should have been eligible slipped through the net. Instead, the *Wehrmacht* opened 50 of its own offices across the country. Then, in 1942, the SS took over the whole operation. The OKW war diary entry for 2 December recorded: 'The *Führer* has transferred to the *Reichsführer-SS* the task of mobilizing those Latvians and Estonians who are fit for military service. For this purpose, *SS-Ergänzungskommandos* [recruiting offices] have been established in Reval [the German name for Tallinn, Estonia] and Riga; they have the authority of the German *Wehrbezirkskommando* [district military headquarters].'

In the end, 32,000 volunteers were recruited. They first saw action at Novo Sokolniki in November 1943, resisting the Soviet winter offensive, where they suffered heavy losses.

By 1944, the *Waffen-SS* had three new divisions – 15. *Waffen-Grenadier-Division der SS* (*lettische Nr 1*), 19. *Waffen-Grenadier-Division der SS* (*lettische Nr 2*) and 20. *Waffen-Grenadier-Division der SS* (*estnische Nr 1*). The *lettische Nr 1* wore the SS runes on its collar patches, even though most of its men were non-German. It also had a collar patch bearing a swastika, which was replaced with three stars surrounded by the sun's rays. Its arm shield carried the Latvian colours of red with white diagonal stripes. The *lettische Nr 2* also wore the swastika collar patch and the Latvian arm shield.

The *estnische Nr 1* wore a collar patch bearing the letter E and a sword. The arm shield bore the Estonian colours of blue, black and white, with three lions couchant superimposed on them.

DESIGNATION

Earlier in the war, SS divisions were identified only by their names, but in 1942 they were given numbers – the lower the number the earlier they had been formed. Where the 'SS' appeared in their title designated their racial profile. An SS-Division such as *3. SS-Panzer-Division 'Totenkopf'* comprised largely native Germans. Formations comprising ethnic Germans or 'Germanic' Western European volunteers were designated *SS-Freiwilligen-Divisione*, such as *11. SS-Freiwilligen-Panzer-Grenadier-Division 'Nordland'*. Those comprising largely non-Germans were designated *Division der SS*, with the nationality given in brackets at the end of the name, as in *15. Waffen-Grenadier-Division der SS (lettische Nr 1)*.

These Baltic divisions fought for the defence of their homelands during the Soviet advance of 1944. It was a lost cause. In the retreat from Leningrad, the Latvian 19th SS Division found itself cut off on the Courland Peninsula, south of the Gulf of Riga, where it remained behind Soviet lines until the end of the war. Most were then executed by the Soviets on the grounds that, as Latvia had been annexed by the Soviet Union before Germany had declared war, siding with the Germans was an act of treason. The division boasted 11 Knight's Cross winners, including one awarded to *Legion-Obersturmbannführer* Voldemars Veiss, commander of the *SS-Freiwilligen-Grenadier-Regiment 42*, the first Latvian to win one. He died of his wounds aged 44 in 1944.

Riga fell to the Soviets on 13 October 1944. The Latvian 15th SS Division, or *15. Waffen-Grenadier-Division der SS (lettische Nr 1)*, was pushed back into Pomerania, where it was decimated. It surrendered to the British in April 1945. There were five winners of the Knight's Cross of the Iron Cross in the division – two of them German and one a Fleming.

The Estonian 20th SS Division, or *20. Waffen-Grenadier-Division der SS (estnische Nr 1)*, was led by *SS-Brigadeführer* Franz Augsberger, an Austrian Nazi who was killed in action in March 1945. With the breakout of the Red Army on the Leningrad front, the Estonian 20th SS Division also found itself cut off in the Courland Pocket, but was successfully evacuated to Germany. In Silesia, it was routed. It fell back into Bohemia, where survivors surrendered at the end of the war.

Those who fell into Soviet hands were killed, but some fought their way westwards to Anglo-American lines. One of them was *Waffen-Standartenführer* Alfons Rebane, who had served in the German Army before winning a Knight's Cross of the Iron Cross with the *Waffen-SS*. He surrendered to the British and was recruited by MI6, organizing the armed resistance to the Soviets in Estonia. Later he moved to Germany, where he died in 1976, aged 67. In 1999 his re-interment in Estonia with full military honours sparked controversy as he was an alleged war criminal. Six members of the division won the Knight's Cross of the Iron Cross.

RACIAL PURITY

Initially, Himmler had refused to have the French and Walloons in the *Waffen-SS* as they were not Germanic. However, even the Germanic legionnaires did not conform to his racial criteria. In July 1942, he ordered Jüttner and the SSFA to ensure that the men from the foreign legions wore national emblems on their collar tabs to distinguish them from those who were racially qualified to be SS men.

'I want purely and simply, for all time, to prevent the admission, as a result of the exigencies of war, of all men who are not from the strictest point of view qualified to be SS men,' he wrote. It was a losing battle and men from Western Europe and the Baltics became regular members of the *Waffen-SS* to all intents and purposes.

The first *Waffen-SS* unit to be formed without regard for race or ethnicity was composed of Muslims from Bosnia and Herzegovina. Hitler ordered is formation in February 1943 as the Muslims had a fanatical hatred of the Serbian Christians who made up the majority of the Communist partisans under Josip Broz Tito, the man who went on to become president of Yugoslavia after the war.

The problem was that the Muslims lived in areas under the control of the puppet Croatian regime. When recruiting proved slow, Himmler discovered they were drafting anyone who showed an interest in joining the *Waffen-SS*, or simply arresting them. Concentration camps were also full of potential recruits.

Himmler wrote to the *Beauftragter des Reichsführers-SS Kroatien* – his representative in Croatia – *SS-Gruppenführer* Konstantin Kammerhofer, asking him to remind the Croatian authorities who was in charge.

'I expect to receive by 1 August 1943, your report that the division, at a strength of about 26,000 men, is completely ready,' Himmler wrote on 1 July. Two days later he ordered Berger to send two million *Reichsmarks* to help Kammerhofer in his recruitment drive. Nevertheless, voluntary enlistment fell short and conscription was introduced. After the war, Kammerhofer appeared at Nuremberg and was extradited to Austria, but escaped. He was found dead in mysterious circumstances in a hostel in Oberstdorf, Germany, in 1958.

Initially, the Bosniak formation was called either the *Kroatischen SS-Freiwilligen-Divisio*n or simply the *Muselmanen-Division* ('Muslim Division'). In October 1943, it was officially designated *13. SS-Freiwilligen b.h. Gebirgs-Division (kroatien)*, then *13. Waffen-Gebirgs-Division der SS 'Handschar' (kroatische Nr 1)*. This was to make the racial make-up of the Mountain Division plain; the 'handschar' was the long fighting knife or sword carried by the Ottoman police in Croatia.

Although Himmler and the SS were very anti-religious, each battalion of the *Handschar* had its own imam and each regiment its own mullah. Hitler afforded them the same privileges they had enjoyed in the old Imperial Austro-Hungarian Army – halal rations and communal prayers. Himmler said that he had 'nothing against Islam because it educates the men in this division for me and promises them heaven if they fight and are killed in action; a practical and attractive religion for soldiers!' But, ever contemptuous, he said that eight weeks' SS training taught Muslim recruits one thing – not to steal from one another.

Although the directive establishing the division encouraged the training of potential leaders among young Muslim recruits, the officers were largely German or *Volksdeutsche*. Like the men under them, they wore a field-grey fez (red with dress uniform) with a tassel, along with the Nazi war eagle carrying a swastika and the SS runes. The right collar tab carried a swastika and a hand grasping a handschar instead of the SS runes.

During training in France, they mutinied. Order was only restored by the personal intervention of the pro-Nazi Grand Mufti of Jerusalem. That done, they were returned to Yugoslavia to take on Tito, who by then had British backing. The Bosniaks were savage in the extreme, killing only with their knives. One man halted to bandage a wound on his arm, then went on to kill 17 more. There were cases where they cut out the heart of a victim. When Hitler heard this, he commented: '*Das ist mir Wurst*' – 'That is sausage to me', meaning 'That means nothing to me', or 'I don't care.'

In October 1944, they were sent to the Hungarian border to prevent the partisans linking up with the advancing Red Army. However, the Bosniaks did not take to fighting outside their local area and deserted in droves. Many took their weapons and joined the partisans. The division was then disbanded.

When the crack 16. *SS-Panzer-Grenadier-Division 'Reichsführer-SS'* was transferred from Italy to the Hungarian front, it took the name 13. *Waffen-Gebirgs-Division der SS 'Handschar'*, so it would not alert the Allies in Italy that the front there had been weakened, while the Red Army would be fooled into thinking that they were facing a motley bunch of Muslim infantrymen rather than an elite mechanized division.

NEW DIVISIONS

During 1944, two more Muslim divisions were raised by the *Waffen-SS*. The first was the Albania-raised 21. *Waffen-Gebirgs-Division der SS 'Skanderbeg' (albanische Nr 1)*, named after the medieval lord George Kastrioti Skanderbeg, who defended Albania against the Ottomans. Recruits wore the Albanian double-headed eagle on their arm shield and a cuff band carrying the word 'Skanderbeg'. It seems that the collar patch with a goat-crested helmet designed for them was never worn.

Italy had invaded Albania in March 1939, before the outbreak of World War II. When Italy surrendered to the Allies in September 1943, Himmler saw the potential of using the Albanian Muslims to fight the partisans, most of whom were Orthodox Christian Serbs. Many recruits came from neighbouring Kosovo, which had been annexed in 1941.

The standard of the recruits was poor and only 6,000 were thought suitable for training. The officers were largely native German or *Volksdeutsche*. Used for police actions, their performance was dire. Most of the Muslims seemed only to be out to settle scores with their Serbian neighbours and there were many atrocities. In just two months, there were 3,500 desertions and 4,000 men were drafted in from the German Navy who, due to the shortage of ships, were surplus to requirements. This did little to improve the division's fighting ability, so it was disbanded. The German cadre was formed into a battle group which joined 7. *SS-Freiwilligen-Gebirgs-Division 'Prinz Eugen'*

The second Muslim force raised was 23. *Waffen-Gebirgs-Division der SS 'Kama' (kroatische Nr 2)* – after the 'kama', a small dagger used by Balkan shepherds. It was similarly plagued with desertions and never went into combat.

SLAVIC MANPOWER

Having breached its own racial regulations by inducting Muslims, the *Waffen-SS* saw no reason not to tap the pool of Slavic manpower. On 28 April 1943, it called for recruits for a 'Galician' SS division. Nearly 100,000 Ukrainians volunteered; less than 30,000 were accepted. This was disappointing because a special effort had been made to concentrate recruiting on the area of German-occupied Poland that had been the Austrian province of Galicia before World War I.

Many of the Ukrainians were nationalists – there had briefly been an independent Ukraine between the collapse of the Imperial Russian Empire in 1917 and the establishment of the Union of Soviet Socialist Republics in 1922. Ukraine had suffered badly under the Soviets and its population greeted the Germans as liberators, at least until the *Einsatzgruppen* got to work.

But the SS leadership also looked down on the recruits as Slavs and, therefore, subhuman. When 14. *SS-Freiwilligen-Division 'Galizien'* – soon after designated 14. *Waffen-Grenadier-Division der SS (galizische Nr 1)* – had finished training in Germany and was on its way to the Eastern Front, it was visited by Himmler, who urged comradeship between the Germans and the Ukrainians, while pointing out the 250 Galician graduates of the *SS-Junkerschule* who had returned to the division as officers. And as Ukraine was largely Catholic, Himmler, a Catholic himself, allowed Ukrainian units to have their own chaplains. Though this was common practice in the Army, it was unheard of in the *Waffen-SS*.

In its first encounter with the Red Army, the *galizische Nr 1* division was encircled, but broke out. However, of the 14,000 men who had gone into action, only 3,000 returned for rest and refitting in Slovakia. A concession was then made to the Ukrainians and 14. *Waffen-Grenadier-Division der SS (galizische Nr 1)* became 14. *Waffen-Grenadier-Division der SS (ukrainische Nr 1)*. Its collar patch showed a rampant lion, with another one in yellow on the blue arm shield also carrying three crowns.

In the autumn of 1944 a regiment was sent to Czechoslovakia to suppress a Slovak uprising. In January 1945, the whole division was sent to Yugoslavia to fight Tito's partisans, but saw little action. Hitler was furious when he learned on 23 March 1945, with only weeks to go before the collapse of the Third Reich, that the division was up to its full strength of 14,000 and well equipped, but far away from the theatre of war.

The division won just one Knight's Cross of the Iron Cross. It was awarded to its commander, *SS-Brigadeführer* Fritz Freitag, who committed suicide on 10 May 1945, two days after the war in Europe ended.

RUSSIAN DIVISIONS

In the summer of 1944, the shortage of manpower forced Himmler to give up his final reservations about admitting non-Germanic *Ostvölker* into the *Waffen-SS*. Ukrainians and Russians in *Schuma-Bataillonen* formed the core of two new divisions – 29. *Waffen-Grenadier-Division der SS (russische Nr 1)* and 30. *Waffen-Grenadier-Division der SS (russische Nr 2)*. Neither of these grew to more than regimental strength.

The *russische Nr 1* was based on a security unit formed in the town of Lokot near the Ukrainian border that was the administrative centre of an autonomous republic under the Nazi occupation. After Red Army units were driven from the area, many took to the forest as partisans to harry the German supply lines. The mayor was granted permission to raise a self-defence force of around 500 men. They were fervent anti-Communists and drastically cut the number of partisan attacks.

The mayor was killed in action and was replaced by Bronislav Kaminski. As a chemical engineer, Kaminski spoke fluent German, since all science text books were then written in German. During the Russian Civil War (1918–20), he had served in the Red Army, but in the Great Purge of 1937 he was thrown out of the Soviet Communist Party. Arrested for criticizing Stalin's farm collectivization policy, he was exiled to the Bryansk oblast. This engendered in him an ardent anti-Communism. He did so well in the role of commander he was allowed to expand the self-defence force into a private army which called itself the *Russkaya Osvoboditelnaya Narodnaya Armiya* ('Russian National Liberation Army', or RONA; POHA in Cyrillic script). As head of the autonomous administration of Lokot, he was ordered to conscript all

Bronislav Kaminski.

able-bodied men, supplemented by Russian 'volunteers' from a nearby concentration camp. The militia was armed with discarded Soviet equipment. Uniforms were supplied by the Germans and bore an arm shield with the letters POHA on a dark green base over a white shield with a red edge enclosing a black Maltese cross.

By January 1943, Kaminski had accrued nearly 1,000 men, plus eight tanks and three armoured cars, which took part in the attack on the Kursk salient. His force also committed a number of atrocities against civilians. The Soviets made efforts to turn Kaminski's troops and several attempts were made on his life.

After the Germans' defeat in the Battle of Kursk, Kaminski's men were evacuated to Belorussia. When his second-in-command tried to defect to the partisans after being offered an amnesty for his entire regiment, Kaminski strangled him and eight others in front of his men. Himmler then awarded Kaminski the Iron Cross First and Second Class. Renamed the *Volksheer-Brigade Kaminski*, his unit undertook more anti-partisan operations. It then became the *Waffen-Sturmbrigade RONA* and Kaminski was given the rank of *Waffen-Brigadeführer der SS*, the only man with such rank. When it became *29. Waffen-Grenadier-Division der SS (russische Nr 1)* Kaminski was promoted to *Waffen-Brigadeführer und Gruppenführer der Waffen-SS*.

He was sent to assist the suppression of the Warsaw Uprising in August 1944. His men killed around 10,000 people in the Ochota area, murdering, looting and raping. German formations that tried to temper their behaviour were met with threats.

After Kaminski's men raped two German women, *SS-Obergrüppenführer* Erich von dem Bach-Zelewski, the SS commander in charge of Warsaw, was inundated with complaints. Himmler used this as an excuse to court martial Kaminski – not for mass murder or rape, but for theft. The property looted by his men belonged to the state and should have been delivered to Himmler, but Kaminski's men had kept it for themselves.

After a brief court martial, Kaminski was shot. To prevent mutiny among his men, they were told he had been killed by Polish partisans. When Kaminski's men refused to accept this explanation, the Gestapo took Kaminski's car, pushed it into a ditch, shot it up with a machine gun, and smeared goose blood all over it in an attempt to convince them.

With the loss of its leader, morale deteriorated and numbers dwindled due to desertion. Remnants joined the Russian Liberation Army of General Andrei Vlasov, also known as 30. *Waffen-Grenadier-Division der SS*.

This division was raised in Belorussia, also known as White Russia or White Ruthen, where much of the population was anti-Soviet and greeted the Germans as liberators. Later, they considered their German occupiers as the lesser of two evils. Even so, many volunteers joined the self-defence force set up in October 1941 by Wilhelm Kube, *Generalkommissar for Weißruthenien* (Commissar General of White Russia). Recruits were keen to defend Belorussia from the Soviets. Conscription was introduced in 1943.

When Belorussia fell to the Red Army the following year, members of the Belorussian Home Defence retreated westwards to Poland to form the *Schutzmannschaft-Brigade 'Siegling'* under the command of *SS-Obersturmbannführer* Hans Siegling. It was then shipped to Germany for training where it became 30. *Waffen-Grenadier-Division der SS (russische Nr 2)*.

As it had experience of anti-partisan operations, the division was sent to France to combat the Maquis, the French resistance that had escaped to the countryside to avoid forced labour in Germany. There were mass defections to the advancing Allies after the D-Day landings; some fled to Switzerland, where they were interned.

With only one regiment left, it was downgraded to brigade status, but redesignated 30. *Waffen-Grenadier-Division der SS (weissßuthenische Nr 1)*. The German officers and NCOs wore SS runes on their collar tabs; the others were thought to have worn blank patches. In spring

1945, the division was disbanded. The German cadre was seconded into the newly formed 38. *SS Panzer-Grenadier-Division 'Nibelungen'* – the Nibelungen being a Scandinavian race of dwarfs from German myth. The Belorussian troops were sent to Vlasov's Russian Liberation Army. Captured by the Red Army in May 1945, they were shot out of hand as traitors.

HUNGARY

During the last month of the war, more *Waffen-SS* formations were created in the east. *25. Waffen-Grenadier-Division der SS 'Hunyadi' (ungarische Nr 1)* was named after the fifteenth-century Hungarian general Janos Hunyadi who fought the Ottomans. Originally designated *25. SS-Freiwilligen-Grenadier-Division*, it was formed from troops drawn from the Royal Hungarian Army's 13th Honvéd Division after Miklós Horthy, the regent of Hungary, was ousted by the Germans in October 1944 for refusing to hand over Hungarian Jews and attempting to make a secret deal with the Allies.

The division was still in training when the Red Army invaded Hungary. As *Hunyadi* retreated into Austria, the battle group rearguard was destroyed. There, the remainder of the division met the US Third Army and, after some fighting, surrendered.

26. Waffen-Grenadier-Division der SS 'Hungaria' (ungarische Nr 2) was raised from 3,000 former Royal Hungarian Army troops, along with 5,000 civilian conscripts in November 1944. It was formed around the nucleus of other units, including *49. SS-Panzer-Grenadier-Brigade 'Gross'* under the command of Knight's Cross-winner *SS-Obersturmbannführer* Martin Gross. Romanians fleeing from the Soviets also joined.

The civilians were yet to be armed or given uniforms and the division was stripped of its heavy weapons by the German Army when the Red Army advanced. Members were reduced to scavenging for food when the division withdrew to Austria, where it surrendered to the Americans. Those left in the rearguard were wiped out.

Raised in the autumn of 1944 from Hungarian *Volksdeutsche*, 31. *SS-Freiwilligen-Grenadier-Division der SS 'Böhemen-Mähren'* was named for Bohemia-Moravia, the German protectorate formed by the rump of the Czech republic after the Sudetenland was annexed by the Third Reich. Its cadre came from the disbanded *Kama* division. It was responsible for the murder of Jews used as slave labour in mines in the village of Cservenka, Hungary (now Crvenka in present day Serbia).

After an initial encounter with the Red Army, it was reinforced with by the *SS-Polizei-Regiment 'Brixen'*, raise in Brixen, northern Italy, where it had an agreement with the partisans not to attack each other. When told they were being posted to the Eastern Front, many deserted. It was still not properly equipped or trained when it was annihilated in Silesia in May 1945.

MORE FORMATIONS

The *Osttürkischer Waffen-Verband der SS* was formed 1944 as 1. *Ostmuselmanisches SS-Regiment* with the support of the Grand Mufti of Jerusalem, Hajj Amin al-Husseini, with the intention of expanding into a division, the *Muselmanischen SS-Division Neu-Turkistan*. The men, largely Azerbaijanis, came from disbanded Turkic units in the German Army, prisoners of war and men working in Germany.

It was used for anti-partisan operations in Belorussia in February 1944. But there were troublesome elements and *SS-Hauptsturmführer* Heinz Billig tried to handle the problem by shooting 78 suspected mutineers, but he was soon removed from command. It fought the Polish Home Army in the Warsaw Uprising, alongside the *SS-Sturmbrigade 'Dirlewanger'*, under *SS-Oberführer* Dr Oskar Dirlewanger, which committed numerous atrocities there.

Posted to Slovakia, it was renamed *Osttürkischen Waffen-Verband der SS*, where it was hit by a number of desertions. Replacements came from the disbanded *Waffen-Gebirgs-Brigade der SS (tatarische Nr 1)*. It was transferred to the *Kaukasischer Waffen-Verband der SS*, also known as *Freiwilligen-Brigade 'Nordkaukasien'*, comprising volunteers from the Caucasus formed around the *Freiwilligen-Stamm-Division*, raised in southern France.

The *Serbisches SS-Freiwilligen Korps* was formed around a Fascist militia in 1941 and numbered around 3,500 men – largely Serbs with a few Croats and Slovenes. After the fall of Belgrade it was taken over by the *Waffen-SS*. It retreated to Austria, where it surrendered to the British. Most of the men were returned to Yugoslavia where they were executed for treason.

ROMANIANS

The *Waffen-Grenadier-Regiment der SS (rumänisches Nr 1)* was formed from members of the 4th Romanian Infantry Division, which had been refitting in Germany territory when Romania signed a ceasefire with the Soviet Union in the hope that it could be made into a division. It included members of the Fascist Iron Guard, which always had a close relationship with the SS.

Attached to the *III Germanisches SS-Panzer Korps*, it fought on the River Oder front, then transferred to the eastern approaches to Berlin where it was smashed by the Soviet offensive launched against the city on the 16 April 1945. Most escapees fled westwards, where they surrendered to the Americans.

A second regiment, the *Waffen-Grenadier-Regiment der SS (rumänisches Nr 2)*, had been formed in Austria, but by this stage in the war there was no fuel for vehicles, little food and no weapons or ammunition for the new regiment. In April 1945, the two battalions raised were used for construction duties.

BULGARIANS

The *Waffen-Grenadier-Regiment der SS (bulgarisches Nr 1)* was formed when Bulgaria quit the Axis and joined the Allies. A small number of pro-German Bulgarians outside Bulgaria was able to join. These included some men from the 5th Army who were engaged in the occupation of Yugoslavia, where they continued to fight, supporting the German retreat. Hitler hoped to raise two divisions of Bulgarians, but its strength only reached a few hundred. Morale slumped when the Red Army took Bulgaria and they were forced to plant potatoes to supplement their rations.

After seeing action on the Eastern Front, the unit was re-equipped with anti-tank weaponry in April 1945 and renamed the *SS-Panzer-Zerstörer-Regiment* (SS Tank Destroyer Regiment). A bunch of deserters was hunted down, and three were killed. Early in May, as the Allies closed in, the regiment disbanded.

The *Waffen-SS* formed two *Kosaken-Kavallerie-Divisionen* from thousands of anti-Soviet Cossack horsemen who fled into the Balkans ahead of the Red Army. Others were recruited from prisoner of war camps. Initially raised by the German Army, they were taken over by the SS which formed them into the *XV SS-Kosaken-Kavallier-Korps*.

It fought in Hungary and against Tito's partisans in Croatia. In May 1945, it withdrew to Austria where it surrendered to the British, who later handed the Cossacks over to the Red Army in exchange for British prisoners of war held by the Soviets. The British were short-changed and the Cossacks were killed.

MORE HUNGARIAN DIVISIONS

Hungary had moved from being an ally to a puppet state. Now it was occupied, Himmler planned to create four fresh Hungarian divisions. Two would be comprised of *Volksdeutsche*, the other two ethnic Hungarians. However, when the *Ungarn* (Hungary) SS division was formed in the autumn of 1943, it was a mixture of *Volksdeutsche* and Hungarians. Not the least of its problems was language. So Himmler ordered the Magyar-speaking contingent to form a battle group under its commander, *Waffen-Obersturmbannführer* Károly Ney. It would remain connected to the division which, by September 1944, would be renamed 22. *SS-Freiwilligen-Kavallerie-Division 'Maria Theresia'*, after the Holy Roman Empress who fought against Prussia in the War of the Austrian Succession.

Though poorly prepared, it took part in the Battle of Budapest, which lasted from November 1944 to February 1945, as part of *IX SS Panzer Korps. General der Kavallerie* Gustav Harteneck, commander of *I Kavallerie-Korps*, wrote: 'While the Corps was still in the process of being transferred, we were once again ordered to take up stationary positions, to our great disappointment. The cavalry divisions of the *Waffen-SS* were fighting in the metropolis of Budapest. Every cavalryman knows that no good could come of that, and, as it turned out, nothing did. The SS divisions were encircled... My cavalry corps launched a night attack in an attempt to relieve them, but it was too late, and the Russian forces were too powerful. Although we managed to fight our way to the city limits, only a hundred or so cavalrymen, under the command of the famous rider Staff Colonel von Mitzlaff, were able to break through to us. The subsequent battles, in the course of which my Corps was under the command of *6. SS-Panzerarmee*, might have turned out quite differently had the two SS cavalry divisions been deployed to full advantage as cavalry divisions, instead of being ordered to hold Budapest.'

Maria Theresia was all but annihilated. In the action three men were awarded Knight's Crosses, two posthumously. The survivor was *SS-Obersturmbannführer* Anton Ameiser, commander of the 52nd SS Cavalry Regiment, who was one of the 170 that escaped. His citation read: 'Ameiser was cut off behind enemy lines with a small *kampfgruppe* that initially consisted of 103 soldiers. However, he and his men managed to make their way back to the *Korps* again following a heroic 23-day long fighting retreat via Köres and Theis.

'The bulk of this small *kampfgruppe* was able to break through without abandoning any weapons along the way, and heavy losses in men and materiel were inflicted on the enemy in the process. This achievement is solely attributable to Ameiser's exemplary personal bravery and skilful leadership.

'He has also acted in a ruthless and praiseworthy fashion in situations that appeared hopeless. By doing so he has repeatedly been able to inspire his men to resist and move forwards despite their exhausted and starved state. Superhuman efforts have been brought about in this way. *SS-Hauptsturmführer* Ameiser has also highly distinguished himself in the heavy combat near Guyla.'

Ameiser went on to command 94. *SS-Freiwilligen-Kavallerie-Regiment* to the end of the war. The other two, *SS-Oberscharführer* Paul Reissmann and *SS-Obersturmführer* Werner Dallmann, both died of wounds sustained in the battle. *Maria Theresia*'s commander *SS-Brigadeführer* August Zehender was also killed in the fighting.

The remnants of the *Florian Geyer* and the *Maria Theresia* were reformed as 37. *SS Freiwilligen-Kavallerie-Division 'Lützow'*, named in honour of the Prussian general from the Napoleonic Wars, Ludwig von Lützow. The entire division never reached the strength of a single regiment. Its battle-ready elements formed *SS-Kampfgruppe 'Keitel'* under the command of *SS-Oberstrumbannführer* Karl-Heinz Keitel, son of *Generalfeldmarschall* Wilhelm Keitel, chief of the OKW and war criminal who was hanged in 1946. It saw heavy action while retreating into Austria, where it surrendered. Its men staged a mass breakout from the Altheim PoW camp on 13 May 1945 when they discovered that regular army troops were being released while they remained in captivity.

The 5,000 men of *Kampfgruppe 'Ney'* made a fighting withdrawal into Austria where they surrendered to the US Army. While the job of the *kampfgruppe* was said to be the 'liquidation of Jews, defeatists, saboteurs and others inside Hungary', Ney was only convicted of the execution of five downed US airmen. While three of his co-defendants were hanged, he was released and went to work for the US Army's Counterintelligence Corps. Sacked for 'operational incompetence', he continued working for French intelligence.

IN ITALY

24. Waffen-Gerbigs-Division de SS 'Karstjäger' ('karst hunter') was formed in July 1944 from the SS volunteer *Karstwehr* battalion, its nominal strength was never more than theoretical and the division was soon reduced to the *Waffen-Gerbirg (Karstjäger) Brigade der SS*. Comprising *Volksdeutsche* from Yugoslavia and the South Tyrol, it was involved with fighting partisans on the Karst Plateau on the frontiers of Yugoslavia, Italy and Austria.

After the Italian surrender, it disarmed the Italian garrison at Tarvisio and kept the passes into Austria open so that German troops could escape from the Balkans and surrender to the British, itself surrendering to the British on 9 May 1945, the day after the war in Europe ended. A joint Italian-German study implicated the division in 23 separate war crimes involving the killing of a total of 277 civilians between the Italian surrender and the end of the war.

When Italy had surrendered to the Allies in September 1943, some 3,000 pro-Fascists who wanted to continue the struggle volunteered for what would become *29. Waffen-Grenadier-Division der SS (italienische Nr 1)* with largely German officers and NCOs. By the end of the year, its strength had swelled to 15,000 in the short-lived *Repubblica Sociale Italiana* established by Mussolini in northern Italy.

Recruits were trained in southern Germany and sent back to Italy as the *Legion Italia* under the command of *SS-Brigadeführer* Peter Hansen. Initially, it was used for anti-partisan activities, but in February 1944 it was re-organized as a *Freiwilligen* brigade and sent back to Germany for retraining as a frontline combat unit. Its collar carried the Italian *fasces* emblem rather that the SS runes.

In April 1944, it found itself in action against the Allies in the abortive landings at Anzio where half the unit's strength was lost. But due to its gallantry, Himmler reluctantly declared: 'Because of the courage and devotion to duty displayed by the volunteers of the Italian SS, they are designated as units of the *Waffen-SS* with all the rights and duties that implies.' However, this applied only to the so-called *Vendetta* Battalion and the *SS Fusilier Bataillon 29* that had fought at Anzio. They then wore the SS runes on their collars.

The brigade was given divisional status in April 1945, but not its strength. Part of the division surrendered to the Americans near Gorgonzola on 30 August. The rest continued fighting partisans until they ran out of ammunition. They then surrendered and were massacred to a man by the partisans. One Italian officer recovering from serious wounds was dragged from his hospital bed and shot.

CHAPTER EIGHT

SS

Becoming an Army

Despite the fact that the German Army had been halted in front of Moscow, in January 1942 Hitler still believed that the war would be a short one and the *Waffen-SS* would return to being an elite, politically reliable police force. However, he had a growing respect for it as a fighting force. 'An extraordinary body of men, devoted to an idea, loyal unto death,' he said. 'The SS knows that its job is to set an example... and that all eyes are upon it.'

Although a Soviet onslaught was expected, German propaganda minister Joseph Goebbels said in his diary: 'If we had twenty men like Sepp Dietrich we wouldn't have to worry at all about the Eastern Front.'

The *Waffen-SS* had proved its worth during that winter. Six divisions, two infantry brigades, one cavalry brigade, four national legions and a number of smaller *Waffen-SS* formations played their part in holding back the Soviet offensive. But when Himmler pushed for its expansion, the only completely new SS division created in the first half of 1942 was the *Volksdeutsche 7. SS Freiwilligen-Gebirgs-Division 'Prinz Eugen'*, which was confined to anti-partisan operations in Yugoslavia.

Fanatical fighting had left the three elite divisions – the *Leibstandarte SS 'Adolf Hitler'*, *Das Reich* and *Totenkopf* – a shadow of their former selves. They were taken out of the line and sent to France for reorganization and retraining. Along with *Wiking*, they were each assigned a tank battalion. They were formed into an SS army corps with an *SS-Generalkommando* under *SS-Obergruppenführer* Hausser.

Without them, the German Army launched its summer offensive in the sector between Kursk and Kharkov. The plan was to make a lightning thrust to seize the oil fields of the Caucasus; oil was a vital resource for mechanized warfare. Once again, the Soviet armies crumbled before *Panzergruppe 'Kleist'*. Within six weeks, the Maikop oilfields and the entire Don River bend were in German hands, with one of the deepest penetrations being made by the *Wiking* SS division.

REVERSES

By the middle of September German troops had reached Stalingrad (Volgograd today). If the city could be taken, the *panzer* army could wheel north along the Volga and roll up the entire Russian front. But, as the city bore his name, Stalin was determined to hold onto it at all costs. The Germans were halted there by a Soviet counteroffensive launched on 19 November 1942 which, within three days, encircled them.

The Third Reich received another fatal blow that month. Erwin Rommel's *Afrika Korps* had swept across North Africa on its way to the oilfields of the Middle East. On 4 November it was thrown back by the British at El-Alamein. Four days later an Anglo-American force landed to Rommel's rear in French North Africa.

As the situation in Russia deteriorated, Hitler agreed to strengthen the *Waffen-SS*. The *SS-Kavallerie-Brigade* was enlarged to form 8. *SS-Kavallerie-Division 'Florian Geyer'*. The *Leibstandarte SS 'Adolf Hitler'*, *Das Reich* and *Totenkopf* were given more tanks, assault guns and armoured personnel carriers and redesignated SS *panzer-grenadier* divisions. Two more SS *panzer-grenadier* divisions were also to be raised, forming a second SS army corps.

Manpower was needed. Recruits were diverted from the Army and the Reich Labour Service. On 1 September 1942, the *Waffen-SS* had 141,975 men in field units with another 45,663 in training and reserve. Within a year this had doubled to a field strength of 280,000, with 70,000 in training and reserve.

DEPLOYMENT

At the beginning of 1943, 1. *SS-Panzer-Grenadier-Division Leibstandarte SS 'Adolf Hitler'*, 2. *SS-Panzer-Grenadier-Division 'Das Reich'* and 3. *SS-Panzer-Grenadier-Division 'Totenkopf'*, along with the *SS-Panzer-General-Kommando* were still in the West, largely in France. 4. *SS-Polizei-Division* and 2. *SS-Brigade* – including the Norwegian, Dutch and Flemish legions – were fighting in Russia with Army Group North. 5. *SS-Division 'Wiking'* was in southern Russia with Army Group Don. 6. *SS-Gebirgs-Division 'Nord'* was on the Finnish front with the German 20. *Gebirgs-Armee*. 7. *Freiwilligen-Gebirgs-Division 'Prinz Eugen'* was in Serbia with Army Group Southeast. 8. *SS-Kavallerie-Division 'Florian Geyer'* and 1. *SS-Brigade*, including *Freikorps 'Danmark'*, were fighting in Russia with Army Group Centre.

9. *SS-Panzer-Grenadier-Division 'Hohenstaufen'* and 10. *SS-Panzer-Grenadier-Division 'Frundsberg'* – named for historical German military leaders – were then being formed, but recruiters were finding it hard to attract volunteers. For the first time, widespread conscription had to be used. The bulk came from the work camps of the *Reichsarbeitsdienst*, or Reich Labour Service, where unemployed youths were indoctrinated with Nazi ideology. The average age of recruits, including officers, was 18.

Letters of complaint came from parents, ministers, bishops and cardinals. Some were addressed to Hitler himself. The authorities made a compromise – recruits were to be kept in training for a month, then offered the choice of volunteering or being released.

'I believe that there were three out of the two entire divisions,' said *SS-Obergruppenführer* Jüttner at the *SS-Führungshauptamt*. 'All the rest said: "No, we stay!" They had not known what the *Waffen-SS* really was, only what ministers and parents had told them.' He claimed both the new divisions turned into crack formations.

HITLER JUGEND

Reichsjugendführer (Reich Youth Leader) Arthur Axmann offered Himmler a division of Hitler Youth for the *Waffen-SS*. Hitler approved. Berger asked to take command, but Himmler refused. Instead, command was given to 35-year-old *SS-Standartenführer* Fritz Witt who had won the Knight's Cross of the Iron Cross as a battalion commander in the SS regiment *Deutschland* in the Battle of France, before being transferred to the *Leibstandarte SS 'Adolf Hitler'*. On 1 July 1943, he was promoted *SS-Oberführer* and, with a cadre from other senior *Waffen-SS* divisions, took command of 12. *SS-Panzer-Division 'Hitlerjugend'* whose first 10,000 volunteers were in training at an SS camp in Belgium.

Hitler would say later: 'The youngsters who come from the Hitler Youth are fanatical fighters... These young German lads, some only 16 years old... fight more fanatically than their older comrades.'

Witt was killed in action in Normandy in 1944 after a massacre of Canadian prisoners of war. Axmann was cleared of war crimes, but sentenced to three years and fined for indoctrinating German youth with National Socialism.

Axmann was in the *Führerbunker* in May 1945 and broke out with Hitler's private secretary Martin Bormann. Bormann was killed. Axmann eluded capture by the Red Army. He was caught by the US Army living under a false name while trying to organize a Nazi underground movement. He faced no war-crimes charges, but a de-

Nazification court sentenced him to three years and three months. He was later heavily fined for indoctrinating German youth with National Socialism.

KHARKOV

Following the surrender of the German 6th Army at Stalingrad on 2 February 1943, Hitler grew disillusioned with the *Wehrmacht. I SS-Panzer Korps* – consisting of the *Leibstandarte SS 'Adolf Hitler', Das Reich* and *Totenkopf* – under the command of *SS-Obergruppenführer* Paul Hausser had been rushed to the Eastern Front as the Red Army surged forward to the Donetsk, overrunning the Italian 8th Army.

Field Marshal von Manstein flew to Hitler's headquarters at Rastenberg to ask permission to short the line to prevent another encirclement. This was refused. Manstein said: 'All Hitler actually had to say about the operational position was to express the belief that the SS *Panzer* Corps would be able to remove the acute threat to the middle of the Donetsk front... His faith in the penetrating power of his newly established SS *Panzer* Corps was apparently unbounded.'

The *Leibstandarte* and *Das Reich* took up positions around Kharkov. The *Leibstandarte* was to hold a defensive bridgehead over 113 km (70 miles) long on the banks of the River Donetsk. In early February, its outer positions were overrun by the Red Army, but the main defensive position held firm with heavy casualties on both sides.

Das Reich was on the east of the river, but was slowly pushed back onto the Donetsk The Army units around it gave way and the division found itself cut off with a 65 km (40 mile) gap between it and the *Leibstandarte* and the Army's 320th Infantry Division, which soon found itself cut off. A *kampfgruppe* under *SS-Sturmbannführer* Joachim Peiper was sent to guide it back to German lines.

Peiper had been Himmler's adjutant during the invasions of Poland and France. In Poland he had witnessed the execution of Polish intellectuals and the mentally defective, along with deportations and

Paul Hausser.

ethnic cleansing. In 1940, he accompanied Himmler on a tour of the concentration camps. During the Battle of France, he got permission to join the *Leibstandarte* as a platoon leader. He won the Iron Cross, second and first class, and was promoted *SS-Hauptsturmführer*.

On 7 September 1940, Himmler addressed the *Leibstandarte* leaders to thank them for their help in expelling Jews from Alsace in eastern France. Returning to work as Himmler's adjutant, he attended a conference in June 1941 with Reinhard Heydrich and Erich von dem Bach-Zelewski where the *Reichsführer-SS* talked of plans to eliminate 30 million Slavs. During Barbarossa, he accompanied Himmler on his inspection of the *Einsatzgruppen* where Heydrich berated one local death squad leader for having shot only 96 Jews in a day. Peiper's job was to provide Himmler with the murder statistics and reports from the *Einsatzgruppen* each morning. He returned to the *Leibstandarte* in October 1941, where his aggressive tactics resulted in heavy casualties. As commander of 11. *Kompanie* he delivered Jews, Roma and others to the death squads.

As commander of 3. *Bataillon*, his rescue of the 320th Infantry Division earned him the German Cross in Gold, soon after the Knight's Cross of the Iron Cross, and his unit earned the nickname the 'Blowtorch Battalion': after two SS officers had been wounded by retreating Soviet forces, Peiper ordered the destruction of two villages and the shooting or burning to death of their inhabitants. Some 240 of these were burned alive in the church of Yefremovka. Peiper was proud of his unit's actions.

'Our reputation precedes us as a wave of terror and is one of our best weapons. Even old Genghis Khan would gladly have hired us as assistants,' he wrote. Indeed, the official SS newspaper *Das Schwarze Korps* ('The Black Corps') described Peiper's actions in Kharkov in glowing terms, calling him 'a born leader, one filled with the highest sense of responsibility for the life of every single one of his men, but who [was] also able to be hard if necessary'.

A larger *kampfgruppe* under *SS-Obergruppenführer* Sepp Dietrich, comprising the *Aufklärungabteilung* of the *Leibstandarte*, the *Das Führer* regiment from *Das Reich*, and the *panzer* regiment and *panzer-grenadier* of *Leibstantarte*, cut across the salient caused by the Soviet advance to make contact with other beleaguered German units in temperatures as low as -20°C. For several days, the fighting went back and forth.

Hausser asked for permission to make a tactical withdrawal. It was refused, but to avoid being encircled he pulled back anyway. On 19 February the Red Army captured Kharkov. But it was exhausted and depleted by heavy casualties, and its supply lines stretched to their limits.

Von Manstein decided to counterattack before the spring thaw gave the Russians time to recover. Hausser's *I SS-Panzer Korps*, now strengthened by the late arrival of the *Totenkopf*, would form the northern thrust of a pincer movement. Within a week, the Soviet 6th Army had been annihilated with over 23,000 killed and 600 tanks and 1,000 guns captured. Nevertheless, the bulk of its manpower had escaped across the frozen Donetsk.

The *Leibstandarte* with the *Totenkopf* covering its flanks encircled the Soviet 5th Guards Army and took Valuyki with huge Soviet losses. Moving north to Polevaya, they forced the enemy back over the Donetsk. During the pursuit of the fleeing Soviets, Theodor Eicke was killed when the reconnaissance aircraft he was flying in was shot down.

I SS-Panzer Korps then attacked Kharkov from the north and west, taking the city after five days' house-to-house fighting at the cost of 11,500 casualties. After the ignominious defeat at Stalingrad, Hitler was delighted. The Soviet advance had been stemmed and the Germans held on to the mineral-rich Donetsk valley.

'The *SS-Panzer Korps* is worth twenty Italian divisions,' he said.

Retaking the city, the *Waffen-SS* butchered 200 wounded in the hospital and set fire to the building. The Soviets claimed that it killed another 20,000 civilians before finally leaving Kharkov in August 1943.

NEW CORPS

I SS-Panzer Korps was reorganized. It now comprised *Leibstandarte* and *Hitlerjugend*. *Das Reich* and *Totenkopf* formed *II SS-Panzer Korps*, while *III SS-Panzer Korps* (*Garmanisches*) comprised *Wiking* and *Nordland*. This division was formed by detaching the *Nordland* regiment from the *Wiking* division and adding the *Norge* and *Danmark* regiments formed by members of the disbanded Norwegian and Danish volunteer formations. Later it got its own *panzer* battalion – the *Hermann von Salza*, named for the grandmaster of the Teutonic Order of German crusaders in the thirteenth century.

Normally such *panzer-grenadier* divisions comprised motorized infantry with no tank component, but the *Leibstandarte* and *Das Reich* were equipped with more and better tanks that most Army *panzer* division. In October they were redesignated SS *panzer* divisions along with the *Totenkopf, Wiking, Hohenstaufen, Frundsberg* and *Hitlerjugend*. By the end of 1943, seven of the 30 *panzer* divisions and six of the 17 *panzer-grenadier* divisions belonged to the SS.

IV SS-Panzer Korps was formed under Herbert Otto Gille, a regimental commander in the *Wiking* division under Felix Steiner who had won the Knight's Cross of the Iron Cross during Operation Barbarossa. While it was intended that each of these corps should have a *panzer* division and a *panzer-grenadier* division, the situation was fluid and divisions were moved from corps to corps. Meanwhile, V *SS-Gebirgs-Korps* was formed in Yugoslavia and VI *Freiwilligen-Korps* (*lettisches*) in Ostland.

Early in 1944, another SS mountain corps, *IX Waffen-Gebirgs-Korps de SS* (*kroatisches*), was formed in the Balkans. By the end of the year, in his new capacity of Commander of the Reserve Army, Himmler had created another six SS army corps – *XI, XII, XIII, XIV, XV* and *XVIII*. These were corps in name only as they had neither the qualified officers to command them nor the divisions to man them. Most of the commanders were police generals and the men came from the

Reserve Army, but Himmler enjoyed empire building and sought to impress Hitler.

Between 1943 and the end of the war, the strength of the *Waffen-SS* more than doubled and the number of divisions grew from 18 to 38. Most were the size of a regiment and only *18. SS-Freiwilligen-Panzer-Grenadier-Division 'Horst Wessel'* could be considered remotely an elite formation.

KURSK

For 12 weeks after the recapture of Kharkov, the Germans consolidated their positions. At this stage of the war, Hitler changed tactics. Against the advice of his field commanders, he abandoned the mobile tactics that had worked earlier in the war and tried to establish rigid defensive lines to stem the Soviet flood, while the *Waffen-SS* staged lightning counterattacks.

Divisions were shuffled from danger spot to danger spot. In the last two years of the war, the *Leibstandarte* yoyoed between the Eastern and Western Fronts seven times, conducting offensive operations after each trip.

A huge Soviet salient around Kursk presented the Germans with an opportunity. The mouth of the salient was just 113 km (70 miles) across. If that could be closed, the frontline could be shortened by some 322 km (200 miles), freeing up troops to counter the expected Allied invasion of southern Europe following the Axis defeat in North Africa. The huge number of Soviet soldiers captured in the encirclement could also be used as forced labour to support the war effort.

In Operation Citadel, Hitler planned a two-pronged attack on the salient with 900,000 men, 10,000 artillery pieces, 200 aircraft 2,700 tanks – including the latest PzKpfw VI Tiger tank and the untried PzKpfw V Panther, equipped with a high-velocity 75 mm gun. Then there was the *Elefant* heavy tank destroyer with its deadly 88 mm gun and the *Brummbär* self-propelled gun, featuring a 150 mm howitzer on a PzKpfw IV chassis.

However, the Soviets spotted the Germans' preparations and brought up 1,300,000 men, 260 aircraft, 3,300 tanks and 20,000 artillery pieces. They also got the local population to dig anti-tank ditches and build strong points, and laid massive minefields to funnel the German attack into well-prepared killing grounds.

After a further reorganization, *II SS-Panzer Korps*, now under *SS-Obergruppenführer* Paul Hausser and comprising the *Leibstandarte* under *SS-Brigadeführer* Theodor 'Teddi' Wisch, *Das Reich* under *SS-Gruppenführer* Walter Kruger and the *Totenkopf* under *SS-Brigadeführer* Herman Priess, were with von Manstein, who would attack from the south. All three had 15 Tiger tanks in their *panzer* regiments.

Tiger tank and grenadiers from the 'Das Reich' division of the Waffen-SS *during Operation Citadel, 1943 (battle of Kursk).*

These Tiger companies formed the tip of each armoured wedge as the divisions advanced in parallel. On 5 July, *II SS-Panzer Korps* broke through the Soviet defences before running into the minefields and anti-tank defences. Nevertheless, with ground-attack support from the *Luftwaffe*, the *Waffen-SS* had penetrated 29 km (18 miles) into Soviet-held territory on the first day.

Although it had outrun the Army units on its flanks, at dawn the following day the *Leibstandarte* engaged in a tank battle with the Red Army's 1st Guards Armoured Brigade, which took a beating as, at long ranges, the Soviet anti-tank guns could not penetrate the thick armour plating on the Tiger tanks.

As a gap opened up in the Soviet lines, Hausser sent his divisions through it, but without Army units in support the *Totenkopf* had to take on flanking duties, weakening the armoured spearhead. Even so, the *Leibstandarte* and *Das Reich* pushed on northwards with the Tiger tanks in the armoured spearheads smashing another gap in the enemy defences which allowed SS assault troops to take huge numbers of Soviet prisoners.

With the *Totenkopf* the *Leibstandarte* prepared to attack the village of Prokhorovka, 87 km (54 miles) southeast of Kursk there was a Soviet build up. On the afternoon of 10 July, the *Totenkopf* had crossed the River Psel. The following day the *Leibstandarte* advanced into the Soviet third defensive belt, taking the Oktyabrsky State Farm.

Six hundred tanks of Hausser's *SS-Korps* then attacked a front that was then only 10 km (6 miles) wide. The Soviets then sent the 5th Guards Tank Army, with 850 tanks and self-propelled guns, into what would become the largest tank battle in history.

To stand a chance against the Tiger tanks, the Soviets had to get in close and attacked at top speed, coming out of the sun. In an area of just a few square miles, 1,500 tanks blasted it out. With the German gunners blinded, the Soviet T-34 tanks attacked the thinner sides of the Tigers and Panthers, blowing them apart. Some Soviet tanks made suicidal attacks, driving at full speed into the *panzers*, blowing up both vehicles. By the end of the day, 700 tanks had been destroyed and their crews killed. The *Totenkopf* held its ground, beating off the Soviet attack, at the cost of half its strength in men and equipment.

During the battle, it was claimed that *SS-Untersturmführer* Michael Wittmann leading a platoon of four Tiger tanks took out 30 enemy tanks, surviving a collision with a burning T-34, and was awarded the Knight's Cross of the Iron Cross. He was killed in action in Normandy in June 1944.

TOO COSTLY

Operation Citadel then began to falter. The northern jaw of the pincer under Field Marshal Günther von Kluge had made little headway, while progress made in the south was too costly in men and materiel. *II SS-Panzer Korps* had started out with 700 tanks. Now only 280 were intact.

Hitler called off the offensive on 13 July. Three days earlier the Allies had landed on Sicily and would soon be threatening Germany's southern flank. A meeting of the Fascist Grand Council on 24 July voted to depose Mussolini. The following day King Victor Emmanuel dismissed Mussolini and had him arrested. In response, Hitler ordered the transfer of the *SS-Panzer Korps* to Italy. Von Kluge flew to Hitler's headquarters, the Wolf's Lair at Rastenburg, East Prussia, to protest, but Hitler remained adamant.

'The point is I can't just take units from anywhere. I have to take politically reliable units,' he said. 'It is a very difficult decision, but I have no choice. Down there, I can only accomplish something with elite formations that are politically close to Fascism. If it weren't for that I could take a couple of Army *panzer* divisions. But as it is, I need a magnet to gather the people together... I must have units down there which come under a political banner.'

A renewed Soviet offensive meant that *Das Reich* and *Totenkopf* had to stay on the Eastern Front. Only *Leibstandarte* was sent to Italy.

SPECIAL COMMENDATION

By the middle of August, a gap of 55 km (34 miles) had opened up in the German lines west of Kursk. Soviet troops poured through and were threatening to retake Kharkov. *Das Reich*, *Totenkopf* and *Wiking* were thrown into a counterattack to hold the city. Though weakened, *Das Reich* had taken over all of the *Leibstandarte*'s armour before it left for Italy and drew special commendation from von Manstein.

'In a daring and energetically led attack along the west flank of the army, the division has destroyed a considerable enemy force, and thus created the necessary condition of further operations,' he wrote on 17 August. 'I convey to the division and its officers my special recognition. Mention of the division in the *Wehrmacht* communiqué has been proposed.'

In just one day of fighting, *Waffen-SS* anti-tank gunners knocked out over 180 Soviet tanks. But on their own they could only delay the advance of the Red Army and on 22 August von Manstein abandoned the city. During the fighting withdrawal the *Waffen-SS* scored some successes against Soviet armour. The. *Wehrmacht* war diary for 26 August records: 'The 6th Army was forced to pull back its front in some places in the face of strong enemy attacks. In this connection the *SS-Panzer-Grenadier-Division 'Das Reich'* achieved an especially successful defensive victory.'

On 12 September, *Das Reich* scored another victory, taking out 78 Soviet tanks in one engagement. However, the Red Army had little problem making good its losses, while the Germans were finding their ranks depleted. Despite fierce resistance by the *Waffen-SS*, the Red Army took Yelnya, Bryansk, Smolensk and Roslavl. By 2 October the Germans had been driven back 193 km (120 miles).

RECALLED

In November 1943, the *Leibstandarte* was recalled from Italy. Re-equipped with the latest tanks, it was sent back into the line south of Kiev with the *XLVIII Panzer Korps* of *4. Panzerarmee*. Despite the best efforts of *Das Reich*, the city fell on 7 November.

The *Leibstandarte* and *Das Reich* took part in a number of counterattacks as part of the *XLVIII Panzer Korps*, but the Soviet reverses were short-lived. At Korosten, 145 km (90 miles) west of Kiev, the *Leibstandarte*, along with 1. and 7. *Panzer-Divisione* encircled a number of Red Army units, but the German line was spread so thin that they narrowly avoided being encircled themselves.

At Brusyliv to the east, *Das Reich*, then attached to *XXIV Panzer Korps*, was overwhelmed in hand-to-hand fighting. The remnants joined the *Leibstandarte* in a fighting withdrawal towards Zhytomyr. The *Leibstandarte* then moved on southwards to link up with 1. *Panzer-Division* at Berdychiv.

Meanwhile, the *Totenkopf* was rushed from one sector to another. In November and early December, it served with *Generaloberst* Hans-Valentin Hube's 1. *Panzerarmee* attempting to hold the Red Army on the Dnieper. Then, on 12 December, *Totenkopf* was switched to *LVII Korps* where, with 11. and 13. *Panzer-Divisione*, it launched a counterattack that temporarily halted the Soviet advance.

But on 13 December, the Red Army broke out of the Nevel salient, overwhelming Army Group Centre. On 24 December, the Soviets pushed forward again from their positions around Kiev. Within a week, they had retaken Zhytomyr and Korosten, pushing southwestwards to reach the pre-war Polish border. Then, on 14 January 1944, the Red Army attacked Army Group North, lifting the siege of Leningrad on 27 January. The Germans withdrew after looting many of the city's art treasures.

MAKING A STAND

The *Wiking* and the *SS-Sturm-Brigade 'Wallonie'*, the Walloon volunteer unit recently transferred from the Army to the control of the *Waffen-SS*, joined the stand the Germans were making at Kirvograd (Kropyvnytski). They held a salient that was a threat to the Soviet forces to the north and the south.

The Red Army then cut them off, encircling 60,000 men – including the *Leibstandarte*, the *Wiking* and a 2,500-man battle group of *Das Reich*. Then there was a sudden thaw, turning the area into a sea of mud and putting the airfield the *Luftwaffe* was using to re-supply the troops out of action. Meanwhile, the Red Army pushed forward, shrinking the pocket near Cherkassy to 104 km^2 (40 miles^2) by 9 February.

Hitler's forces were surrounded by 35 Soviet divisions. Hitler urged von Manstein to relieve them in a renewed offensive. When this proved impossible Hitler reluctantly gave his permission for the encircled troops to break out. This would be led by *5. SS-Panzer-Division 'Wiking'*, commanded by *SS-Obergruppenführer* Hebert Gille, with the *SS-Sturm-Brigade 'Wallonie'*, under *SS-Hauptsturmführer* Léon Degrelle, forming the rearguard.

The breakout began on 16 February. Making slow progress over the waterlogged land, the Germans came under murderous artillery and rocket attack from the Soviets. The wounded were left behind and artillery and heavy equipment abandoned. *Wiking* lost its remaining tanks, all of its equipment and half its personnel.

Things were worse for *Wallonie*, which left 70 per cent of its strength dead on the battlefield. As the remnants drew near German lines, *Wiking* turned back to hold off the Soviets during their extraction. Some 32,000 men escaped. Gille and Degrelle were summoned to the Wolf's Lair where Gille was awarded the Oakleaves and Swords to his Knight's Cross, while Degrelle got the Knight's Cross. Gille later received Diamonds to the Knight's Cross, making him the most highly decorated *Waffen-SS* member of the war.

Das Reich was exhausted and sent for rest and refitting in France in February 1944, though a battle group under *SS-Oberführer* Heinz Lammerding remained on the Eastern Front. Lammerding won the Knight's Cross of the Iron Cross there. After the war, he was sentenced to death *in absentia* by a French court for the murder of 750 civilians at Tulle and Oradour-sur-Glane, but was not extradited from West Germany as he was already serving a prison sentence for war crimes there. After he was released, he became a founder member of HIAG. When he died of cancer in 1971, aged 65, 200 former SS men turned out for his funeral.

While Army Group South withdrew across the Dnieper into Romania, the *Totenkopf* was airlifted to Balta on the border of Moldova to form a new defensive line, but was quickly overrun by the Red Army. After fighting off the Soviet spearhead, the *Totenkopf* pulled back into the Carpathian mountains to avoid encirclement. As the Soviet offensive ran out of steam, the *Totenkopf* was pulled out of the line for rest and refitting. It was given new tanks and armoured vehicles along with 6,000 replacement troops. Some were *Totenkopf* veterans returning to the division after recovering from wounds, but three-quarters were raw recruits from the recently formed 16. *Panzer-Grenadier-Division 'Reichsführer-SS'*.

UNTRIED IN BATTLE

To the north, the *Leibstandarte* and Lammerding's *Das Reich Kampfgruppe* was surrounded with 1. *Panzerarmee* in the Kamenets-Podolsk pocket. To rescue them, Hitler had to release the last of his SS reserve. The reconstituted *II SS-Panzer Korps*, comprising 9. *SS-Panzer-Division 'Hohenstaufen'* under *SS-Brigadeführer* Willi Bittrich and 10. *SS-Panzer-Division 'Frundsberg'* under *SS-Brigadeführer* Karl von Treuenfeld, were rushed from France to the Eastern Front.

Although untried in battle, the *Reichsdeutsche* of these two divisions had been in training for a year and had been formed around a cadre from the *Leibstandarte* and *Das Reich*. Bittrich had been Sepp Dietrich's Chief of Staff in Poland and commanded the *Deutschland* SS regiment in France, before commanding 8. *SS-Kavallerie-Division 'Florian Geyer'* in security operations that included the collective punishment against villages suspected of supporting partisans, an automatic death sentence for immediate families of suspected partisans, the deportation of women and children to death and labour camps, and the confiscation of property for the state. He assumed temporary command of *Das Reich* while Paul Hausser was recovering from wounds.

Von Treuenfeld had been SS and Police Leader of the *Waffen-SS* in occupied Western Europe until he was given command of the 2nd SS Infantry Brigade for Operation Barbarossa. Then he was given command of the 1st SS Infantry Brigade. Both were engaged in rear-area security, killing Jews, Communists and other civilians. A deputy to Reinhard Heydrich in Bohemia and Moravia, he was in command of the troops that stormed the church where Heydrich's assassins had taken refuge. In reprisal, in the villages of Lidice and Ležáky, the men were murdered, the women and children sent to death camps, and the villages razed. He then took charge of the *Waffen-SS* in southern Russia and Ukraine, before being given command of *Frundsberg*. After being wounded, he was sent to Italy. He committed suicide while in an American prisoner of war camp in 1946.

II *SS-Panzer Korps* quickly launched a flank attack that neatly amputated the tip of the Soviet spearhead. This allowed 1. *Panzerarmee* to withdraw under the cover of a blizzard with minimal losses. Meanwhile, hundreds of Soviet armoured vehicles were destroyed.

After its rescue, the *Leibstandarte* was sent to Belgium for refitting before being stationed in France. What was left of Lammerding's *kampfgruppe* rejoined *Das Reich* in France, awaiting the anticipated Allied invasion, while *Hohenstaufen* and *Frundsberg* were held in reserve in Poland, ready for any renewed Soviet advance.

The survivors of the *Wiking* division were withdrawn for rest and refitting while a 4,000-man *kampfgruppe* was left behind. *Totenkopf* continued its year-long defence of the south-central front. But the Red Army was soon in striking distance of Hungary. In late March 1944, Hitler unleashed Operation Margarethe – the occupation of Hungary – and 16. *SS-Panzer-Grenadier-Divsion 'Reichführer-SS'*, 18. *SS-Panzer-Grenadier-Division 'Horst Wessel'* and 8. *Kavallerie-Division 'Florian Geyer'* took over the country.

THE BATTLE OF NARVA

After lifting the siege of Leningrad, the Red Army pushed the Germans back towards Estonia and Latvia. The principal *Waffen-SS* unit in the area was *III SS-Panzer Korps (germanisches)* under *SS-Gruppenführer* Felix Steiner. At the time it comprised 11. *SS-Freiwilligen-Division 'Nordland'* and *SS-Freiwilligen-Brigade 'Nederland'*. Their volunteers came from Norway, Denmark, the Netherlands, France, Sweden and Switzerland. Also in that sector were the 15. and 19. *Waffen-Grenadier-Divisione* from Latvia, 20. *Waffen-Grenadier-Division* from Estonia, the Flemish *Langemarck* brigade and the Walloon *Sturm-Brigade 'Wallonie'*.

By the end of January, the Red Army had reached the city of Narva, which lay in a natural choke point between Lake Peipus and the Gulf of Finland. Lying on the Estonian border, Narva had been strategically important for hundreds of years and the Germans established defences along the west bank of the River Narva with the *Nordland* and *Nederland* dug in on a bridgehead on the east bank in what would be called the Battle of Narva, or the Battle of the European SS.

The Red Army began softening up the defences with heavy artillery. It forced a crossing of the river to the north of Narva, establishing a small bridgehead. But the *Waffen-SS* grenadiers threw it back. *Nordland*'s 11. *Panzer-Battalion 'Hermann von Salza'* repulsed a second attempt. A third attempt managed to establish a bridgehead to the northwest of the city, but a concerted assault by *Nordland* and *Nederland* destroyed it.

A fourth attempt by the Soviets to claw a foothold on the west bank was supported by heavy artillery. But in hand-to-hand combat 19. *Waffen-Grenadier Division* thwarted that too. In the fighting 22-year-old Estonian volunteer *Waffen-Unterscharführer* Haralt Nugiseks took over when his commanding officer was killed. After capturing the bridgehead, he was awarded the Knight's Cross of the Iron Cross, the second Estonian to have won it. Captured by Czech partisans in May 1945, he was handed over to the Soviets and spent ten years in the Gulag before returning to Estonia in 1958.

The Soviets then sought to get behind the defenders by making an amphibious assault on the beaches 8 km (5 miles) down the Baltic coast near Meriküla. They reached the town, where they were halted by *Waffen-SS* grenadiers and Stuka ground-attack aircraft, and the invasion was crushed with heavy losses.

SS Battalion Narwa June 1944 in Estonia.

The Red Army did manage to establish a bridgehead to the south in an area held by the *Wehrmacht*. By 24 February, it looked as though the Soviets were about to break out and sweep around the rear of *III SS-Panzer Korps* (*germanisches*). *Nordland* moved quickly to prevent this. After initial successes, the division got bogged down in hand-to-hand fighting. Only the arrival of some Army Tiger tanks allowed them to disentangle themselves.

On 7 March, the Red Air Force launched a 12-hour air raid on Narva, followed by heavy shelling. The civilian population had been evacuated and the *Waffen-SS* defenders dug themselves deeper into the rubble. The main attack came on an area held by the Dutch volunteer *General Seyffardt* regiment – named for Dutch collaborator Hendrik Seyffardt, a figurehead for the Dutch Legion who had been shot by the Resistance at his home in The Hague on 5 February 1943. It held off the Soviet attack and its commander *SS-Obersturmbannführer* Wolfgang Joerhel was awarded the Knight's Cross of the Iron Cross. He was commander of the *SS-Junkerschule* in May 1945 when he was captured by Czech partisans and killed.

However, the Soviets managed to break through another Dutch volunteer *panzer-grenadier* regiment, *De Ruyter* – named for a successful Dutch admiral in the Anglo-Dutch Wars. But they were driven back by reinforcements from *Nordland*'s *Danmark* and *Norge* regiments. They managed to hold onto the bridgehead on the east of the Narva, though it shrank under Soviet pressure until, on 24 July 1944, 20. *Waffen-Grenadier-Division der SS* was forced back over the River Narva, destroying the bridges behind it.

With news of the disasters to the south and the increasing strength of the Red Army, it pulled back 16 km (10 miles) to Sinimäe and the so-called Tannenberg Line, named for one of Germany's early victories on the Eastern Front in World War I. During the fighting, the *General Seyffardt* regiment was cut off while withdrawing and annihilated by the Red Army.

THE TANNENBERG LINE

The Soviet assault on the Tannenberg Line began on 26 July with the Red Army taking Orphanage Hill on the east of the line, but *Danmark* took it back the following night. *III SS-Panzer Korps (germanisches)* repulsed Soviet attempts to take the hill back the next day. A counterattack was launched by an SS reconnaissance battalion and an Estonian battalion, but this collapsed under fire from Soviet tanks which destroyed the Estonian battalion.

The Soviets retook Orphanage Hill on 29 July, but suffered heavy losses on their assault on Grenadier Hill in the centre. Soviet tanks surrounded Grenadier Hill and Tower Hill to the west. Steiner sent out his remaining seven tanks. These caught the Soviet armour by surprise and forced them back.

An improvised battle group led by *Hauptsturmführer* Paul Maitla launched a counterattack which recaptured Grenadier Hill. Maitla was awarded the Knight's Cross of the Iron Cross. He too was captured by Czech partisans in May 1945 and killed.

The Soviets reinforced and attacked once more. Again they were repulsed and on 10 August the offensive was called off. But it was a brief respite. On 14 September, the Soviets launched the Riga Offensive. After months of holding the line, the exhausted men of *III SS-Panzer Korps* joined the withdrawal. Some of the Estonians stayed behind to conduct guerrilla warfare against the occupying Soviet forces.

CHAPTER NINE

SS

In Retreat

By the time German forces on the Eastern Front were in full retreat, Hitler had other things to think about. His forces had been soundly defeated in North Africa and driven out of Sicily. On 3 September 1943, Allied forces had landed on mainland Italy. Although Italy had changed sides, Germany had sent forces there and the Allies found themselves involved in a long hard slog to fight their way up the long, narrow Italian peninsula.

That summer a new division was created in Corsica. *16. SS-Panzer-Grenadier-Division 'Reichsführer-SS'* was formed around a cadre from the *SS-Sturm-Brigade 'Reichsführer-SS'*, itself built from personnel from the *Leibstandarte*. Its commander was *SS-Brigadeführer* Max Simon, a regimental commander from *Totenkopf*. When the Allies took Sardinia and Corsica in October 1943, it was transferred to the mainland where elements helped hold back Allied troops that had landed at Anzio. They fought alongside the Italian Legion, which became *29. Waffen-Grenadier-Division der SS (italische Nr 1)*. They were transferred to bitter anti-partisan operations. Other Italians joined 24. *SS-Gebirgs-Division 'Karstjäger'*, which also fought partisans in northern Italy and along the Adriatic coast.

The rest of the *Reichsführer-SS* division was sent to Hungary in Operation Margarethe, but returned when the Allies continued their advance. It was involved in anti-partisan actions that resulted in the massacre of 560 civilians, including 130 children, at the village of Sant'Anna di Stazzema, and 770 civilians at Marzabotto, the worst mass-shootings of the war in Italy.

The commander of the *Reichsführer-SS's Aufklärungsabteilung 16*, *SS-Sturmbannführer* Walter Reder, was identified as the main culprit. Extradited to Italy in 1948, he was sentenced to life imprisonment. He was released in 1985 and returned unrepentant to his native Austria.

Simon was awarded the Oakleaves for his Knight's Cross and the German Cross in Gold. He was given command of *XIII SS-Panzer Korps*, where he ordered the execution of three Germans in the village of Brettheim in Baden-Württemberg for 'undermining military morale' after they had confiscated the weapons of the Hitler Youth.

Command of the *Reichsführer-SS* division passed to *SS-Oberführer* Otto Baum, also a regimental commander in the *Totenkopf*. After the war, Simon was sentenced to death for the massacre in Marzabotto, but this was commuted to life imprisonment. He was released in 1954 and subsequently acquitted for other war crimes.

Although the *Waffen-SS* did not play a significant role in the campaign against the Allies in Italy, its security activities left an indelible mark. The Chief of the Security Police and Security Service *SS-Obersturmbannführer* Herbert Kappler deported over 2,000 Jews to the Nazi death camps and he was responsible for the Ardeatine massacre. In reprisal for partisans killing 32 members of an SS Police Regiment, he ordered the murder of 335 civilians in the ancient Ardeatine caves outside Rome, which were then dynamited to hide the evidence. After the war, Kappler was sentenced to life imprisonment by an Italian military tribunal. Diagnosed with terminal cancer, he escaped in 1977, dying aged 70 in West Germany shortly after.

THE BATTLE OF NORMANDY

On D-Day, 6 June 1944, the *Leibstandarte* was near Bruges in Belgium. While Hitler still thought that the landings in Normandy were a feint, the *Leibstandarte* was not allowed to move without the *Führer*'s express permission. Eleven days later was it committed to combat at Caen, where the left flank of the Allied invasion had stalled.

The *Hitlerjugend* division, based at Dreux on the road to Paris, was the first *Waffen-SS* formation to go into action in Normandy a day after the landings, while 17. *SS-Panzer-Grenadier-Division* 'Götz von Berlichingen' sprang into action from Tours. *Das Reich* was near Toulouse in the south, expecting an invasion on the Cote d'Azur which did not come until 15 August. But soon after D-Day it was ordered north to take on the Maquis in the area between Tulle and Limoges. Lammerding ordered his men to use the same brutal methods they had used in the East.

Following the D-Day landings the Maquis had gone on the offensive. When *Das Reich* reached Tulle, the Maquis fled, but the SS arrested every man between 16 and 60. Ninety-nine were hanged and 149 were sent to the Dachau concentration camp, where a further 101 died. In response to a last-minute plea from the prefect to save the victims from hanging, *SS-Sturmbannführer* Aurel Kowatsch responded that 'we have developed on the Russian Front the practice of hanging. We have hanged over a hundred thousand men in Kharkov and in Kiev, this is nothing to us'.

Nooses were hung from trees, lampposts and balconies by the pioneer section under *SS-Hauptsturmführer* Otto Hoff who had volunteered to be the executioners. The victims were brought in groups of ten. Each of them was led to the foot of the step ladders set next to the nooses. Two SS stood by each noose. One of them climbed the stepladder with the condemned and put the noose around the prisoner's neck. When he was clear, the other SS man removed the prisoner's stepladder. In some cases, the executioners, all volunteers, hung from the legs of the victim, struck them or finished them off with a submachine gun or a pistol. 'Sometimes, to speed up the execution, the killers would shove their victims with rifle butts and, with terrible screams, kicked their stepladder over,' said an eyewitness.

The following day the *Der Führer* regiment of *Das Reich* reached the small hamlet of Oradour-sur-Glane. The Resistance in a nearby village had kidnapped a soldier. Women and children were herded into the church. Grenades were thrown in after them and it was set on fire. The men were locked in a barn. Machine-gunners shot them in the legs. They were doused with petrol and set alight. In all, 642 died, including 207 children, and the hamlet was completely destroyed. In 1953, 65 of the 200 *Waffen-SS* men involved were brought to trial. Only 21 appeared as many were in East Germany, which did not allow extradition. Twenty were convicted, but those from Alsace who claimed to have been forcibly conscripted into the *Waffen-SS* were released after a week, others soon after. All of the German defendants were also released by 1958.

Kowatsch died on the Eastern Front in March 1945. Hoff was given ten years' hard labour, but released after five. Lammerding was sentenced to death *in absentia*, but escaped punishment for these particular crimes.

In 1983, *SS-Obersturmführer* Heinz Barth was tracked down in East Germany. He had been the leader of a 45-man platoon in the *Der Führer* regiment at Oradour-sur-Glane. Charged with ordering the shooting of 20 men in a garage, he was sentenced to life imprisonment, but was released in 1997. The village of Oradour-sur-Glane was not rebuilt and was left as a memorial to the cruelty of the Nazi occupation.

On 11 June Hitler cancelled a planned offensive at Kowel on the Eastern Front and sent *II SS-Panzer Korps* to France. With *Hohenstaufen* and *Frundsberg* there were six crack *Waffen-SS* divisions facing the Anglo-American forces, but they failed to push the Allies back into the sea. The Red Army seized the opportunity to launch its main summer offensive on 22 June. By the end of the month, it had reached the Gulf of Riga in the north, the suburbs of Warsaw in the south and the San River in western Ukraine.

CAEN

As the British tried to take Caen, the *Hitlerjugend* moved into position. *SS-Standartenführer* Kurt 'Panzer' Meyer formed a *kampfgruppe* with three battalions of infantry and a number of tanks from the division's *panzer* regiment. Together with the Army's 21. *Panzer-Division*, they went into the attack. With over 30 Allied tanks destroyed for just two German losses, the British advance was brought to a halt, but the battle group was not strong enough to push them back. For his actions in Normandy Meyer was awarded the Swords to his Knight's Cross with Oak Leaves. He was also sentenced to death by a Canadian court for ordering the murder of Canadian prisoners of war. No charges were laid against him for previous war crimes in Poland or Ukraine as the court was constituted to deal only with crimes committed against Canadian nationals. The sentence was commuted to life imprisonment. He was released in 1954 and became a leading member of HIAG.

With Caen now heavily defended, the British spotted a gap in the German line between Caumont-l'Éventé and Villers-Bocage and sent the 7th Armoured Division of the Eighth Army, veterans of the campaign in North Africa. However, when four of their Cromwell tanks entered the village of Villers-Bocage, they met 2. *Kompanie, schwere* (heavy) *SS-Panzer-Abteilung 101* under *SS-Obersturmführer* Michael Wittmann with four Tiger tanks and one PzKpfw IV with its deadly 88mm gun.

They quickly knocked out the four Cromwells, then went on to attack the armoured column of the British 22nd Armoured Brigade,

Kurt Meyer.

knocking out a further 14 tanks and 15 personnel carriers, along with two anti-tank guns, within the space of 15 minutes. The British had no defence, as their shells bounced off the Tiger's heavy armour plating.

By the time Wittmann's company returned to Villers-Bocage, the British were waiting for them with six-pounder anti-tank guns which took out all five vehicles, hitting their weaker sides at close range, although all of the German crews managed to escape. But Wittmann's action had saved the flanks of the *Panzer 'Lehr'* division defending Caen. He was awarded the Oak Leaves and Swords to his Knight's Cross. Wittmann died in battle the following month when his batallion and its seven Tiger tanks were destroyed by Canadian forces. A shell penetrated the upper hull of his Tiger and ignited the ammunition, blowing up the tank. Wittmann and this crew were buried in an unmarked grave.

17. SS-Panzer-Grenadier-Division 'Götz von Berlichingen' moved to reinforce a paratroop regiment facing American paratroops who had taken Carentan at the foot of the Cherbourg peninsula. But the *Waffen-SS* division was delayed by transport shortages and attacks by Allied aircraft. While the German Army was forced back, *Götz von Berlichingen* staged a counterattack that was initially successful. Warned of the extent of the opposition, Combat Command A of the US 2nd Armored Division forced it back in what became known as the Battle of Bloody Gulch.

Arriving in Normandy on 25 June, *Hohenstaufen* and *Frundsberg* joined the line between Villers-Bocage and Caen. The following day the British renewed their efforts to take Caen. They crossed the Odon River and took the crucial Hill 112 on 29 June. *Hohenstaufen* and *Frundsberg* counterattacked, retaking the hill. Meanwhile *Hitlerjugend* held on in Caen itself, though it was forced back by heavy artillery, and aerial and naval bombardment.

The British eventually reached the River Orne that ran through the centre of the city, but only at the cost of heavy casualties. *Hitlerjugend* still held the rest of the city, until it was relieved by *Leibstandarte* and sent to the reserve north of Falaise.

On 18 July the Allies made another attempt to take Caen. A three-hour bombardment was followed by an armoured assault. *Leibstandarte* was forced back to the edge of the city, but took out over 400 tanks and managed to hold the German line of defence intact.

BARKMANN CORNER

Arriving in Normandy, *Das Reich* joined *Götz von Berlichingen* in trying to prevent the Americans driving inland after taking Cherbourg. With *Das Reich* was *panzer* ace *SS-Oberscharführer* Ernst Barkmann, who had served in Poland and on the Eastern Front. On 8 July, the 23-year-old tank commander scored his first kill in the West when he took out an American M4 Sherman tank with the high-velocity 75mm gun on his Panther. On 13 July he took out three more M4s. But his claim to fame came on 27 July at an isolated intersection on the St Lô-Coutances road that became known as 'Barkmann Corner'.

Taking shelter under a large oak tree, Barkmann watched as a large American armoured column approached. He opened fire, taking out the first two Shermans. He then hit the petrol tanker following behind. A Sherman finding its way around the blaze was hit. A second loosed off a couple of shots that made little impression on the Panther's thick armour. The second Sherman was soon ablaze.

His Panther then came under air attack. A track was blown off and the ventilation system damaged. During the strafing, two more Shermans moved in. Soon they were ablaze too. At this point, Barkmann decided to quit while he was ahead. The badly damaged Panther reversed out of danger and made it safely back to German lines.

Barkmann was awarded the Knight's Cross of the Iron Cross for the action. In all, Barkmann and his crew were credited with the destruction of at least 82 Soviet, British and US tanks, 43 anti-tank guns and 136 miscellaneous armoured fighting vehicles. However, military historian Steven Zaloga failed to find the losses claimed at Barkmann corner in the Allied war records and attributes the story to *Waffen-SS* propaganda. Barkmann survived the war and died in 2009, aged 89.

ALLIED AIRCRAFT

While the *Waffen-SS* and *Wehrmacht* were fully engaged with the British and Canadians around Caen, the Americans made another attempt to break out of their bridgehead to the west. The operation was to begin with an Allied air attack. Some 1,600 aircraft took off from England for Normandy, but by the time they got there the weather had closed in and the bombardment killed 25 Americans and wounded 130 in friendly fire.

The *Götz von Berlichingen* put up a stubborn defence, but found itself dangerously exposed and was forced to withdraw. The *panzers* were particularly vulnerable to Allied aircraft firing rockets at them as they negotiated the bocage country of Normandy, where narrow roads run between high wooded banks. Tank movements had to be made under the cover of darkness. This led to accidents. The *Leibstandarte*'s *SS-Obersturmführer* Georg Karck, who won the Knight's Cross on the Eastern Front, was killed when his jeep ran into an unlit ammunition truck.

On their right, the Americans were held back by the badly battered *Das Reich*. But after three days of heavy fighting they managed to break through to Coutances. The following day, *Das Reich* and *Götz von Berlichingen* counterattacked, smashing through the US 67th Armored Regiment and the 41st Armored Infantry near St Denis le Gast. But, by then, the Americans had an overwhelming numerical superiority and the Germans were forced to withdraw towards Avranches, which fell to the US 4th Armored Division. This created a gap. General George S. 'Old Blood and Guts' Patton's Third Army poured through, quickly overrunning most of Brittany.

Waffen SS troops in retreat, France 1944.

Elements of the *Leibstandarte* and *Das Reich* launched a counter-attack that aimed to split the American force in two on the night of 6 August. *Das Reich* took the town of Mortain and the high ground around Saint-Hilaire-du-Harcouët. However, the Army's *panzer* divisions got bogged down and the advance faltered.

General Eisenhower described the situation to his Combined Chiefs of Staff, saying: 'The enemy infantry was in no condition to resist us, and only weary, badly battered armor put up any considerable fight.' While the *Wehrmacht* pulled back 'in a state of complete disorganization, only the *Waffen-SS* divisions put up any fight'. After heavy fighting, on 2 August the Allies entered Vire, only for it to be recaptured by two SS *panzer* divisions the following day. There was a bitter struggle for some days before the Germans were finally forced from this sector.

ENCIRCLEMENT

The Germans were now in danger of being encircled, so Hitler uncharacteristically allowed them to withdraw from Mortain on 11 August, while the *Leibstandarte* and 116. *Panzer-Division* assembled at Carrouges for a counterattack on the advancing Americans. While 116. *Panzer-Division* temporarily halted the Americans, the *Leibstandarte* and 2. *Panzer-Division* were forced to abandon the counterattack at Argentan.

For the first time, Hitler noted, the *Waffen-SS* had failed him, though Sepp Dietrich and Hausser had both protested the order to renew the attack. But now, in Hitler's eyes, they had proved unreliable. In reality, the SS divisions had made almost superhuman efforts to hold back the Allies in the face of heavy naval fire, air attacks, superior artillery and endless streams of tanks and motorized infantry being brought across the Channel. Even the blind determination of the *Waffen-SS* to carry out directives from Berlin was a mistake, according to Eisenhower.

'As on former occasions,' he wrote, 'the fanatical tenacity of the Nazi leaders and the ingrained toughness of their men had led the Germans to cling too long to a position from which military wisdom would have dictated an earlier retreat.'

Meanwhile, the Supreme Commander West Field Marshal Günther von Kluge had been cut off from his headquarters for 12 hours by an enemy artillery barrage. Paranoid after the attempt on his life on 20 July 1944, Hitler suspected treason, saying that the failure of the counterattack came about because Kluge did not want it to be successful. He concluded that Kluge had been making contact with the Allies in order to surrender. Kluge was dismissed and *SS-Oberstgruppenführer* Hausser replaced him temporarily, before Field Marshal Walter Model took over.

Hausser was seriously injured in Normandy, but was given several commands before being relieved on 3 April 1945. At the Nuremberg Trials, he claimed that the *Waffen-SS* only had a military role and denied that it was involved in war crimes and atrocities. Hausser continued to take this line as a prominent member of HIAG, publishing his memoirs *Waffen-SS im Einsatz* (*Waffen-SS in Action*) in 1953. Convinced that Hitler thought he was implicated in the 20 July plot, Kluge committed suicide after being recalled to Berlin.

Field Marshal Gerd von Rundstedt, who returned as Supreme Commander West, said later: 'As far as I was concerned the war was ended in September.' He appeared as a witness for the defence at Nuremberg. Rundstedt was later investigated for war crimes, including 'the maltreatment and killing of civilians and prisoners of war... killing hostages, illegal employment of prisoners of war, deportation of forced labour to Germany... mass execution of Jews... and other war crimes, yet to be specified,' according to the indictment. But he was judged by the British to be too old and feeble to stand trial. He was released, but America and the Soviet Union still sought his extradition. Confined to the British Zone of occupied Germany, he died in Hanover in 1953, aged 77.

THE FALAISE GAP

Having broken through down the coast, the Americans swung inland in a pincer movement with the British and Canadians moving south after Caen fell on 6 August. The *Frundsberg* tried to hold the Americans at Domfront, but it soon became clear that the Germans in Normandy could only save themselves by retreating immediately through the gap between Falaise and Argentan. This began on 16 August.

Between the 4th Canadian and 1st Polish Armoured Divisions pushing south and General Patton's Third Army sweeping north, it was left to the *Hitlerjugend* to hold open the Falaise gap, committing a number of atrocities there. Part of *Frundsberg* was trapped in the pocket and annihilated. *Das Reich* and *Hohenstaufen* had escaped, but turned to launch a counterattack. It did no good. The German forces were caught in the ever-shrinking Falaise pocket where they were annihilated by Allied fighter-bombers.

Although British and American units finally joined up at Chambois on the night of 19 August, what remained of the *Götz von Berlichingen* managed to escape through a lightly held section of the line north of Mont Ormel. The gap was sealed on 21 August.

'While the SS elements usually fought to annihilation, the ordinary German infantry gave themselves up in increasing numbers,' Eisenhower wrote. Some 50,000 prisoners were taken and 10,000 corpses were found on the battlefield.

By then, the *Leibstandarte* had only weakened infantry elements left. All its tanks and artillery had been destroyed. It was withdrawn to Aachen in Germany for rebuilding. *Das Reich* still had 15 tanks, but only 450 men. It was withdrawn to the Schnee Eifel area of central Germany. *Hitlerjugend* had ten tanks left, no artillery and just 300 men, just 20 per cent of those committed. It was withdrawn east of the Maas.

To make its escape, *Götz von Berlichingen* had been broken up into four *kampfgruppen*, which were withdrawn to Metz. In early September, the division absorbed what was left of the *SS-Panzer-Grenadier-Brigade 49* and *SS Panzer-Grenadier-Brigade 51*, raising its infantry strength. Replacements for missing tanks and assault guns arrived slowly. On 8 September, the division was put back into the line and was tasked with destroying the American bridgehead over the Moselle River. After heavy fighting for the American bridgeheads, the division fell back and began to prepare to defend Metz itself.

The *Hohenstaufen* had 25 tanks and 460 men, while *Frundsberg* had no tanks or artillery and only four battalions of infantry. They were withdrawn to Arnhem in The Netherlands where it was thought they would have a quiet time.

DEFENDING ARNHEM

However, on 17 September the newly promoted Field Marshal Bernard Montgomery launched Operation Market Garden, a push through Belgium and The Netherlands with British paratroops tasked to take the bridge at Arnhem, just 16 km (10 miles) from the German border. *Hohenstaufen* and *Frundsberg* – together forming *II SS-Panzer Korps* under *SS-Obergruppenführer* Willi Bittrich – though decimated by the fighting in Normandy were waiting. They had been sent there for refitting.

Kampfgruppe 'Hohenstaufen' was in place to halt the British airborne troops at Arnhem, while *Kampfgruppe 'Frundsberg'* was sent to block the advance of the British XXX Corps 19 km (12 miles) to the south at Nijmegen where American paratroops had taken the bridge. Also joining the battle at Arnhem was a smaller *kampfgruppe* made up from the staff of the *SS-Unterführerschule* at Wolfheze, 400 troops from 16. *SS-Stammbattalion* and a number of Dutch SS police.

While some 600 British paratroops reached the northern end of the bridge, they were not strong enough to displace the *Waffen-SS panzer-grenadiere* holding the southern end. The situation for the British deteriorated further when *Waffen-SS* reconnaissance troops advanced from the south. To the north was the *Hohenstaufen* division under *SS-Obersturmbannführer* Walter Harzer, while the *SS-Kampfgruppe 'Spindler'* under *SS-Obersturmbannführer* Ludwig Spindler and *SS-Kampfgruppe 'Krafft'* under *SS-Sturmbannführer* Sepp Krafft were to the west.

When *SS-Panzer-Aufklärungsabteilung 9* turned up, their commander *SS-Hauptsturmführer* Victor-Eberhard Grabner, who had won the Knight's Cross in Normandy, led a frontal assault across the bridge. Grabner was killed and 20 of the unit's vehicles were left ablaze.

On 19 September, *SS-Kampfgruppe 'Spindler'* helped hold off an attempt by the British paras to take the bridge, while *SS-Kampfgruppe 'Krafft'* destroyed the Polish glider-borne troops that landed to the west.

At midday on 21 September *SS-Kampfgruppe 'Knaust'* under Army *panzer* officer *Oberst* Hans-Peter Knaust forced its way across the bridge, ending British resistance. *SS-Kampfgruppe 'Knaust'* was then sent south to meet XXX Corps at Nijmegen. Meanwhile *SS-Obersturmbannführer* Walter Harzer assembled a blocking force comprising Army, Navy, *Luftwaffe*, Coastal Defence troops and Dutch SS men to face the 1st Polish Parachute Brigade.

Both sides were exhausted, but the Germans were reinforced by *Panzer Ableilung 506* with a full complement of King Tiger tanks. Two companies were sent to *Kampfgruppe 'Frundsberg'* to hold back the British XXX Corps. The third was sent to deal with the survivors of the British assault force to the west at Oosterbeek.

Leaving the wounded and some medical staff, the British withdrew southwards. Clearly this was a victory for the Germans. But it was short-lived. Ten days later, Bittrich's *II SS-Panzer Korps* – a corps in name only – gave up its attempt to halt XXX Corps and the bridge at Arnhem was bombed, denying its use to fleeing German forces.

Harzer was awarded the Knight's Cross for his actions at Arnhem. He went on to become Chief of Staff of *V SS-Gebirgs Korps*, then took command of *4. SS-Polizei-Division* which surrendered to the Americans on 8 May 1945. After the war he became the official historian of HIAG and died in 1982, aged 69. Spindler remained with the *Hohenstaufen* and was killed in an air attack on his car during the Battle of the Bulge. Krafft survived the war and returned to police work.

BATTLE OF THE BULGE

After the British attempt to take the crossing at Arnhem had proved a 'bridge too far' Hitler realized that the Western Allies with their over-extended supply lines could still be halted, especially if they were denied the ports of northern Europe.

On 16 September, while listening to a situation report on the Western Front, Hitler suddenly announced: 'I shall go on the offensive... out of the Ardennes, with the objective, Antwerp.' After all, the attack through the Ardennes had proved spectacularly successful in 1940.

The operation was called *Wacht am Rhein* ('Watch on the Rhine'), later *Herbstnebl* ('Autumn Fog') when the attack was delayed from 25 November to 10 December, then again to 16 December, in order to build up enough armour for the offensive. If it succeeded it would weaken the Western Allies and shatter their hope of total victory, drop their insistence on unconditional surrender and open peace negotiations. If it failed, there would be no stopping the Anglo-American armies in the west.

The lead element would be the newly formed *6. Panzerarmee*. Although it did not receive the SS designation, it was commanded by *SS-Oberstgruppenführer* Sepp Dietrich and comprised what was left of *I SS-Panzer Korps* – that is, *Leibstandarte* and *Hitlerjugend*. Dietrich said: 'We call ourselves the 6th *Panzer* Army, because we've only got six *Panzer*s left.' *II SS-Panzer Korps* – *Das Reich* and *Hohenstaufen* – were held in reserve.

To blunt any counteroffensive, a hand-picked force of English-speaking Germans would be sent behind the Allies' lines wearing American uniforms and carrying American weapons. They would disrupt Allied forces by switching signposts and misdirecting traffic. They would be commanded by *SS-Hauptsturmführer* Otto Skorzeny. In September 1943, he had led German paratroops and *Waffen-SS* commandos on a daring raid to rescue Mussolini from Gran Sasso, the remote and defendable mountain plateau where he had been held after his fall from power.

I SS-Panzer Korps would form the spearhead with *Leibstandarte* on the left and *Hitlerjugend* on the right. They were led by *SS-Obersturmführer* Joachim Peiper, who had seen action at Kursk and in Northern Italy.

While the *Waffen-SS* was given the best equipment, the men were not of the standard they had been earlier in the war. Many had been drafted from the *Luftwaffe* and the *Kriegsmarine* and had no training in tank or infantry warfare. Nevertheless, *Kampfgruppe 'Peiper'* – comprising 140 tanks and a battalion of motorized infantry – punched through the weak American defences around Losheim. In the lead were two companies of PzKpfw IV tanks, followed by two companies of PzKpfw V Panthers, with the King Tiger tanks of *SS-Panzer-Abteilung 501* bringing up the rear.

Despite being impeded by slower Army units, *Kampfgruppe 'Peiper'* overtook retreating American troops, who surrendered after offering token resistance. At Honsfeld, Peiper's men shot 19 GIs and robbed their bodies. At an airfield near Büllingen, Peiper forced captured Americans to refuel his tanks. Afterwards, he shot them. Eight more US prisoners of war were killed at Ligneuville. A hundred American prisoners were machine-gunned in Malmédy. Twenty who miraculously escaped the slaughter were found hiding in a café. It was set on fire and those who ran out were machine-gunned.

The advance slowed when Peiper stayed behind at Ligneuville to confer with *SS-Oberführer* Wilhelm Mohnke, who was commanding the *Leibstandarte*. When Peiper returned to his unit, it took the bridge at Stavelot. However, the Americans had blown the bridge over the River Amblève at Trois Ponts, forcing them to turn northwards, finding an alternative bridge at Cheneux.

The battle group was now coming under attack by fighter-bombers and the bridge at Neuf Moulin was blown as Peiper's troops approached. Two alternative bridges were too small to support heavy tanks and Peiper had no heavy bridging equipment. Meanwhile, the Americans had retaken Stavelot, threatening to cut off Peiper's force. The *Leibstandarte* counterattacked but failed to dislodge the Americans there.

On 19 December, after a two-hour battle, Peiper's tanks took Stoumont. He pursued the retreating Americans out of town but ran into a roadblock, losing several tanks. By 21 December, the Allies had recovered somewhat from the initial surprise of the German attack and resistance stiffened. Battle raged around Cheneux, leaving 200 Americans dead before the Germans were driven out.

The following day, Peiper's force found itself out of fuel and short on ammunition. Supplies dropped by the *Luftwaffe* fell into American hands. On 23 December, Peiper was given permission to withdraw to the east. He destroyed his vehicles and the remaining 1,000 men crossed the River Salm and linked up with the *Leibstandarte* on Christmas Day.

Peiper was sentenced to death for the massacre at Malmédy, but this was commuted to life imprisonment and he served 12 years in jail. Other charges against him were dropped. Maintaining contacts with HIAG, he moved to France where he was murdered when his house was set on fire after flyers revealing his membership of the *Waffen-SS* and the war crimes he committed were distributed. Mohnke was investigated for war crimes, but no charges were brought.

Hitlerjugend ran into heavy resistance on Elsenborn ridge. After three days' fighting, it was diverted to the *Leibstandarte*'s southern flank to take on the US 7th Armored Division. After sustaining heavy losses, it was forced to withdraw to regroup.

Das Reich was attached to 5. *Panzerarmee* under General Hasso von Manteuffel. On 23 December it took the vital crossroads at Baraque de Fraiture, taking Manhay the following night. However, after determined actions, the Americans retook Manhay on 27 December.

Hitlerjugend and *Hohenstaufen* joined *Das Reich* in the Manhay area, but failed to penetrate the American lines. However, *SS-Oberscharführer* Barkmann came to the fore again, credited with destroying another four M4 Shermans. His comrade, *SS-Hauptscharführer* Franz Frauscher, was awarded the Knight's Cross to the Iron Cross for taking out nine Shermans. However, by the end of the year, the operation stalled. As there was no chance of it reaching its objective – the port of Antwerp – Hitler turned his attention elsewhere.

On 1 January he launched Operation *Nordwind*, attacking weak US forces in Alsace. Taking part would be 17. *SS-Panzer-Grenadier-Division 'Götz von Berlichingen'* and 6. *SS-Gebirgs-Division 'Nord'*, recently evacuated from the northern sector of the Eastern Front. The Allies were again caught by surprise and several hundred American prisoners were taken. But the attack soon foundered and a fresh assault by the *Frundsberg* aimed at Strasbourg also ground to a halt.

Meanwhile, in the Ardennes, the *Leibstandarte*, the *Hitlerjugend* and the *Hohenstaufen* were involved in the attempt to take Bastogne which was held by the 101st Airborne Division under Brigadier-General Anthony McAuliffe. Finding himself completely surrounded, he was asked to surrender and famously replied: 'Nuts.' The 101st held out for six days, supplied by air, blocking the German supply lines, until it was relieved by Patton's Third Army.

By 24 January, *Waffen-SS* divisions were withdrawn. Six *panzer-grenadier* troops seized the opportunity to desert and the commander of their battalion issued this order of the day:

> Traitors from our ranks have deserted to the enemy... These bastards have given away important military secrets. The result is that for the past few days the Americans have been laying quite accurate artillery fire on your positions, your bunkers, your company and platoon headquarters, your field kitchens and your messenger routes. Deceitful Jewish mud-slingers

taunt you with their pamphlets and try to entice you into becoming bastards also. Let them spew their poison! We stand watch over Germany's frontier. Death and destruction to all enemies who tread on German soil. As for the contemptible traitors who have forgotten their honour, rest assured that they never see home and loved ones again. Their families will have to atone for their treason. The destiny of a people has never depended on traitors and bastards. The true German soldier was and is the best in the world. Unwavering behind him is the Fatherland. And at the end is our Victory. Long live Germany: Heil to the *Führer!*'

CHAPTER TEN

ᛋᛋ

Last Gasp

While the Ardennes offensive was Hitler's last gasp in the West, things were looking no better in the East. In the spring of 1944, Stalin decided that it was time to kick the Germans off Soviet soil. On the night of 22 June, the Red Army smashed through Army Group Centre. Within weeks they had eliminated 350,000 German troops, the equivalent of 28 divisions. *3. SS-Panzer-Division 'Totenkopf'* was sent from Romania to fend off the Soviet attack west of Minsk. It held Grodno for 11 days, before being ordered to withdraw to Warsaw.

As the Red Army approached Warsaw in July 1944, the Soviet authorities encouraged the Polish Home Army resistance under Major-General Tadeusz Bór-Komorowski to stage an uprising against the German occupiers. However, the Red Army halted at the gates of Warsaw and offered no help. The *Waffen-SS* was sent to deal with the uprising in the guise of the *Waffen-Sturm-Brigade RONA* and the *SS-Sturm-Brigade 'Dirlewanger'*. During the battle, the *RONA* was responsible for the Ochota massacre, an orgy of mass murder, looting, arson, torture and rape that took some 10,000 lives.

The *Dirlewanger* behaved even more atrociously, encouraged by their commander *SS-Oberführer* Oskar Dirlewanger, who told them to take no prisoners. Hitler had ordered the city to be razed. The *Dirlewanger* looted, gang-raped women and young girls, played 'bayonet catch' with live babies and tortured captives by hacking off their arms, dousing them with petrol and setting them alight to run flaming down the street. The unit's behaviour was so bad that Himmler detailed a battalion of SS military police to ensure they did not turn on their own leaders or nearby German units.

On 2 October 1944, Bór-Komorowski surrendered to *SS-Obergruppenführer* Erich von dem Bach-Zelewski, commanding the suppression of the uprising, after Nazi Germany agreed to treat the Home Army fighters as prisoners of war. After the end of the war, Bach-Zelewski went into hiding and tried to flee the country, but was arrested by the Americans on 1 August 1945. At Nuremberg, he escaped punishment by testifying for the prosecution. He boasted that he had supplied the cyanide Hermann Göring used to commit suicide. Later, he was imprisoned for murdering a former SS officer during the Night of the Long Knives and for the murder of six Communists in the 1930s. His confession to mass murder in Poland, as an *Einsatzgruppe* leader in the Soviet Union, killing at least 30,000 civilians, and in establishing the death camp at Auschwitz were overlooked. He died in prison aged 72.

BUDAPEST

8. *SS-Kavallerie-Division 'Florian Geyer'*, 22. *SS-Freiwilligen-Kavallerie-Division 'Maria Theresia'* and 18. *SS-Freiwilligen-Panzer-Grenadier-Division 'Horst Wessel'* were committed to the defence of Budapest, though elements of *Horst Wessel* were involved in the German defence in Galicia and in helping suppress the uprising in Slovakia.

When it became clear that Horthy intended to put out peace feelers to the Allies, *SS-Obersturmbannführer* Otto Skorzeny organized a coup d'etat by kidnapping his son and forcing him to resign, then installing a pro-Nazi puppet government. But nothing could halt the advance of the Red Army, which had crossed the border at the beginning of October.

Skorzeny was captured by the Americans on 15 May 1945. He was tried for violating the laws of war by directing German troops to infiltrate Allied lines in American uniforms, but was acquitted. While waiting a West German denazification trial in 1949, he escaped and sought refuge in Spain. The court declared him *entnazifiziert* ('denazified') *in absentia* anyway. With other former *Waffen-SS*

Waffen SS soldiers fighting in Hungary, winter 1944.

officers he went on to train the Egyptian Army in the 1950s. There were rumours that he set up a secret organization call *Die Spinne* ('The Spider') to help former SS men escape from Germany and even that he worked for Mossad to spy on former German rocket scientists working on weapons programmes for Egypt.

On 14 August, the Soviets renewed their offensive, launching attacks across the Vistula to the north and west of Warsaw. But *IV SS-Panzer Korps – Totenkopf* and *Wiking* – managed to hold them back for a week. On 25 August, the Red Army tried again, this time concentrating on *Totenkopf* positions, forcing the *Waffen-SS* back on Warsaw. The *Totenkopf* struck back on 11 September, but could only halt the Soviet onslaught temporarily. A renewed attack on 10 October forced the Germans back to the edge of the city, where the *Waffen-SS* managed to stabilize its line.

By the end of the month, both Romania and Bulgaria had switched sides, allowing the Red Army to continue its advance unhindered. The ethnic volunteer SS divisions *Skanderbeg*, *Kama* and *Prinz Eugen* were soon confined in Yugoslavia where they faced not only the oncoming Soviets but also Tito's guerrilla army.

MUTINY

On 1 September 1944, members of the *Skanderbeg* division stationed in Tetovo and Gostivar mutinied, killing their German officers and NCOs. Half its strength deserted. Himmler brought in 3,000–4,000 members of the *Kriegsmarine* from Greece, but the division remained around a third of its intended strength. By 24 October, all remaining Albanian personnel were disarmed and the division was disbanded on 1 November. It continued the fight against the partisans in Kosovo, where tens of thousands died.

The remaining German troops and former naval personnel were reorganized as the regimental *Kampfgruppe 'Skanderbeg'* under the command of *SS-Obersturmbannführer* Alfred Graf. It made a fighting withdrawal from Yugoslavia. The survivors of the naval personnel were transferred to 32. *SS-Freiwilligen-Grenadier-Division '30 Januar'*. The rest of the former division was reorganized as *II Battalion* of *14 Regiment* of *7. SS-Freiwilligen-Gebirgs-Division 'Prinz Eugen'*.

Skanderbeg's commander *SS-Standartenführer* August Schmidhuber was promoted *SS-Brigadeführer und Generalmajor der Waffen-SS* and placed in command of *Prinz Eugen*. After the war, he was found guilty of killing civilians and hanged. In military terms the division was a failure. Not one member was awarded the Iron Cross while serving in it. It was better known for deporting Jews to their deaths in extermination camps and committing atrocities against Serbs.

The Bosnians in *23. Waffen-Gebirgs Division der SS 'Kama'* (kroatische Nr 2) mutinied on 17 October 1945. Its commander *SS-Standartenführer* Helmuth Raithel quickly regained control. Some Bosnians deemed to be reliable were transferred to *13. Waffen-Gebirgs-Division der SS 'Handschar'* (*kroatische Nr 1*). The numerical designator '23' was given to *23. SS-Freiwilligen-Panzer-Grenadier-Division 'Nederland'*, and Raithel went on to command *11. SS-Gebirgsjäger-Regiment 'Reinhard Heydrich'* of *6. SS-Gebirgs-Division 'Nord'* in southern Germany in the final months of World War II. Wounded, he was captured by the Americans and survived the war, dying in a traffic accident in 1982, aged 82.

PRINZ EUGEN

7. Freiwilligen-Gebirgs-Division 'Prinz Eugen' was known for its brutality. According to evidence submitted at the Nuremberg Trials: 'Everything they came across they burnt down, they murdered and pillaged.... The victims were shot, slaughtered and tortured, or burnt to death in burning houses. Where a victim was found not in his house but on the road or in the fields some distance away, he was murdered and burnt there. Infants with their mothers, pregnant women and frail old people were also murdered. In short, every civilian met by these troops in these villages was murdered. In many cases, whole families who, not expecting such treatment or lacking the time for escape, had remained quietly in their homes were annihilated and murdered. Whole families were thrown into burning houses in many cases and thus burnt.... The villages were burnt down and razed to the ground.'

When *Prinz Eugen* surrendered to the Yugoslav Army three days after the capitulation of Germany, members were executed wholesale. Family members were also killed during the ethnic cleansing of the German-speaking populations throughout Eastern Europe following the war.

Two of its commanders, *SS-Brigadeführer und Generalmajor der Waffen-SS* Karl Reichsritter von Oberkamp and *SS-Brigadeführer und Generalmajor der Waffen-SS* August Schmidthuber, were hanged for war crimes in Belgrade. A third, winner of the Knight's Cross with Oak Leaves and Swords *SS-Brigadeführer und Generalmajor der Waffen-SS* Otto Kumm, avoided extradition to Yugoslavia by escaping from the US internment camp at Dachau. He went on to became a founder member and the first head of HIAG. And he was unapologetic, writing in the in-house magazine *Wiking-Ruf* (*Viking Call*): 'Even during the war, and especially after the war, infamous and lying propagandists have been able to make use of all the unfortunate events connected to the Third Reich and also with the SS to destroy and drag through the mud all of what was and is sacred to us... Let us be clear about it: the battle was directed not only against the authoritarian regime of the Third Reich, but, above all, against the resurgence of the strength of the German people.' He died in 2004, aged 94.

BUDAPEST SURRENDERS

By 20 December 1944, the Red Army had crossed the Danube and went on to encircle Budapest. The *IV SS-Panzer Korps* was sent from Warsaw to relieve the city. It made two attempts to break through before being forced back.

The garrison held out until 11 February 1945 when 3,000 German troops tried to break out to the west. The *Florian Geyer* and *Maria Theresia* were cut to pieces. Just 700 men managed to make it back to German lines. Budapest surrendered the following day.

Meanwhile, the Red Army drove through the Baltic states, trapping two German armies in the Courland peninsula – 33 divisions in all. Twelve escaped by sea. The *Nederland* brigade was on a ship that was attacked and sunk. Some of the Dutch SS men survived to form the core of 23. *SS-Freiwilligen-Panzer-Grenadier-Division 'Nederland'* which was sent back into action on the Eastern Front.

This was just a sideshow. The Red Army's main priority was to drive the Germans out of Poland. The advance began on 12 April. After taking Warsaw, the Red Army drove on into Silesia, seizing the coal fields and factories there. By early February, it had reached the River Oder which would form the eastern border of post-war East Germany as part of the Oder-Neisse line.

With the surrender of Budapest, thousands of Soviet troops were freed up for a fresh offensive against the German Army. The German-held oilfields at Nagykanizsa in Hungary were now in jeopardy. Horrified at the prospect of losing vital oil supplies, Hitler decided on a new offensive which, he hoped, would throw the Red Army back over the Danube and stabilize the situation in Hungary.

SPRING AWAKENING

While *IV SS-Panzer Korps* remained in defensive positions around Lake Balaton in the west of Hungary, 6. *SS-Panzerarmee* joined the pincer movement of General Otto Wöhler's Army Group South. Under the command of *SS-Oberstgruppenführer* Sepp Dietrich, 6. *SS-Panzerarmee* now comprised the *Leibstandarte*, the *Das Reich*, the *Hohenstaufen* and the *Hitlerjugend*, whose strength had been depleted in the fighting in the Ardennes.

The *Leibstandarte* under *SS-Brigadeführer* Otto Kumm and the *Hitlerjugend* under *SS-Oberführer* Hugo Kraas formed *I SS-Panzer Korps*.

A winner of the Knight's Cross of the Iron Cross with Oak Leaves, Kraas surrendered to the Americans in Austria on 8 May 1945. He was tried *in absentia* in Italy for the murder of dozens of Italian Jews and found guilty 1955. Ten years later similar charges were dropped in West Germany due to lack of evidence.

II *SS-Panzer Korps* comprised *Das Reich* under the command of *SS-Standartenführer* Rudolf Lehmann and the *Hohenstaufen* under *SS-Oberführer* Sylvester Stadler. Lehmann was awarded the Oak Leaves to his Knight's Cross of the Iron Cross by Sepp Dietrich. After the war he wrote two volumes of the history of the *Leibstandarte* for HIAG. Stadler also won the Knight's Cross with Oak Leaves. He surrendered his division to the Americans in May 1945. He died in 1995, aged 84.

Hitler's plan was called *Unternehmen Frühlingserwachen*, 'Operation Spring Awakening'. Spearheading the attack would be 6. *SS-Panzerarmee*, which was pulled out of the Ardennes. 16. *SS-Panzer-Grenadier-Division* 'Reichsführer-SS' was brought up from Italy through the Brenner Pass and attached to 2. *SS-Panzerarmee*. 9.

SS-Panzer-Grenadier-Division 'Hohenstaufen' arrived just days before the operation was to start. 6. *SS-Panzerarmee* also took command of the Hungarian II Corps, along with its 20th Hungarian Division and 9th Replacement Division.

Fanatical about secrecy, Hitler would not even allow his trusted SS commanders to stage preliminary reconnaissance missions in the areas where they were to operate in case it alerted the enemy. Unit names were changed. They were not to appear on situation maps. Movements were to take place at night and troops were ordered to cover all identifying insignia.

The element of surprise was thrown away when Hitler ordered a preliminary attack. I *SS-Panzer Korps* was to smash the Red Army's bridgehead at Estergom, which threatened 6. *SS-Panzerarmee*'s push to secure the oilfields. It did this with little difficulty. But seeing a large formation of elite SS troops, the Soviets realized that a major offensive was on its way and began strengthening their defences.

The vain attempts at secrecy continued on 6 March, the day the main assault was to begin. The soldiers going to the front were dropped 19 km (12 miles) behind the launch point. They were to proceed on foot in heavy snow. By the time they were in position, the *Waffen-SS* grenadiers were cold, wet and exhausted. Some reached the launch point late, long after the preliminary artillery barrage had again alerted the enemy that an attack was coming.

There had been an early thaw that year and *II SS-Panzer Korps* foundered in the mud. It suffered heavy losses and managed to advance just 8 km (5 miles). *I SS-Panzer Korps* did better, driving the enemy back 40 km (25 miles), again with heavy losses. The Soviets had an overwhelming numerical superiority, while the *Waffen-SS* was being reinforced with ill-equipped and poorly trained men recruited from the *Luftwaffe* and the *Kriegsmarine*.

By 14 March, Operation Spring Awakening was in serious trouble. Two days later the Soviets began a counterattack in strength. Within 24 hours the Germans were driven back to their start position. *6. SS-Panzerarmee* was soon in danger of becoming encircled and withdrew towards Vienna with the Red Army in hot pursuit.

Hitler was so annoyed by the retreat that he issued an order saying that the troops, particularly the *Leibstandarte*, 'did not fight as the situation demanded'. As a punishment, *Leibstandarte* members were ordered to remove their coveted cuff titles that bore his name. Dietrich did not pass on the order.

SURRENDER IN AUSTRIA

The *Totenkopf*, *Das Reich* and *Hitlerjugend* defended Vienna, along with the remnants of *Hohenstaufen*, which was formed into a small *kampfgruppe*. The *Wiking* was decimated. The rest of *6. SS-Panzerarmee* withdrew to defend Germany itself with *Reichführer-SS* heading for the Untersteiermark in the south of Austria, where it surrendered. The *Hitlerjugend* travelled a further 97 km (60 miles) to surrender to the Americans at Linz.

The *Leibstandarte* and what was left of *Hohenstaufen* surrendered to the Americans on 8 May at Steyr in Austria. *Totenkopf* surrendered to the Americans northwest of Vienna the following day. However, its men were handed over to the Soviets. Few survived captivity.

The remnants of *Das Reich* withdrew to the area east of Dresden. However, at the end of April, *SS-Obersturmbannführer* Otto Weidinger, commander of the *Der Führer* regiment, was summoned to Prague where the senior SS commander asked him to cover the evacuation of the German population of the city in the event of an expected Czech uprising.

When the revolt came, Weidinger returned with a *kampfgruppe*. Cut off from its parent unit, this was placed under the command of Field Marshal Ferdinand Schörner, a dedicated Nazi who again ordered Weidinger to crush the uprising. *Der Führer* entered the city on 6 May to find itself confronted with a roadblock so big it could not be shifted with explosives. Instead it had to be dismantled by hand under the harassment of snipers.

After a brief gunfight, Weidinger negotiated a truce with local Czech officers, allowing *Der Führer* to enter the city unmolested. Transportation was at a premium, but Weidinger assembled a convoy of 1,000 vehicles to carry out of the city civilians, a group of female signals' auxiliaries, stragglers and a train full of German wounded who had been abandoned in a railway siding. They headed for Pilsen, where they surrendered to the Americans.

Weidinger, who had been a guard at Dachau concentration camp before winning the Knight's Cross of the Iron Cross with Oak Leaves, was interned in Dachau after the war. In 1947, he was handed over to the French to be tried on charges relating to the Oradour-sur-Glane massacre, but was acquitted. At subsequent trials, he appeared as a witness for the defence. He went on to write a five-volume history of *Das Reich* published by HIAG and a revisionist account of the massacres at Tulle and Oradour. He died in 1990, aged 75.

Although Schörner also surrendered to the Americans, he too was handed over to the Soviets. He was convicted of war crimes and served time in prison in the Soviet Union, East Germany and West Germany. Named as his successor as commander-in-chief of the German Army in Hitler's will, Schörner was particularly harsh on deserters, executing anyone caught behind the lines without written orders. Joseph Goebbels wrote: 'They are hanged from the nearest tree with a placard round their necks saying "I am a deserter. I have declined to defend German women and children and therefore I have been hanged".... Naturally such methods are effective. Every man in Schörner's area knows that he may die at the front but will inevitably die in the rear.' Released in 1960, he died in obscurity in 1973, aged 81.

14. *Waffen-Grenadier-Division der SS (ukrainische Nr 1)* and 20. *Waffen-Grenadier-Division der SS (estnische Nr 1)* surrendered to the Soviets in Czechoslovakia. Most of them were executed on the spot. *Horst Wessel* also surrendered in Czechoslovakia, while *Nordland* and the Latvians of 15. *Waffen-Grenadier-Division der SS (lettische Nr 1)* perished in the Battle of Berlin along with *Nederland*, which was down to regimental strength, and the remnants of *Charlemagne*, *Langemarck* and *Wallonien*. The Russian volunteers of 30. *Waffen-Grenadier-Division der SS (weissßuthenische Nr 1)* were sent to General Vlasov's Free Russian Army. It is not difficult to imagine their fate when they fell into the hands of the Soviets.

KNIGHT'S CROSSES

Members of these foreign legions won a substantial number of Knight's Crosses of the Iron Cross. They included the Latvian *Waffen-Hauptsturmführer* Robert Ancans, who was injured in the last days of the war and evacuated, saving him from capture by the Soviets. In the 1950s, he emigrated to the US.

Another Latvian, *Waffen-Hauptscharführer* Zanis Ansons, was awarded the Knight's Cross in the Courland Pocket. He spent ten years in the Gulag before being allowed to return to Latvia. *Waffen-Obersturmführer* Nikolas Galdins was also captured in the Courland Pocket, but he was executed by firing squad in Leningrad in October 1945.

The Latvian *Waffen-Hauptsturmführer* Miervaldis Adamsons was in command of *6. Kompanie, 44. Waffen-Grenadier-Regiment, 19. Waffen-Grenadier-Division der SS (lettische Nr 2)* when he won the Knight's Cross of the Iron Cross in the Courland Pocket in January 1945. Although wounded several times, he refused a place on a boat evacuating German troops and civilians to Sweden, choosing to remain in Latvia. He was still in hospital when he was taken into Soviet custody. Claiming to be German, he was sent to work in the nickel mines at Murmansk. With several German officers, he tried to escape in the winter of 1945-46. They were recaptured on the Finnish border. When it became clear that he was Latvian, he was sentenced to death for homeland betrayal in May 1946 and executed by firing squad on 23 August in Riga. In 1993 Adamsons was fully exonerated by Latvia's supreme court.

SS-Obersturmführer Søren Kam, a member of the Danish Nazi Party, served on the Eastern Front and as an SS instructor training Danish recruits, before participating in a robbery where the *Waffen-SS* stole the birth records of the Jewish community in Denmark, making it easier for the German authorities to deport or murder Danish Jews. Kam and two others killed unarmed newspaper editor Carl Henrik Clemmensen, who was hit by eight bullets fired from three different pistols. He claimed he had acted in self-defence.

On 15 February 1945, Kam, then a company commander of the *SS-Panzer-Grenadier-Regiment 'Germania'*, won the Knight's Cross for 'especially decisive action in the battle against the enemy'. After the war, Kam disappeared. The Danish authorities assumed he was dead. He was living in West Germany under the name Peter Müller. In 1956, he was granted German citizenship.

In 1968, the public prosecutor investigated his part in the murder of Clemmensen, but dropped the charges due to lack of evidence. But the Danes still had a warrant out on him. In 1998, Kam was interrogated again. He admitted to shooting Clemmensen, but only when he was dead on the ground as an act of solidarity with the other assassins. However, the post-mortem report showed that all the bullets hit Clemmensen while he was standing. Again, Kam claimed they had fired in self-defence, though Clemmensen was unarmed.

The Danish minister of justice requested Kam's extradition, but this was refused by Germany. In 2007, he was arrested in Bavaria on a European arrest warrant issued by Denmark. However, a German court decided that Kam's part in Clemmensen's death was not murder by manslaughter – thus falling under the statute of limitations which had then expired. He regularly appeared at rallies of ex-SS men. He was also closely associated with Heinrich Himmler's daughter Gudrun Burwitz and her network *Stille Hilfe* (Silent Aid), set up to support former SS men who had been arrested or were on the run. In 2014, he was number five on the Simon Wiesenthal Center's list of most wanted Nazi war criminals. He died in Bavaria in 2015, aged 93.

A former Danish soldier, *SS-Hauptsturmführer* Johannes Helmers was wounded twice holding the line in Latvia when he won the Knight's Cross on 5 March 1945 as the commander of *6. Kompanie* in *2. Bataillon, 49. Freiwilligen-Panzer-Grenadier der SS 'De Ruyter', 23. SS-Panzer-Grenadier-Division 'Nederland'*. A nationalist not a Nazi, he managed to retire into private life in Denmark where he died in 1999, aged 81.

SS-Obersturmführer Jacques Leroy, a Belgian, lost his right eye and right arm with the *SS-Sturmbrigade 'Wallonien'* in November 1944. In

March 1945, as commander of I *Bataillon, SS-Grenadier-Regiment 69* he led 40 survivors in the defence of Altdamm at the mouth of the River Oder. For three days and nights this band of Walloon volunteers held off sizable enemy assaults, even turning back an attack by 19 Soviet tanks on 17 March 1945, destroying many of them. When they were finally relieved, only eight of the defenders were still alive – 32 had been killed in action, including Jacques Leroy's younger brother Claude. His other brother, a platoon leader, would fall in the defence of the Finkenwalde railway station, three days before the Soviet offensive on the Oder sector temporarily halted.

Leroy was awarded the Knight's Cross of the Iron Cross. Captured by the British, he spent a long time in prison in Belgium. Released, he moved to Bavaria where he became a German citizen. Plagued by the wounds he had suffered during the war, he died there in 1996, aged 72.

Waffen-Unterscharführer Eugène Vaulot, a Frenchman with the *Waffen-Grenadier-Division der SS 'Charlemagne'*, volunteered to fight in the Battle of Berlin. He was awarded the Knight's Cross for destroying six tanks with a *Panzerfaust* anti-tank grenade launcher on 29 April 1945 near Hitler's bunker. Three days later he was killed by a sniper.

Fellow Frenchman, *Waffen-Oberscharführer* François Apollot was also at the Battle of Berlin, winning the Knight's Cross for singlehandedly destroying six tanks and temporarily halting the attack on the Reich Chancellery. It was thought that he was killed by a sniper, though other accounts say he was still alive in France in 1997.

Another Frenchman, *Waffen-Hauptsturmführer* Henri Fenet, also won the Knight's Cross at the Battle of Berlin where his unit destroyed 21 Soviet tanks. Although he surrendered to the British, he was handed over to the Soviets, though he was released after his wounded foot had been treated. Returning to France, he was sentenced to 20 years with hard labour for being a collaborator, serving only ten. He died in 2002, aged 83.

Five more Latvian *Waffen-SS* men won the Knight's Cross of the Iron Cross in the last few weeks of the war. They included *Waffen-Unterscharführer* Karlis Sensberg, who was missing presumably killed with 19. *Waffen-Grenadier-Division der SS* (*lettische Nr 2*) at the Battle of Berlin.

Waffen-Obersturmführer Roberts Gaigals led a badly depleted company in a counterattack against the Red Army in the forests of Latvia, though he was injured in the jaw and could only issue orders with hand signals. Taken prisoner by the Soviets, he returned to Latvia in 1954, dying in Riga in 1982, aged 69.

Waffen-Sturmbannführer Voldemars Reinholds was awarded the Knight's Cross fighting in the Courland Pocket, though he never received it. He did not surrender to the Soviets and disappeared into the forest, but was arrested soon after. He escaped the firing squad and lived under an alias in Riga until a former colleague revealed his identity to the Soviet authorities. Sentenced to 25 years in the Gulag, he served just ten before returning to Latvia where he died in 1986, aged 83.

LAST DITCH

Although the war was clearly lost, the *Waffen-SS* fought on. *Frundsberg* battled on in the rearguard action in Pomerania in early 1945 with 11. *SS-Panzerarmee* commanded by Felix Steiner, now an *SS-Obergruppenführer*.

During the Battle of Berlin, Steiner disobeyed Hitler's orders to attack the incoming Red Army as he did not have the manpower. After the surrender, he faced charges at Nuremberg, but they were dropped for lack of evidence. He went on to work with the CIA and was a founding member of HIAG, publishing a number of apologist books before his death in 1966, aged 69.

On 16 February 1945, *Frundsberg* joined *Nordland*, *Nederland* and *Wallonien* in an attack on the Red Army under the command of Marshal

Georgy Zhukov. These weakened divisions stood no chance and were driven back in a couple of days.

Soon Steiner's '*panzer* army' existed on paper only. The Walloons had been sacrificed trying to hold the bridgehead at Altdamm, while *Nederland* was sent to the south to contain the Soviet attack and *Nordland* was brought back to defend Berlin. The *Waffen-SS* – now largely non-German volunteers – joined the last-ditch defence of the city, along with children from the Hitler Youth and old men and the unfit from the *Volkssturm*. There were two under-strength divisions of the German Army, along with the depleted *Nordland* and *Charlemagne* divisions, a battalion of Latvians from 15. *Waffen-Grenadier-Division der SS (lettische Nr 1)* and 600 men from Himmler's escort battalion, the *Begleit-Bataillon Reichsführer-SS*.

Earlier plans that Hitler should leave Berlin for Obersalzberg in Bavaria were abandoned. It had been thought he could establish an alpine redoubt there, defended by *6. SS-Panzerarmee*. Instead, Hitler dedicated his time to an even less practical plan: the relief of the capital.

When Steiner explained that he did not have the divisions to perform the attack Hitler had ordered, General Gotthard Heinrici, who had replaced Himmler as Commander-in-Chief of Army Group Vistula, made it clear that if Hitler did not allow the IX Army to retreat to the west he would tender his resignation. On 22 April, at his afternoon situation conference, Hitler fell into a tearful rage. He declared that the war was lost, blaming the generals for the defeat and that he would remain in Berlin until the end and then kill himself.

According to Gerhard Herrgesell, stenographer to Germany's Supreme Headquarters Staff, Hitler had given up all hope because he had been 'betrayed by the *Waffen-SS*'.

'He had lost confidence in the *Wehrmacht* quite a while ago,' said Herrgesell. 'This afternoon he said that he was losing confidence in the

Waffen-SS for the first time. He had always counted on the *Waffen-SS* as elite troops that would never fail him.... the failure of the SS troops to hold the Russians north of Berlin had apparently convinced Hitler that his elite troops had lost heart.'

Herrgesell added: 'The *Führer* always maintained that no force, however well trained and equipped, could fight if it lost heart, and now his last reserve [the *Waffen-SS*] was gone.'

But the hearts of the rank-and-file *Waffen-SS* men were far from gone. Many were still true to their motto – *Meine Ehre heist Treue* (My Honour is my Loyalty) – engraved on the belt buckle of every SS man. They fought on ferociously. However, some of their senior officers, including the *Reichführer-SS* himself, had ceased to believe in their eventual victory.

One of those who had lost heart was Steiner himself. He had defied a direct order and failed to launch his attack. As far as Hitler was concerned, he had foresworn his oath. Steiner lacked the strength to take on the Red Army effectively. The 11th Army amounted to little more than a small headquarters staff attempting to create a battle group out of sailors, airmen and whatever stragglers they could lay their hands on. The Hitler Youth was sent, along with a battalion of *Luftwaffe* troops that guarded Göring's Karinhall estate who were 'to be put unconditionally under the command of *SS-Obergruppenführer* Steiner'.

Hitler told *Luftwaffe* Chief of Staff General de Flieger Karl Koller: 'All *Luftwaffe* personnel available for action on the ground must immediately be sent to Steiner. Any commander who holds back his troops will forfeit his life in five hours. You yourself will guarantee with your head that the last man is thrown in.'

When Koller phoned the *Führerbunker* to report that he had issued the necessary instructions, Hitler reassured him: 'You'll see, the Russians will suffer the greatest and bloodiest defeat in history at the gates of Berlin.'

These reinforcements amounted to less than 5,000 *Luftwaffe* personnel and a small band of Hitler Youth armed only with hand weapons. Steiner sent them back.

'Their commitment would have been irresponsible,' he said. 'Considering the situation, the operation seemed ridiculous.'

Hitler ordered that Steiner be stripped of his command and replaced with Lieutenant-General Rudolf Holste, a corps commander in the badly battered 12th Army. However, Steiner and Holste decided to ignore this order and continued commanding their own units.

On 25 April, Steiner did attack, establishing a bridgehead across the Ruppiner Canal west of Oranienburg, north of Berlin. Soviet armoured units were quickly sent to halt its advance. The Red Army then broke into its rear. The OKW's war diary recorded that 'as difficult as it is, there remains no choice other than to give up the Steiner attack'. No one dared tell Hitler.

He only discovered the truth on 28 April when General Hans Krebs, Chief of the Army General Staff, called from the *Führerbunker* to ask Field Marshal Wilhelm Keitel at the new Supreme Command Headquarters in Fürstenberg about the progress of the relief operation.

'The *Führer* is mainly interested in the attack west of Oranienburg. What's the situation there? Is the attack moving forward? The *Führer* removes Steiner from command there. Has Holste taken over the command there yet? If we are not helped in the next 36 to 48 hours, it will be too late.'

Keitel replied that the bridgehead was not large enough for German tanks to operate, while the Red Army was attacking from three sides.

'A further continuation of the attack will in any case lead to defeat,' Keitel said.

'Why is Holste not in command there?' asked Krebs. 'The *Führer* has no trust in Steiner.'

'Holste is on the western wing of his very broad front and I have not been able to bring him over,' said Keitel. 'At the moment, the way things stand, there is nothing that can be done about it.'

'The *Führer* awaits immediate help,' Krebs replied. 'There remains at most 48 more hours. If help doesn't come by then it will be too late. The *Führer* asks me to remind you of that.'

Keitel reassured him 'there still lies the possibility of rescue by a northerly advance'. There wasn't. That was the last phone call from the OKW to the *Führerbunker*. After that the lines were cut.

BETRAYAL

News of Hitler's outburst on 22 April – particularly his comments about being 'betrayed by the *Waffen-SS*' – reached Himmler's ears. He then succumbed to the appeals of *SS-Gruppenführer* Walter Schellenberg, Head of Military Intelligence, to negotiate an armistice. Schellenberg survived the war and testified against the SS at Nuremberg. But he was sentenced to six years for ordering the murder of Soviet PoWs, and released after two years due to ill health.

Himmler contacted Count Bernadotte at the Swedish consulate at Lübeck. This leaked to the press and was reported by the BBC. The broadcast was picked up by the Propaganda Ministry in the ruins of Berlin. When the news reached Hitler, 'his colour rose to a heated red and his face was unrecognizable... After a lengthy outburst, Hitler sank into a stupor and for a time the bunker was silent,' said aviator Hanna Reitsch, who was thought to have landed at an improvised airstrip near the Brandenburg Gate in a last-ditch attempt to rescue Hitler.

It now seemed clear to Hitler that not only had the *Waffen-SS* betrayed him in the field, its leader 'loyal Heinrich' had been trying to surrender to the Allies. The man who would pay the price was Himmler's adjutant *SS-Obergruppenführer* Fegelein.

Hitler ordered the new commander-in-chief of the *Luftwaffe* Field Marshal Ritter von Greim to fly out of Berlin with Reitsch and arrest Himmler, telling him: 'A traitor must never succeed me as *Führer*. You must go out to make sure he does not.'

Greim and Reitsch caught up with Himmler at the headquarters of Admiral Karl Dönitz, Hitler's short-lived successor, at Plön in Schleswig-Holstein, but they were in no position to arrest him. Greim committed suicide after being captured by the Americans. Himmler did the same in British custody. Dönitz served ten years for crimes against humanity, while Reitsch was held for interrogation for 18 months. Asked about her flight with von Greim, she said: 'It was the blackest day when we could not die at our *Führer*'s side.' Reitsch also said: 'We should all kneel down in reverence and prayer before the altar of the Fatherland.' When the interviewers asked what she meant by 'Altar of the Fatherland' she answered, 'Why, the *Führer*'s bunker in Berlin ...'

Despite Hitler's distrust of the SS, to the very end he surrounded himself with adjutants and guards from the *Leibstandarte*, recognizing that there were some last-ditch loyalist. He had little choice. Indeed, members of Himmler's Escort Battalion, which the *Reichsführer-SS* had sent to Berlin at the last moment, formed a *Fliegende Feld-Standgerichte* ('flying courts-martial') that hanged from lampposts those they considered shirkers and deserters. A German Army officer in Berlin said they were 'mostly very young SS officers. Hardly a decoration. Blind and fanatical.'

Even when it heard that Hitler was dead and Berlin was about to surrender, the *Nordland* continued to fight. When the division was reduced to just 100 men, it tried to break out, only to be cut down by enemy fire.

IN THE *FÜHRERBUNKER*

SS-Brigadeführer Wilhelm Mohnke was appointed Battle Commander for the central government district that included the Reich Chancellery and *Führerbunker*. Fanatically loyal to Hitler, Mohnke had become a member of the Nazi Party in 1931 and the *SS-Stabswache Berlin* when it was formed as Hitler's personal guard in 1933, going on to serve in the *SS-Sonderkommando Berlin*. He fought with the *Leibstandarte* in Poland and France. He was appointed to command a regiment in the *Hitlerjugend* SS division in 1943, receiving the Knight's Cross of the Iron Cross on 11 July 1944 during the Battle for Caen. Mohnke returned to the *Leibstandarte* as commander during the Battle of the Bulge in December 1944.

Kampfgruppe 'Mohnke' was divided into two weak regiments. These were made up of the *Leibstandarte* Flak Company, replacements from the *Leibstandarte Ausbildungs-und Ersatz Bataillon* from Spreenhagen under *SS-Standartenführer* Günther Anhalt, the 600 men from the *Begleit-Bataillon Reichsführer-SS* and the *Führer-Begleit-Kompanie*, Hitler's Escort Company, formed around a core group of 800 men from the *Leibstandarte SS 'Adolf Hitler'* that was assigned to guard Hitler. As the Reich Chancellery and *Führerbunker* were potent political symbols they were the Red Army's principal targets.

With the Battle for Berlin raging around them, Hitler ordered Mohnke to set up a military tribunal to try *SS-Gruppenführer* Hermann Fegelein for desertion. Later Mohnke described the scene to James O'Donnell, author of *The Bunker*:

> I was to preside over it myself... I decided the accused man deserved trial by high-ranking officers... We set up the court-martial... We military judges took our seats at the table with the standard *German Army Manual of Courts-Martial* before us. No sooner were we seated than defendant Fegelein began acting up in such an outrageous manner that the trial could not even commence.
>
> Roaring drunk... Fegelein first brazenly challenged the competence of the court. He kept blubbering that he was responsible to... Himmler alone, not Hitler... He refused to defend himself. The man was in wretched shape – bawling, whining, vomiting, shaking like an aspen leaf...

I was now faced with an impossible situation. On the one hand, based on all available evidence, including his own earlier statements, this miserable excuse for an officer was guilty of flagrant desertion... Yet the *German Army Manual* states clearly that no German soldier can be tried unless he is clearly of sound mind and body, in a condition to hear the evidence against him... In my opinion and that of my fellow officers, Hermann Fegelein was in no condition to stand trial... I closed the proceedings... So I turned Fegelein over to SS General Rattenhuber and his security squad. I never saw the man again.

The following day *SS-Gruppenführer* Johann Rattenhuber was called to see Hitler.

'About 10 o'clock at night Hitler summoned me to his room,' he later recalled. 'Hitler said: "You have served me faithfully for many years. Tomorrow is your birthday and I want to congratulate you and thank you for your faithful service, because I shall not be able to do so tomorrow... I have taken the decision... I must leave this world..." I went over to Hitler and told him how necessary his survival was for Germany, that there was still a chance to try and escape from Berlin and save his life. "What for?" Hitler argued. "Everything is ruined... and to flee means falling into the hands of the Russians."'

Rattenhuber himself was attempting to flee Berlin with Mohnke the day after Hitler killed himself when they were captured by the Red Army. In August 1951 the Soviet Ministry of State Security charged that 'from the early days of the Nazi dictatorship in Germany in 1933 and until the defeat of the latter in 1945, being an *SS-Gruppenführer*, Police Lieutenant-General and the chief of the Reich Security Service, he ensured the personal security of Hitler and other Reich leaders'. More seriously, in January 1942, his unit murdered 227 Jews at Strizhavka in Ukraine. Rattenhuber was sentenced to 25 years' imprisonment after giving the Soviet authorities a description of the last days of Hitler and the Nazi leadership in the bunker complex. He was released from prison in 1955 and handed over to the East German authorities, who allowed him to go to West Germany. He died in Munich in 1957, aged 60.

Following their capture, Mohnke and other senior German officers from *Kampfgruppe 'Mohnke'* were treated to a banquet by the Chief of Staff of the 8th Guards Army. Afterwards, he was flown to Moscow for interrogation and kept in solitary confinement for six years, then spent another four years in a prison camp for high-ranking German officers. After his release in 1955, he was investigated by the Canadian, British and German authorities for the murder of three Canadian prisoners of war in Normandy in 1944. He died in West Germany in 2001, aged 90. *SS-Standartenführer* Günther Anhalt died on 27 April in the Battle for Berlin.

THE REICHSTAG

The Red Army broke through Berlin's defences on 28 April and headed for Germany's parliament building, the Reichstag. The *Waffen-SS* counterattacked, forcing the Soviets to withdraw from the Gestapo headquarters on Prinz-Albrechtstrasse. By 30 April, the Soviets had repaired the bridges over the Spree and were able to bring up artillery to support their attack on the Reichstag, which had not been repaired since it had been set on fire in February 1933 and had since been damaged in Allied air raids. The rubble provided useful cover for the defenders.

In the battle for the building, there was fierce room-to-room fighting. The *Waffen-SS* had turned the basement into a fortress which repelled the Soviets for two days. When the building was finally taken on 2 May, the Red Army famously flew a Soviet flag from the roof.

By then Hitler was dead and General Helmuth Weidling had surrendered the city. Nevertheless, small groups of *Waffen-SS* men continued to fight until all the formal surrender negotiations had been completed on 7 May 1945. Indeed, some continued fighting a guerrilla war against the Soviets for years to come as men from Ukraine and the Baltic states knew what awaited them if they surrendered.

SURRENDER

Waffen-SS troops could expect little quarter in the West too. As advancing Allied troops liberated concentration and death camps, they found that the guards wore the same uniforms as the *Waffen-SS* men they had met on the battlefield. Nevertheless, they conducted themselves with dignity.

The surrender signed by the *Wehrmacht* in Rheims on 7 May was to take effect two days later. But the generals had not forgotten the formidable *Waffen-SS* forces still concentrated in Austria. The OKW war diary for 9 May said: 'Field Marshal Kesselring informed *SS-Oberstgruffenführer* Dietrich that the terms of the ceasefire are also binding on the formations of the *Waffen-SS* [and] expects that, like the entire *Wehrmacht*, the *Waffen-SS* will also conduct itself in an irreproachably correct manner.'

The same day, the *SS-Panzer-Grenadier-Regiment 'Deutschland'*, the oldest regiment in the *Waffen-SS*, sent a message to the headquarters of the *Das Reich* division saying: 'The Regiment *Deutschland* – now completely cut off, without supplies, with losses of 70 per cent in personnel and equipment, at the end of its strength – must capitulate. Tomorrow the regiment will march into captivity with all heads held high. The regiment which had the honour of bearing the name "*Deutschland*" is now signing off.'

A former SS officer said that, during the final ride, the vehicles kept 'a more exact formation than usual. The grenadiers sat stiffly at attention. With exemplary bearing we drove westwards. There were the Americans.'

The *Hitlerjugend* followed suit. They ignored the American order to drape their vehicles in white flags, which they described as 'demeaning'.

Less than 1.6 km (1 mile) from the demarcation line where they were to surrender, they passed in review in front of their commander. Then the division drove into captivity 'disciplined and with proud bearing'.

CHAPTER ELEVEN

⚡⚡

Criminal Organization

fter the war many former *Waffen-SS* men claimed that they were just regular soldiers and had taken no part in the crimes committed by the other parts of the organization. The International Military Tribunal at Nuremberg in 1946 thought otherwise. The panel of judges agreed with British prosecutor Sir David Maxwell-Fyfe who said it 'was in theory and in practice as much an integral part of the SS organization as any other branch of the SS'. This was because, even in battle, members were under the jurisdiction of Himmler and the SS Main Legal Office, not the Army.

The *Waffen-SS* was, he said, 'involved in the deportation of Jews and other foreign nationals... in the widespread murder and ill-treatment of the civilian population of occupied territories. Under the guise of combating partisan units, units of the SS exterminated Jews and people deemed politically undesirable by the SS, and their reports record the execution of enormous numbers of persons. *Waffen-SS* divisions were responsible for many massacres and atrocities in occupied territories such as the massacres at Oradour and Lidice.'

What's more 'SS units were active participants in the steps leading up to aggressive war. The *Verfuegungstruppe* was used in the occupation of the Sudetenland, of Bohemia and Moravia [Czechoslovakia] and of Memel' – part of East Prussia given to Lithuania after World War I.

In respect of charges of war crimes and crimes against humanity, the Tribunal concluded: 'Units of the *Waffen-SS* were directly involved in the killing of prisoners of war and atrocities in occupied countries. It supplied personnel for the *Einsatzgruppen*, and had command over the concentration camp guards after its absorption of the *Totenkopf-SS*, which originally controlled the system.'

The *Waffen-SS* was judged to be a criminal organization due to its connection to the Nazi Party and its direct involvement in numerous war crimes and crimes against humanity. Former *Waffen-SS* members, with the exception of conscripts who comprised about one third of the membership, were denied many of the rights afforded other military veterans.

The judgement did not automatically mean that all individual members were convicted war criminals. Individuals appeared in front of other Allied military tribunals on specific charges. A few hundred *Waffen-SS* members, including members of fighting formations, were convicted of specific criminal acts. Otherwise, officers and NCOs were kept in prison camps for four years, before appearing before German de-Nazification Courts. While 99 per cent were found free of personal guilt, some were convicted of being a member of a criminal organization and stripped of their civil rights.

Members of the *Wehrmacht* took the opportunity to blame their own misdeeds on the *Waffen-SS*. Some even blamed them for the defeat of Germany. To fight back, SS veterans set up the *Hilfsorganization auf Gegenseitigkelt* [HIAG] *der Waffen SS*, the Mutual Aid Society of the *Waffen SS*. They published a magazine called *Der Freiwillige* (*The Volunteer*) and books by former *Waffen-SS* men, and they maintained a library of neo-Nazi tracts, putting former members in touch with each other and fighting for the civil rights of members who had been stripped of them.

MALMÉDY

The lobby to rehabilitate the *Waffen-SS* got under way after the conviction of Sepp Dietrich and 72 members of *Kampfgruppe 'Peiper'* at an American Military Tribunal held at the former Dachau concentration camp in 1946 for the massacre of American prisoners of war at Malmédy during the Ardennes Campaign. Forty-three of the defendants, including Joachim Peiper, were sentenced to death by hanging; 22, including Dietrich, were given life imprisonment, two were given 20 years; one 15 years; and five ten years.

A campaign was started in right-wing newspapers to get the convicted men lighter sentences. Senator Joseph McCarthy, the anti-Communist campaigner, took up the case. It was appealed to the United States Supreme Court, which made no decision. The US Senate set up a subcommittee to investigate allegations that the defendants had been beaten, tortured and subjected to mock trials to get them to confess. Almost all the defendants presented affidavits repudiating their former confessions and alleging aggravated duress of all types.

Most of the death sentences had already been commuted. Life sentences were commuted to a few years. Peiper was released in 1956. Dietrich was released in 1955, only to be re-arrested and serve another 19 months for his role in the Night of the Long Knives.

While the fighting abilities of the *Waffen-SS* had been impugned by other *Wehrmacht* officers, Heinz Guderian, the architect of *blitzkrieg* warfare, rode to their rescue. When Paul Hausser published the first history of the *Waffen-SS* – *Waffen-SS im Einsatz* (*Waffen-SS in Action*) in 1953, Guderian contributed a foreword saying: "'Our Honour is our Loyalty." This was the motto the *Waffen-SS* trained to, and it was the motto they fought by. Whoever saw them in battle is bound to

Defendants for Malmédy Massacre including Joachim Peiper (third from left, first row), Fritz Kraemer and Herman Priess.

confirm that. After the collapse this formation faced exceptionally heavy and unjust charges.... Since so many untrue and unjust things have been said and written about them, I welcome most cordially the initiative of their pre-war teacher and one of the most outstanding wartime commanders, who has taken up his pen to give evidence of the truth. His book will help disperse the clouds of lies and calumnies piled up around the *Waffen-SS* and will help those gallant men to resume the place they deserve alongside the other branches of the *Wehrmacht.*'

This soon had an effect. In August 1953, West Germany's first post-war Chancellor, Konrad Adenauer, made a speech saying that members of the combat formations of the *Waffen-SS* had been soldiers like any others. Soon after, a number of former *Waffen-SS* men imprisoned for war crimes were released. One of these was Kurt '*Panzer*' Meyer who had been commander of the *Hitlerjugend* during the Allied invasion of Normandy and had originally been sentenced to death for the murder of Canadian prisoners of war. He became a leading spokesman for HIAG. Released war criminals were then granted returnee compensation such as was given to former prisoners of war.

Hasso Von Manteuffel, the former Army general who was by then a member of West Germany's parliament, the *Bundestag*, called for the rehabilitation of the *Waffen-SS*. Then, in 1956, the German Ministry of Defence announced that former members of the *Waffen-SS* could join the new *Bundeswehr*, the West German armed forces, at their old rank. However, the German Federal Government refused to give former *Waffen-SS* men the pensions provided for career soldiers of the *Wehrmacht*.

In 1957, Kurt Meyer addressed 8,000 ex-*Waffen-SS* men at a HIAG convention in Bavaria, claiming: 'SS troops committed no crimes except the massacre at Oradour, and that was the action of a single man. He was scheduled to go before a court-martial, but he died a hero's death before he could be tried.'

He also denied the Nuremberg Tribunal's finding that the *Waffen-SS* had been responsible for the massacre at Ludice and its destruction.

'The *Waffen-SS* was as much a regular army outfit as any other in the *Wehrmacht*,' he insisted. Making the *Waffen-SS* a criminal organization was imposing collective guilt on all its former members. The government should not 'treat former SS troops as second-class citizens [when] they did nothing more than fight for their country'.

He maintained that the charge *Waffen-SS* units had been assigned to carry out extermination operations was 'designed to defame the formation'. However, he did not deny that crimes had been committed.

'In the interests of historical truth nothing must be glossed over,' he wrote. 'Things happened during the war that are unworthy of the German nation. The former soldiers of the *Waffen-SS* are men enough to recognize and deplore actual cases of inhuman behaviour. It would be foolish to label all charges laid at our doorstep as the propaganda of our former enemies. Of course they made propaganda of it... but crimes were committed. It is useless to argue about the toll of victims – the facts are burdensome enough.'

He also said that the *Waffen-SS* had been blamed for what went on in the concentration camps, but the guards there had been budgeted as combat troops who 'knew no more and no less about these activities in the homeland than the mass of the German people'. What's more ex-*Waffen-SS* men had been 'subjected to inhuman suffering for crimes which they neither committed, nor were able to prevent'. Passing off concentration camp guards as combat troops was a betrayal by 'leading personalities of the state'.

TOTENKOPFVERBÄNDE

Despite Meyer's protest, the *Waffen-SS* and the concentration camps were intimately connected. Some 6,500 members of the *SS-Totenkopfverbände* – the Death's Head Units who guarded the concentration camps – were transferred to the newly established *Totenkopf-division* in October 1939. So, concentration camp guards formed the core of one of the elite *Waffen-SS* combat formations.

Its leader was Theodor Eicke who had served on the Western Front in World War I, winning the Iron Cross Second Class. Between the wars he worked as a policeman and a security officer at IG Farben, an international chemical company that supported the Nazis and used slave labour from concentration camps. Thirteen of its directors were convicted of war crimes.

Eicke had joined the Nazi Party in 1928 and the SS in 1930, quickly rising to the rank of *SS-Standartenführer*. After a short period of exile in Fascist Italy, he returned to Germany when Hitler took power. He was sent to a mental asylum. Himmler arranged his release and appointed him commandant of the first official concentration camp at Dachau after the first commandant, *SS-Sturmbannführer* Hilmar Wäckerle, faced criminal charges for murdering inmates.

With Himmler's permission he formed a dedicated Guard Unit, the *SS-Wachverbände*, which was subjected to rigid discipline and inflicted it on the inmates. He was responsible for the adoption of the death's head insignia on the guards' collars and the blue and white striped pyjamas worn by the inmates.

During the Night of the Long Knives, he assisted Sepp Dietrich in arresting SA commanders and, with Michael Lippert, murdered Ernst Röhm. The SS then took over the remaining SA-run camps. As Inspector of Concentration Camps, Eicke reorganized them with Dachau as their model. As commander of the *SS-Totenkopfverbände*, he taught the guards to hate their charges. Human sympathy was considered a weakness. Men were to renounce any church or religious organization they belonged to. Their loyalty was only to be to the *SS-Totenkopfverbände* and to Eicke himself.

Unlike membership of the *SS-Verfügungstruppe*, service in the *SS-Totenkopfverbände* was not considered an alternative to military service and members had to spend two years in the *Wehrmacht* before returning to duty in the camps. At the outbreak of war, those of military age were called up, leaving the old, the infirm and those under 20 as guards. Their duties grew as new camps for political enemies were established in the occupied territories. Meanwhile, Eicke moved on as commander of the *SS-Totenkopfdivision* at the front. The new Inspectorate of Concentration Camps under *SS-Brigadeführer* Richard Glücks came under the authority of Himmler's new main office, the *SS-Führungshauptamt*, making the concentration-camp system nominally part of the *Waffen-SS*. Indeed, Himmler issued directives controlling the concentration camps and dressed its guards in *Waffen-SS* uniforms. They carried *Waffen-SS* paybooks.

Despite further reorganization, Glücks and his staff continued to hold nominal *Waffen-SS* ranks and went on to implement the forced labour of camp inmates, human medical experiments and the gassing of Jews and others. Glücks committed suicide in 1945 after the surrender of Germany.

Throughout the war, there was a continuous exchange of personnel between concentration camp guards and combat formations. *SS-Obersturmbannführer* Rudolf Höss, commandant of Auschwitz from May 1940 and December 1943, said that 2,500 members of his staff were sent to the front and replaced with others who had served. Some 1,500 guards at Sachsenhausen concentration camp were similarly transferred. Even trainees were co-opted. In April 1945, a British general saw Hungarian *Volksdeutsch* recruits from the nearby *Waffen-SS panzer-grenadier* school 'shooting indiscriminately among the mob of gibbering skeletons' at Belsen.

Höss admitted gassing and burning 2,500,000 victims, while at least another half million under his supervision died of starvation and disease. He was hanged.

Waffen-SS officers who proved incompetent at field command were also given camp assignments. Friedrich Hartjenstein, who was transferred voluntarily from the *Wehrmacht* to the *SS-Totenkopfverbände* in 1938, commanded a guard company at Sachsenhausen. He served as an officer in the *SS-Totenkopfdivision* from 1940 to 1942, but was dismissed for incompetence and sent to Auschwitz as commander of a guard detachment. He went on to be commandant of the Birkenau extermination camp, then the Natzweiler camp in France. He died of a heart attack while awaiting execution.

In the first years of the war, men of the *SS-Totenkopfstandarten* were used for 'special police tasks' in occupied Europe. These included deportations and executions in accordance with Hitler's racial policies.

When Germany invaded the Soviet Union, these tasks were handed over to other SS or Police formations. While the *Totenkopfstandarten* then converted into *SS-Totenkopf* infantry regiments, some were retained by Himmler for operations against partisans which often involved the mass extermination of civilians. Tens of thousands of men serving with *Waffen-SS* frontline formations had witnessed, if not participated in, these crimes.

EINSATZGRUPPEN

Then there were the *Einsatzgruppen*, or deployment groups, who committed mass shootings of Jews and others in occupied territories. They were often manned by *Waffen-SS* personnel and were under the control of Himmler. Prior to the invasion of Russia, there were four *Einsatzgruppen* comprising just 3,000 men, but they managed to murder nearly half-a-million people in just six months. Combat troops were posted to the *Einsatzgruppen* as a regular part of *Waffen-SS* discipline.

Knight's Cross winner *SS-Obergruppenführer* Georg Keppler, commander variously of the *Das Reich* and *Totenkopf* divisions, *I SS-Panzer Korps, III SS-Panzer Korps* and the *XVIII SS-Armee Korps*, explained how candidates were picked: 'They were late or fell asleep on duty. They were court-martialled but were told they could escape by volunteering for Special Commandos. For fear of punishment and in the belief that their career was ruined anyway, these young men asked to be transferred to the Special Commandos. Well, these commandos, where they were first put through special training, were murder commandos. When the young men realized what they were being asked to do and refused to take part in mass murder, they were told the orders were given them as a form of punishment. Either they can obey and take that punishment or they can disobey and be shot. In any case their career is over and done with. By such methods decent young men were frequently turned into criminals.'

DENIAL

Some 1,500 *Waffen-SS* men were responsible for the murder of hundreds of thousands of civilians. Senior *Waffen-SS* officers such as Paul Hausser, Gottlob Berger and Erich von dem Bach-Zelewski distanced themselves from the atrocities committed by the *Kaminski* and *Dirlewanger SS-Sonderkommandos*, or Special Commandos, denying these formations were ever part of the *Waffen-SS*. However, Kaminski's Russian National Liberation Army became 29. *Waffen-Grenadier-Division der SS (russische Nr 1)* in 1944. Kaminski was promoted *Waffen-Brigadeführer und Gruppenführer der Waffen-SS* and was decorated by Himmler.

There were 6,500 men under Kaminski's command, the largest single unit deployed by the Germans to suppress the Warsaw Uprising. They were largely Ukrainians who had a traditional antipathy towards the Poles. Four thousand men in SS-*Sturmbrigade 'Dirlewanger'* also took part in the suppression of the Warsaw Uprising. The brigade had been formed in 1940 when Berger suggested establishing a special unit comprising convicted poachers in SS-controlled prisons and concentration camps. Himmler liked the idea, but was in two minds about accepting Berger's friend Oskar Dirlewanger as its commander. But Dirlewanger was an irreproachable Nazi.

A veteran of the *Freikorps*, Dirlewanger was a vicious anti-Semite and had been a member of the Nazi Party since 1923. A police report described him as 'a mentally unstable, violent fanatic and alcoholic, who had the habit of erupting into violence under the influence of drugs'. With a long record for the illegal possession of guns and embezzlement, in 1934, while a Nazi Party official, he was sentenced to two years for raping a 14-year-old girl from the League of German Maidens, the female branch of the Hitler Youth. Arrested again upon his release, he was sent to Welzheim concentration camp as a sexual deviant.

When Berger got him released, he went to Spain where he served in the Spanish Foreign Legion during the Civil War, before transferring into the German Condor Legion. At the beginning of World War II, Dirlewanger volunteered for the *Waffen-SS* and was given the rank of *SS-Obersturmführer*. Alongside poachers, Dirlewanger recruited other criminals and concentration camp inmates, court-martialled *Waffen-SS* men, convicts from military prisons, mental asylum patients, homosexuals, interned Romani people and eventually even political prisoners sentenced for their anti-Nazi activities.

Serving as the commandant of a labour camp, Dirlewanger was accused of murder, corruption and 'racial defilement'. He would have young Jewish women stripped, whipped and injected with strychnine so he and his friends could enjoy watching their death throes. Their bodies were cut up and boiled to make soap. He also repeatedly pillaged the ghetto in Lublin, extorting ransoms. His leadership was 'characterized by continued alcohol abuse, looting, sadistic atrocities, rape and murder'. This was tolerated by Berger and Himmler as he was just the sort of man they needed commanding their Special Commandos.

In anti-partisan operations, 'Dirlewanger's preferred method was to herd the local population inside a barn, set the barn on fire, and then shoot with machine guns anyone who tried to escape.' Civilians were routinely used as human shields and marched over minefields. Dirlewanger and his force 'raped and tortured young women and slaughtered Jews *Einsatzgruppen*-style in Byelorussia beginning in 1942,' said American historian Richard Rhodes. It is estimated that his *Sonderkommando*, by then regiment-sized, killed at least 30,000 Belorussian civilians.

In Warsaw, Dirlewanger participated in the Wola massacre where some 40,000 civilians were rounded up and shot in just two days. He had three hospitals burned down with patients inside, while the nurses were whipped, gang-raped and finally hanged naked, together with the doctors to the accompaniment of the popular song '*In München steht ein Hofbräuhaus*'. Later, his men 'drank, raped and murdered their way through the Old Town, slaughtering civilians and fighters alike without distinction of age or sex'. Some 30,000 civilians were killed, along with several thousand wounded in field hospitals who were shot and set on fire with flamethrowers. He shot his own men, with his own pistol, if they displeased him or he wanted whatever they had looted. There were even attempts by the Main SS Legal Office to prosecute him that were thwarted by Berger. Instead, he was awarded the Knight's Cross.

As his unit ended the war as 36. *Waffen-Grenadier-Division der SS*, the Nuremberg Tribunal concluded that it was part of the *Waffen-SS*. Dirlewanger was arrested after being spotted by a former concentration camp inmate and is thought to have died in custody, though rumours persisted that he escaped.

FRONTLINE TROOPS

While it is clear that atrocities were committed by concentration camp guards, members of the *Einsatzgruppen* and other *Sonderkommandos*, frontline *Waffen-SS* men also committed appalling crimes. On 19 September 1939, during the invasion of Poland, a *Waffen-SS* private named Ernst in the SS Artillery Regiment attached to *Panzer-Division* 'Kempf' and a military policeman herded a work detail of 50 Jews into a synagogue and shot them. The two men were arrested, court-martialled and found guilty of manslaughter. Ernst was sentenced to three years imprisonment, while the military policeman got nine years' hard labour.

The prosecuting officer had wanted the death penalty for murder and appealed the sentences. However, the lighter sentences were upheld as Ernst was an 'excellent soldier' who had never been punished before. The judge said: 'He was in a state of irritation as a result of the many atrocities committed by Poles against ethnic Germans. As an SS man he was also particularly sensitive to the sight of Jews and the hostile attitude of Jewry to Germans; and thus acted quite unpremeditatedly in a spirit of youthful enthusiasm.'

The higher court reduced the military policeman's sentence to three years. An amnesty then rescinded both sentences and neither man served a single day in prison. Much play was made of this case at Nuremberg, where the Tribunal considered that three-years' imprisonment was insufficient punishment for the murder of 50 people. But it was surprising that charges had been brought at all.

To avoid such things happening again, Himmler set up a separate court system for the SS. When members of the SS-*Totenkopfdivision* murdered 99 British soldiers at Le Paradis during the Battle for Flanders in 1940, the Army wanted to prosecute, but the matter was taken over by the *Hauptamt SS-Gericht*, or SS Court Main Office. Nothing happened until after the war, when *SS-Obersturmführer* Fritz Knöchlien, the man accused to ordering the massacre, was convicted of a war crime and hanged.

Granted impunity by the SS Courts, the massacres continued on the Eastern Front where *Waffen-SS* men were told they were involved in an ideological and racial war against an enemy that was subhuman. Thus, they had a free hand.

Two weeks after Germany invaded the Soviet Union, the *Wiking* division murdered 600 Galician Jews, ostensibly in 'reprisal for Soviet cruelties'. Then came the murder of 4,000 prisoners in reprisal for the killing of six members of the *Leibstandarte* in the GPU headquarters in Taganrog. Colonel-General Georg Lindemann of the German 18th Army filed a complaint with SS Headquarters, naming members of the 2nd SS-Infantry Brigade who had shot prisoners of war. Himmler defended his men and refused to take disciplinary action against them. However, such atrocities were so commonplace that they usually went unrecorded.

At Nuremberg, the Soviets introduced charges that 'units of the SS – particularly the SS Division of Adolf Hitler [1. *Panzer-Division Leibstandarte SS 'Adolf Hitler'*] under the leadership of *Obergruppenführer* Dieterich, and the SS Division *Totenkopf* (Death's Head) under the leadership of *Obergruppenführer* Simon, are responsible for the extermination of more than 20,000 peaceful citizens of Kharkov, for the shooting and burning alive of prisoners of war'. Although this does not sound unlikely, they could produce no supporting evidence. Kharkov may have been the *Waffen-SS*'s greatest military victory, but it may also have been its greatest military atrocity.

Evidence against the *7. SS-Freiwilligen-Gebirgs-Division 'Prinz Eugen'* was more forthcoming. The Yugoslav delegation offered detailed descriptions of the torture and murder of captured partisans, along with the burning of villages and the murder of their inhabitants. One captured *Waffen-SS* soldier was found to be carrying a photograph of a Yugoslav being beheaded with an axe while grinning *Waffen-SS* men looked on. No one denied that these atrocities took place, but senior SS officers such as *SS-Obergruppenführer* Paul Hausser said that the division comprised ethnic Germans from Yugoslavia and that fighting in the Balkans was traditionally brutal. However, the officers and NCOs of *Prinz Eugen* were Germans from the Reich.

Even elite *Waffen-SS* divisions found themselves involved in atrocities behind the lines. In September 1941, a reserve company of *Das Reich*, then on the move from one area of the front to another, joined an SS extermination squad in shooting 920 Jews near Minsk. *Waffen-SS* men still in training were involved in the destruction of the Warsaw Ghetto in the spring of 1943.

Himmler sometimes held back combat units of the *Waffen-SS* for use in these so-called pacification operations. The *SS Kavallerie-Brigade* went to work in the area around the Pripet Marshes in southern Belorussia in the summer of 1941. One regiment reported shooting 259 Soviet prisoners of war and 6,504 civilians.

ATROCITIES IN ITALY

The *Waffen-SS* committed atrocities in Italy, too. After the capitulation of Italy on 8 September 1943, Joachim Peiper was in northern Italy with the *Leibstandarte* to disarm the Italian military. The division took to looting Jewish property. Their corps commander Paul Hausser ordered them to stop as only the security police and the *Sicherheitsdienst*, or SD, the SS's intelligence wing, were allowed to do that. Nevertheless, Peiper's unit continued hunting down Jews and was pursuing a thousand who had fled the former Italian zone of occupation in France when another unit from the division killed 54 Jewish civilians and disposed of their bodies in Lake Maggiore.

Then two of Peiper's men were captured by partisans near the town of Boves. He threatened to destroy the town unless they were freed. A local businessman and a parish priest negotiated their release. For their pains, they were doused in petrol and burned alive. His men then opened fire on the town with artillery. Some 350 house were destroyed and 24 people killed. They were largely the elderly or infirm who had been unable to flee. One was an 87-year-old women who could not move from her bed and was burnt alive when Peiper's men set her house on fire. The deputy parish priest was shot dead while giving absolution to an old man who had been shot by a German soldier.

Peiper and Lieutenants Otto Heinrich Dinse and Erhard Gührs were charged with these crimes but in 1968 an Italian court found there was 'insufficient suspicion of criminal activity on the part of any of the accused to warrant prosecution'. A German district court came to a similar conclusion and the prosecution was dropped, though Peiper served ten years for the massacre at Malmédy when he had been leading a battlegroup detached from the *Leibstandarte SS 'Adolf Hitler'* in the Ardennes Offensive.

At the trial, Peiper and his fellow defendants gave conflicting testimony. Some said that the men shot down had been mistaken in the fog for an attacking force. Others said that they were shot when attempting a mass escape from the field where they were being held. However, First Lieutenant Virgil T. Lary Jr, the only American officer to survive the massacre, testified:

It was decided that it would be best to surrender to this overwhelming force, the 1st Adolf Hitler SS *Panzer* Division, as we learned later. This we did... We were all placed in this field, approximately 150 to 160, maybe 175 men... The Germans then, at a particular time, were continuing to advance in a southerly direction toward Bastogne, and one of their self-propelled 88mm guns was ordered to stop, and it was backed around facing the group of personnel as they were standing in the field. After what happened, I have no doubt today that if they had been able to depress the muzzle of the gun into our group, they would have fired at point-blank range with their artillery into that group of men. They were not able to do that, however, because we were more or less in a depression below the gun and they couldn't lower it. So this particular self-propelled weapon was blocking their advance and it was ordered off. At that time they drove up two halftracks and parked them facing the group, at a fifteen- or twenty-foot interval between the two. A man stood up in this vehicle, who I later identified at Dachau, and fired a pistol... into the group. At the time we ordered our men to stand fast because we knew if they made a break that they would have a right then to cut loose on us with their machine guns. His first shot killed my driver. The second shot that he fired into the group then set off a group of machine guns firing into this helpless group of unarmed American prisoners of war. Those of us who were not killed immediately in the initial burst fell to the ground.... We continued to lay on the ground and the fire continued to come into us.... When they ceased firing after approximately five minutes, maybe three minutes, they came into the group to those men who were still alive and, of course, writhing in agony, and they shot them in the head.... During the initial firing I was only hit one time.

Lary and perhaps 20 others were overlooked. They lay in the field for hours. Vehicles full of Germans drove by. Lary said he 'could hear them laughing and every once in a while they would fire into the group of men as they lay on the ground, more or less as target practice'.

When darkness fell, the survivors jumped up and ran towards nearby woods. SS guards shot them down. Some escaped but were shot after they were found in a house where they had sought shelter. Lary hid in a shed. Later, he reached American troops at Malmédy. When the Allies retook the ground some weeks later the bodies of the dead lay frozen in the snow where they had fallen.

Das Reich was also responsible for the atrocities at Tulle and Oradour-sur-Glane, where the regimental records reported the massacre of unarmed men, women and children as if it was a military operation. In this 'cleansing action', there were '548 enemy dead' at the cost of 'two men wounded'. *4. SS-Polizei-Panzer-Grenadier-Division* took similar reprisals against local residents in Greece when it was attacked by partisans near Klisura.

The *Hitlerjugend* division shot 64 unarmed British and Canadian prisoners of war in Normandy. An Allied court of enquiry established that some units had been given orders to shoot prisoners after they had been interrogated. This was the policy throughout the division. Kurt Meyer was sentenced to death for this and for denying quarter to Allied soldiers who were surrendering. This was commuted to life and he served ten years. Other charges concerning atrocities in Poland and the Ukraine were dropped.

SS-Obergruppenführer Max Simon served eight years for ordering the murder of some 2,700 civilians when he was in Italy with *16. SS-Panzer-Grenadier-Division 'Reichsführer-SS'*. He was tried three times in German Federal courts and found not guilty of other crimes, including three murders in the German village of Brettheim in the last days of the war. On 10 April 1945, a farmer named Friedrich

Hanselmann had taken away the weapons of 15-year-old members of the Hitler Youth and threw them in a pond. The boys reported this to their commanding officer, *SS-Sturmbannführer* Gottschalk, who had Hanselmann arrested. Gottschalk sentenced Hanselmann to death and asked the mayor of Brettheim Leohard Gackstatter and a teacher called Leonhard Wolfmeyer to confirm the sentence. The two men refused and Simon ordered their execution for *Wehrkraftzersetzung* – 'undermining military morale'. Their bodies were left hanging for four days. A week later American tanks approached the village, but the SS had declared Brettheim a 'cornerstone of the German defence', preventing the hoisting of white flags. Seventeen civilians were killed. Two weeks after that, Simon and his corps surrendered to the Americans. Simon was acquitted on the grounds that he was obeying a legal order Himmler had issued as Minister of the Interior and Chief of the SS and Police.

In the last days of the war, young *Waffen-SS* officers from Hitler's and Himmler's bodyguard detachments conducted drumhead courts martial that led to the summary execution of soldiers or conscripted civilian for cowardice, desertion or 'resisting the war effort'. Some even shot at Germans surrendering to the oncoming Soviets, even though Hitler was already dead.

WAR CONTRIBUTION

At the beginning of the war, the *Waffen-SS* comprised just 28,000 men. At its peak, there were 600,000 men in 38 divisions. The *Leibstandarte*, particularly, fought in all theatres of Hitler's war of aggression, from the militarization of the Rhineland, the annexation of Austria, the Sudetenland, Czechoslovakia, Poland, the campaign in the West, the Balkans and the invasion on the Soviet Union. However, it never came to rival the Army.

Even in 1944, the strength of the *Waffen-SS* was less than a twentieth of that of the *Wehrmacht*. But it had nearly a quarter of the *panzer* divisions and a third of the mechanized *panzer-grenadier* divisions. Despite this it did not achieve independence of command and none of its officers were in the German High Command. Its funds came out of the police budget of the Ministry of the Interior, though pay and conditions paralleled those of the Army. When the German surrender was signed in Berlin on 9 May 1945 by representatives of the Army, Navy and Air Force, the *Waffen-SS* was not present, nor even mentioned.

Although the *Waffen-SS* spearheaded Hitler's military adventures, his victories would have been won without them. During the early years of the war, Hitler resisted Himmler's efforts to expand it. Where the *Waffen-SS* proved itself invaluable was in temporarily halting or even rolling back the Allied advance.

From the autumn of 1942 until the end of the war, the *Waffen-SS* doubled in size each year. This was done by relaxing many of its initial racial criteria. Recruits from Eastern Europe performed poorly. Those from the West discharged themselves better. On the whole, they were a formidable force because of their commitment. Eisenhower told his Chiefs of Staff that even in defeat SS 'morale, backed by a blind confidence in ultimate Nazi victory, was extremely good, and whether in attack or defense they fought to a man with fanatical courage'.

Of the million men who passed through its ranks, a third were killed or seriously wounded in battle. Thirty-six general officers were killed – nearly one for each division. This was because due to the *Waffen-SS*'s fearsome reputation, they were more often sent to the front line and given dangerous assignments – rather than an indication that they were committed Nazis. Most active Nazis from the party itself, the SA and the Hitler Youth served in the *Wehrmacht*. Many members were soldiers of fortune who did not even speak German, let alone understand the ideology of National Socialism. Few of the German recruits would have been old enough to have been involved in the *Freikorps* movement that spawned the Nazi Party after World War I.

Though there were a number of butchers such as Theodor Eicke, Erich von dem Bach-Zelewski and Oskar Dirlewanger who achieved their positions through a stroke of Himmler's pen, the backbone of the *Waffen-SS* was commanded by Army veterans such as Paul Hausser, Felix Steiner and Georg Keppler. Below them were young officers who had graduated from *Junkerschulen*, steeped in blind obedience to the *Führer*. They were tough and loyal, and put no value on human life – including their own. They led from the front, putting their own lives on the line, and were respected by their men, if not loved.

On top of everything, they could barely envisage defeat. Towards the end of the war, they staged last-ditch stands and shot anyone who did not show a similar commitment out of hand. Many were in their thirties. Kurt Meyer was only 33 and commanding a division when he ordered his men to murder prisoners of war.

While the killing of his victims was not motivated by racial ideology, the *Waffen-SS* did not shirk when called upon to murder Jews or Slavs, who they considered to be inferior. They were supermen, while the rest were subhuman. One can only imagine what they thought of the civilians they killed in Boves or Oradour. While apologists from HIAG claimed that they were 'soldiers like any others', they consistently violated the rules of war.

PERSECUTION OF THE JEWS

Clearly the *Waffen-SS* was anti-Semitic. But then so were many in Europe at the time. In the countries Germany occupied, they found many collaborators willing and eager to assist in the persecution of Jews. Many of the atrocities were carried out by foreigners working for the Germans.

The persecution of the Jews in Germany was underway long before the beginning of World War II. Although Jews were well integrated into German society, with many serving in the German Army during World War I, they became scapegoats for Germany's defeat in 1918.

Many of the Communist agitators against the continuation of the war were Jewish. This was the source of the Nazi theory that Germany had been defeated by a Jewish-Bolshevik conspiracy. This was ironic as the Bolshevik revolution in Russia in 1917 had resulted in an armistice on the Eastern Front, allowing the German High Command to move troops to the Western Front. Germany's Spring Offensive of 1918 gave the nation its deepest advances into Allied territory since 1914. However, the prospect of victory was snatched from Germany when strikes in armaments factories left troops temporarily short of materiel.

War weary German troops faced fresh American soldiers who were arriving in increasing numbers. They were also subjected to the Allied deployment of tanks. Meanwhile, the Royal Navy's blockade of Germany brought about hunger and unrest at home. Republican politicians forced the resignation of the Kaiser and sued for peace. This led to the myth that the German Army had not been defeated on the battlefield. Rather, it had been stabbed in the back by the 'November criminals'. The capitulation of the Central Powers was blamed upon the unpatriotic populace, Socialists, Bolsheviks, the Weimar Republic, and especially the Jews. Jewish bankers and businessmen were also thought to have profiteered during the war.

Young Germans growing up after World War I became used to the idea that Jews were responsible for their nation's woes. This was reinforced with anti-Semitic propaganda when Hitler came to power. The Nazis implemented laws that stripped Jews of their citizenship and civil rights, and excluded them from the legal profession and the civil service. Their businesses were boycotted and those who had intermarried were put in concentration camps. The effect was to exclude Jews from society. Hitler also maintained the Slavs were subhuman. Their land was to be taken to give the German people *lebensraum* or 'living space', where Slavs could be employed as slaves.

The *Waffen-SS* was steeped in this philosophy. The mass murders began with the Jews and intellectuals in Poland. Warned by the Commander-in-Chief in Occupied Poland General Johannes Blaskowitz that this would result in 'tremendous brutalization and moral depravity', Himmler responded by evoking the Prussian military virtue of 'hardness'.

'An execution must always be the hardest thing for our men,' he said. 'And despite it, they must never become weak, but must do it with pursed lips. In the beginning it was necessary. The shock which the Poles had to have, they have had.'

In the autumn of 1940, he addressed the officers of the *Leibstandarte* about events in Poland, saying: 'In a temperature of forty degrees below zero, we had to drag away thousands, tens of thousands, hundreds of thousands... to shoot thousands of leaving Poles, where we had to have hardness, otherwise it would rebound on us later.'

He was unequivocal about the reason for this: 'We must be clear about one thing. We are firmly convinced of it. I believe it exactly as I believe in God. I believe that our blood, Nordic blood, is actually the best blood on this earth.... In hundreds of thousands of years this Nordic blood will always be the best. Over all others, we are superior.'

And enemies were everywhere: 'We, a *Volk* of seventy-five million are, despite our great numbers, a minority in the world. We have very, very many against us, as you yourselves as National Socialists know very well. All capital, the whole of Jewry, the whole of freemasonry, all the democrats and philistines of the world, all the Bolshevism of the world, all the Jesuits of the world, and not least all the peoples who regret not having completely killed us off in 1918, and who make only one vow: if we once get Germany in our hands again it won't be another 1918, it will be the end.'

When the Germans entered the Soviet Union, the *Einsatzgruppen* activities began almost immediately. Execution centres were set up in Minsk and Lvov where Jews and anyone else on Heydrich's death list had to report. They were march out to nearby woods where they were forced to hand over their valuables and undress. Then they were marched in single file to a long grave and shot. Indoctrinated to hate Jews and other 'lower races', the SS men felt no remorse. An SS NCO involved in the killings said: 'What can they be thinking? I believe each still has the hope of not being shot. I don't feel the slightest pity. That is how it is and how it has got to be.'

An Army witness to the shootings in Dubno in October 1942 said: 'We heard shots from the vicinity of the pit. Those Jews who were still alive had been ordered to throw the corpses into the pit, then they themselves had to lie down in the pit to be shot in the neck.'

Not all the victims were shot. An *Einsatzgruppen* report made shortly after the invasion of Russia said: 'Only the children were not shot. They were caught by the legs, their heads hit against stones, and they were thereupon buried alive.'

CHAPTER TWELVE

⚡⚡

The Worst of the Worst

One of the worst mass killings of the war took place in a ravine called Babi Yar outside Kiev, the capital of Ukraine, where the Nazis butchered possibly more than 30,000 Jews. When the Germans marched into Kiev on 19 September 1941, many Ukrainians had rejoiced, seeing it as the end of Soviet/Russian rule. Since the Soviets had taken over in 1919, Ukraine had been decimated by collectivization, purges and famine. Even the Jews welcomed the Germans. The Soviet newspapers carried no word of the Nazi atrocities in Poland and France. Right up to Hitler's sudden attack in June 1941, the Soviet press had heaped praise on Stalin's ally Hitler. Nothing was said of the treatment of Jews in Germany and Poland. Some Jews even praised Hitler for being an able statesman. The older people recalled that, when the Germans had been in Ukraine in World War I, they had behaved very well – much better than the Russians. They had not been anti-Semitic then. The Germans were civilized Europeans with a respect for order. Most of all they were renowned for their consistency. Soon the Ukrainian Jews would discover they were tragically wrong.

When the Germans entered the city, they headed straight for the Kreshchatik. This was the main street in Kiev where the party officials and secret policemen lived and worked. Naturally, they had already departed. The Germans set up their headquarters there. They took over the Continental Hotel and converted the Doctors' Club into a club for German officers. Germans filled the boulevard cafés. Two enterprising Jewish barbers set up shop and did a roaring trade, cutting German officers' hair.

The first ominous note was sounded when the Germans took over the radio station. All Jews working there were ordered out. On 24 September, the new boss of the radio station was just telling his staff that he wanted the world to hear 'the voice of free Kiev' when there was a massive explosion. The German headquarters had been blown up. Explosions continued for the next five days, setting the whole of the centre of Kiev on fire. Nobody knows how many Germans were killed. Neither the Nazis nor the Soviets would say. Long after the war, the Soviets denied blowing up the Kreshchatik, blaming it on the Germans. It is clear now that the Soviet authorities mined the whole area before leaving. A few soldiers had been left behind to detonate the bombs, but word spread that the Jews were to blame.

Two days later, the military commander of Kiev Major General Kurt Eberhard, who was also a *Brigadeführer* in the *Waffen-SS*, met with *SS-Obergruppenführer* Friedrich Jeckeln, the SS and Police Leader, to plan the extermination of the Jews of Kiev, ostensibly in retaliation for the explosion. Also present were *SS-Standartenführer* Paul Blobel, commander of *Sonderkommando 4a*, and his superior, *SS-Brigadeführer* Dr Otto Rasch, commander of *Einsatzgruppe C*.

The killings were to be carried out by *Sonderkommando 4a*, commanded by Blobel, under the general command of Jeckeln. This unit consisted of *Sicherheitsdienst* (SD) and *Sicherheitspolizei* (SiPo), the third company of the Special Duties *Waffen-SS* battalion, and a platoon of *9. Polizei-Bataillon*. *Polizei-Bataillon 45*, commanded by

Major Besser, conducted the massacre, supported by members of a *Waffen-SS* battalion.

On the morning of 28 September, a notice went up. It said in Russian, Ukrainian and German:

'All Yids living in the city of Kiev and its vicinity are to report by eight o'clock on the morning of Monday, 29 September 1941, at the corner of Melnikovsky and Dokhturov Streets (near the cemetery). Bring documents, money and valuables, and also warm clothing, linen, etc. Any Yid not carrying out this instruction and who is found elsewhere will be shot. Any civilian entering flats evacuated by Yids and stealing property will be shot.'

Ukrainians assumed that the Jews were being deported to Palestine, possibly as a reprisal for the Kreshchatik bombings. Most Jews thought so too and they did what they were told. The following morning the streets near the cemetery were full of women and children, the sick and the elderly. Able-bodied young men had already been conscripted into the Red Army. They were poor people too. Anyone with enough money to leave Kiev was long gone. Some had even managed to bribe their way out of the city after it had been occupied.

Nevertheless, many more Jews turned out than were expected. The commander of the *Einsatzkommando* reported two days later: 'The difficulties resulting from such a large-scale action – in particular concerning the seizure – were overcome in Kiev by requesting the Jewish population through wall posters to move. Although only a participation of approximately 5,000 to 6,000 Jews had been expected at first, more than 30,000 Jews arrived who, until the very moment of their execution, still believed in their resettlement, thanks to an extremely clever organization.'

Some Ukrainians had no great love for the Jews and hurled insults at them. Others called for them to be confined in a ghetto. Some Jews already feared that they were going to their deaths. One woman had poisoned herself and her children. A young girl had thrown herself from an upper storey window. Her body lay in the street covered with a sheet. Nobody bothered to remove it.

As the crowd moved off, the word was that they were heading for the railway station. People carried suitcases. Some seemed to have the entire contents of their houses strapped to their backs. Others had clubbed together to hire a truck to carry their possessions.

The Russians and Ukrainians were not universally hostile to the Jews. Some had come to see old friends off. Others helped them with their bags. German soldiers looked on, keeping an eye out for pretty Jewish girls.

The dense crowd edged along until it got to the Jewish cemetery. The entrance was guarded by German soldiers and Ukrainian policemen who told the crowd that anyone who entered would not be allowed back – with the exception of cabbies who could drop their fare and go back for another one. Jews were separated from non-Jews, husbands from wives.

Still most people assumed that they were being taken to a train. There was a war on and they were being evacuated somewhere safer. The Jews were going first, they reasoned, because they were more closely related ethnically to the Germans than the Russians or Ukrainians.

Once inside the cemetery everyone was told to drop what they were carrying – foodstuffs on the right, baggage on the left. They would have to sort things out when they got to their destination. By now they could hear the occasional burst of machine-gun fire nearby. But people could not admit to themselves that they were going to be shot. For one thing, there was such an enormous mass of people. Such things did not happen, they told themselves.

By the time they realized what was happening, it was too late. They found themselves walking through a narrow corridor lined by soldiers and dogs. The soldiers stood shoulder to shoulder. They had their sleeves rolled up and they were armed with clubs and sticks. As the crowd passed through, the soldiers beat them savagely, aiming for the ribs, the stomach and the groin, drawing blood. Those who fell to the ground were set upon by the dogs and trampled by those coming from behind.

Young women were propositioned by German soldiers who said that they could save them in return for sex. Ukrainian policemen then ordered everyone to strip. Those who hesitated had their clothes ripped off. They were still being kicked and hit with knuckle dusters and clubs by Germans who seemed to be in a sadistic frenzy. This was being done to keep the huge mass of people disorientated. Some people laughed hysterically. Some went grey in minutes.

Bleeding naked people formed up in lines at a gap that had been dug in the steep wall of sand there. Some Ukrainians who had got mixed up with the Jews stood to one side, but an officer ordered that they be shot anyway. If word got out what was happening, he was afraid no Jews would turn up the next day.

The lines of naked people were marched into the ravine and were lined up on a narrow ledge in the quarry. It had been cut especially for the executions and was so narrow that victims automatically leant back against the sandstone. Below them was a sea of bodies covered in blood. On the other side, the machine-gun crews had built a fire where they brewed coffee. When the ledge was full, they left the fire and returned to their guns. Then they loosed off a burst along the line. As each person was hit they fell into the sea of bodies below. According to an *Einsatzgruppen* report 33,771 people were killed that day.

One woman escaped to tell the tale. Her name was Dina Mironovna Pronichev. She was an actress and the mother of two. Her husband was Russian. She did not look Jewish, spoke Ukrainian and could have passed as one. When she read the notice, she decided not to go. However, she said she would see her parents to the train, then return home to look after the children. When she realized what was happening, her parents told her she should save herself. She approached one of the Ukrainian policemen and showed him her union card which did not mention her ethnic group. He set her to one side with the Ukrainians who had got mixed in with the Jews.

'We'll shoot the Jews first, then let you out,' he said.

But when a German officer turned up, he ordered that she should be shot anyway. They were the last batch that day.

When she stood on the ledge, she felt the bullets coming towards her. Before they reached her, she jumped. It was a long drop, but she landed softly on the bodies below and was splattered with blood. Beneath her, she could feel people moving. The Germans climbed down and walked over the corpses, shooting anyone who was still alive. One SS man caught his foot on Dina. He shone a torch in her face, then picked her up and punched her. But she hung limp and lifeless. He kicked her in the chest and trod on her hand so the bones cracked. Then he walked away.

Earth was then piled on top of the bodies. Sand went in her mouth. Dina realized that she would rather be shot than buried alive. She held her breath to stop herself coughing and wriggled free. It had been a long day for the Ukrainian policemen and they only covered the corpses with a light sprinkling of sand. In the dark, she crawled to the edge of the pit.

She dug hand-holds in the sandy sides and hauled herself out. She nearly jumped back in when she heard a whisper. It was a young boy who had somehow escaped too. Together, they crawled off into the night.

They made little progress. When it grew light they hid in some bushes on the edge of another ravine. From there, they watched the Germans sorting out people's belongings. An old woman and her six-year-old grandson came by. The Germans shot them. Six or seven Germans led two young women out on to a ledge on the other side of the ravine and gang-raped them. When they had finished, they bayoneted them, leaving their bodies naked with their legs spread. All the time, in the background, was the sound of shooting.

Dina fell into a trance and saw her mother, father and sister in long white robes. She was awoken by the boy who said plaintively: 'Don't die, lady, don't leave me.'

When it grew dark again, they crawled on. Towards dawn, the boy crawled ahead as a lookout. She heard him shout: 'Don't move, lady, there are Germans here.'

Then she heard him being shot. Luckily, the Germans had not understood what he had said and they did not come looking for her. She was so distraught that she temporarily lost her mind, digging a small hole, then filling it up with sand as if she was burying the boy who had saved her.

The next day she took refuge in a rubbish tip, covering herself with rags and boxes. Occasionally, she heard Germans coming by. Across the road, she saw tomatoes growing in a garden. When it was dark, she crawled over and ate them. She crawled on. Around dawn she saw a barn behind a cottage and crawled into it. But a dog started barking. A woman came out of the cottage and sent her son to fetch the Germans. They took Dina to a guardhouse where soldiers were drinking coffee. She tried to sit on a chair, but they shouted at her and made her sit on the floor.

When the soldiers went, they left one behind on duty. He was sympathetic and let Dina sit on the chair. Later he gave her a rag and indicated that she should clean the window. He told her to look out of the window and pick out the way she had to run. But before she could escape, an officer turned up with two 15-year-old girls. They were sobbing, kissing his boots and telling him he could do anything he liked with them – including have sex with them – if he did not shoot them. The officer took them and Dina back to the place where the victims had been stripped. Around 40 old men and women were sitting among the clothes. One was lying paralyzed. They were guarded by a single sentry.

'Don't look at me,' he shouted at Dina. 'I can't do anything for you. I have children too.'

A girl in a soldier's tunic and greatcoat came up. She put the coat around Dina, who was shivering in the cold. She was a 19-year-old Russian nurse who had been left behind in the Soviet retreat.

A lorry arrived and they got on. It took them to a garage which was being used as a temporary prison. When they arrived, an old woman got off and squatted down to relieve herself. A German soldier shot her in the head. The garage was already filled with people rounded up on the streets, waiting to be shot. The lorry pulled off again. It seemed to be heading for the Brest-Litovsk highway. It was going full tilt when Dina threw herself off. Either the guards did not see her, or did not care. The lorry did not stop. A group of people gathered around her. She explained that she had meant to go to the market, but had missed her stop and jumped off. They did not believe her, but took her into a nearby farmhouse anyway. Half an hour later she found refuge with her brother's wife, who was Polish.

Over the next two years, the slaughter continued. Between 100,000 and 200,000 Jews, Communist officials and Russian prisoners of war were killed at Babi Yar. When the Germans retreated in August 1943, they had bodies exhumed by slave labour and burnt in huge pyres in an attempt to conceal what they had done. But Dina survived the war and testified to a war-crimes trial about what had happened at Babi Yar on 29 September 1941.

Eberhard was captured by the Americans in November 1945. He committed suicide in captivity on 8 September 1947. Jeckeln had earlier murdered another 23,600 Jews at Kamianets-Podilskyi in Ukraine in August 1941, wiping out the entire Jewish community along with 16,000 deportees from Hungary.

He went on to commit other massacres and developed what became known as the 'Jeckeln system' or *sadinenpackung* – sardine packing – where victims were forced to line up along a trench or on top of the bodies of those who had already been shot. The executioner would then walk along the edge of the excavation and shoot victims in the back of the head, using a Russian machine gun set on single shot. Those who did not die were buried alive.

Jeckeln was responsible for the Rumbula massacre where 25,000 Jews were murdered in the forest outside Riga. Three people survived. One of them was Frida Michelson, who remembered: 'Young women, women with infants in their arms, old women, the handicapped helped by their neighbours, young boys and girls – all marching, marching. Suddenly, in front of our window, a German SS man started firing with an automatic gun point blank into the crowd. People were mowed down by the shots, and fell on the cobblestones. There was confusion in the column. People were trampling over those who had fallen, they were pushing forward, away from the wildly shooting SS man. Some were throwing away their packs so they could run faster.... I stood by the window and watched until about midday when the horror of the march ended.... Now the street was quiet, nothing moved. Corpses were scattered all over, rivulets of blood still oozing from the lifeless bodies. They were mostly old people, pregnant women, children, handicapped – all those who could not keep up with the inhuman tempo of the march.'

She survived by pretending to be dead and hiding under a heap of the victims' shoes.

'A mountain of footwear was pressing down on me. My body was numb from cold and immobility,' she said. 'However, I was fully conscious now. The snow under me had melted from the heat of my body.... Quiet for a while. Then from the direction of the trench a child's cry: "Mama! Mama! Mama!". A few shots. Quiet. Killed.'

Jeckeln commended the troops that committed this slaughter. He was captured by the Red Army on 28 April 1945. At his trial in Riga the following year he admitted his guilt, and even admitted to taking part in the killing himself to encourage the others. He was sentenced to death and hanged in front of an audience of 40,000.

Blobel went on to use gas vans to kill Jews at Poltava in Ukraine. In June 1942 he was put in charge of destroying the evidence of Nazi atrocities in Eastern Europe. This entailed digging up the mass graves and burning the bodies. Blobel was sentenced to death at Nuremberg and hanged on 7 June 1951. Rasch also appeared at Nuremberg, but the case against him was ended in February 1948 when he showed symptoms of Parkinson's disease. He died the following year.

THE ANGEL OF DEATH

There were other war criminals in the *Waffen-SS*. One such was Dr Josef Mengele, whose experiments on prisoners at Auschwitz led him to be called the Angel of Death. Born in 1911, he earned a PhD in anthropology before going to work at the Institute for Hereditary Biology and Racial Hygiene in Frankfurt, where he worked for Dr Otmar Freiherr von Verschuer, a German geneticist with a particular interest in researching twins.

Mengele joined the Nazi Party in 1937 and the SS in 1938. Called up for service in the *Wehrmacht* in 1940, he volunteered for medical service in the *Waffen-SS* with the rank of *SS-Untersturmführer*. Posted to Ukraine in June 1941, he joined *5. SS-Division 'Wiking'* in January 1942, earning the Iron Cross First Class for rescuing two German soldiers from a burning tank.

Wounded the following year, he was declared unfit for active service. He was promoted to the rank of *SS-Hauptsturmführer* in 1943 and applied for a transfer to the concentration camp service. He was posted to Auschwitz where he became chief physician of the *Zigeunerfamilienlager* (Romani family camp) at Birkenau. His duties there included making weekly visits to the hospital barracks where anyone who had not recovered within two weeks was sent to the gas chambers.

He also carried out selections where arrivals were divided into those fit enough to work from the elderly, infirm, pregnant women, women with small children and children themselves who were sent immediately to the gas chambers. He supervised the administration of Zyklon B himself, while also keeping an eye out for twins he could experiment on.

An outbreak of noma – a gangrenous bacterial disease of the mouth and face – struck the Romani camp in 1943. Mengele initiated a study to determine the cause of the disease and develop a treatment. He enlisted the assistance of prisoner Berthold Epstein, a Jewish paediatrician and professor at Prague University. The patients were isolated in separate barracks. About 3,000 people died due to this research, which included deliberately infecting healthy individuals. Several afflicted children were killed so that their preserved heads and organs could be sent to the SS Medical Academy in Graz and other facilities for study. This research was still ongoing when the Romani camp was liquidated and its remaining occupants killed in 1944.

When an epidemic of typhus broke out in the women's camp, Mengele sent 600 women from one block to the gas chambers. The building was then disinfected. Inmates from another block were bathed, de-loused and given clean clothing before being moved in. Epidemics of scarlet fever and other diseases were treated the same way, with those infected being killed. For this, Mengele was awarded the War Merit Cross (Second Class with Swords) and was promoted in 1944 to First Physician of the Birkenau subcamp.

At Auschwitz, Mengele took the opportunity to continue his anthropological studies and research into heredity by using inmates for human experimentation. His medical procedures showed no consideration for the victims' health, safety, or physical and emotional suffering. He was particularly interested in identical twins, people with heterochromia iridum (eyes of two different colours), dwarfs, and people with physical abnormalities.

A grant was provided by the German Research Foundation at the request of von Verschuer, who received regular reports and shipments of specimens from Mengele. The grant was used to build a pathology laboratory attached to Crematorium II at Auschwitz II-Birkenau.

Dr Miklós Nyiszli, a Hungarian-Jewish pathologist who arrived in Auschwitz on 29 May 1944, performed dissections and prepared specimens for shipment in this laboratory. The twin research was in part intended to prove the supremacy of heredity over environment to strengthen the Nazi premise of the genetic superiority of the Aryan race. His experiments included the unnecessary amputation of limbs. He would infect one twin with a disease, then transfuse blood into the other. When one died he would kill the other to make a comparative post mortem. He sewed two Romani twins together, back to back, in a crude attempt to create conjoined twins. Both children died of gangrene after several days of suffering.

Nyiszli and others reported that the twin studies may also have been motivated by an intention to increase the reproduction rate of the German race by improving the chances of racially desirable people having twins. The fate of his victims meant nothing to Mengele as he was a fanatical anti-Semite.

He would try changing the colour of victim's eyes by injecting dye into the eyes of the living. People with heterochromatic eyes also had their eyes removed to be sent to Berlin for study. He would also conduct experiments on pregnant women. Operations would be carried out without anaesthetic.

Mengele's research subjects were better fed and housed than the other prisoners. When visiting his young subjects, he introduced himself as 'Uncle Mengele' and offered them sweets, though they could be sent to the gas chambers at any time. He also killed an unknown number of victims with lethal injections, shootings, beatings and his deadly experiments. His son Rolf said that his father showed no remorse for his wartime activities.

Mengele left Auschwitz ten days before the Soviets arrived, fleeing westwards in a *Wehrmacht* uniform. He was captured but escaped identification because he had been spared the SS blood group tattoo. Through the ratline network of former SS members, he managed to reach Genoa. Using a passport provided by the International Committee of the Red Cross, he reached Argentina. With Nazi hunters on his tail, he moved on to Paraguay and then Brazil, where he drowned after having a stroke while swimming in 1979, aged 67.

THE DOCTOR'S TRIAL

Other doctors in the *Waffen-SS* did not escape punishment and were brought to justice at that so-called Doctors' Trial, technically known as the *United States of America v Karl Brandt, et al*. This was not held before the International Military Tribunal, but before a US military court in the same rooms at the Palace of Justice in Nuremberg. The accused were charged with:

1 Conspiracy to commit war crimes and crimes against humanity as described in counts 2 and 3.

2 War crimes: performing medical experiments, without the subjects' consent, on prisoners of war and civilians of occupied countries, in the course of which experiments the defendants committed murders, brutalities, cruelties, tortures, atrocities, and other inhuman acts. Also planning and performing the mass murder of prisoners of war and civilians of occupied countries, stigmatized as aged, insane, incurably ill, deformed, and so on, by gas, lethal injections, and diverse other means in nursing homes, hospitals, and asylums during the Euthanasia Program and participating in the mass murder of concentration camp inmates.

3 Crimes against humanity: committing crimes described under count 2 also on German nationals.

4 Membership in a criminal organization, the SS.

Count 1 was dropped as the charge was considered beyond its jurisdiction.

One of those charged was Hitler's personal physician Karl Brandt. He was a *Gruppenführer* in the SS and *Generalleutnant* in the *Waffen-SS*. With Viktor Brack, a *Waffen-SS* officer and Chief Administrative Officer in the Chancellery of the *Führer* of the NSDAP, he had been chosen to head the *Aktion T4* euthanasia programme.

Brandt became a medical doctor and surgeon in 1928, specializing in head and spinal injuries. After joining the Nazi Party in 1932, he met Hitler. He became a member of the SA in 1933 and a member of the SS on 29 July 1934 with the rank of *Untersturmführer*. From the summer of 1934, he was Hitler's 'escort physician' and a close confidant.

Nazi Germany enacted the Law for the Prevention of Hereditarily Diseased Offspring. This legalized the compulsory sterilization of anyone suffering from a hereditary disease or anyone who was likely to produce children with a serious physical or mental defect. Conditions cited included congenital mental deficiency, schizophrenia, manic-depression, epilepsy, Huntington's disease, blindness, deafness, deformity and alcoholism. It aped the Model Eugenical Sterilization Law enacted in many American states in the 1920s. In Germany, over 400,000 people were sterilized against their will.

Amendments to the German law made in 1935 also enforced sterilization on the so-called 'Rhineland bastards', the mixed-race children of German civilians and French African soldiers who had occupied the Rhineland. Hitler also decriminalized the abortion of foetuses with racial or hereditary defects, though the abortion of pure German or Aryan children remained forbidden. Brandt carried out many of these abortions.

In September 1939, Brandt was appointed co-head of the *Aktion T4* euthanasia programme with *Reichsleiter* Philipp Bouhler. This involved the mass murder of between 275,000 to 300,000 people from psychiatric hospitals in Germany and Austria, occupied Poland and the Protectorate of Bohemia and Moravia, now the Czech Republic. Hitler and Brandt discussed methods of giving a 'merciful death' to those they considered 'useless eaters'. Gassing them with carbon monoxide was considered the most humane way.

The first victim was a child who Brandt said 'was born blind, an idiot – at least it seemed to be an idiot – and it lacked one leg and part of one arm'. It was claimed that its parents had petitioned Hitler, asking for the child to be 'put to sleep'.

Brandt was also charged with ordering experimentation on human beings. These included experiments involving freezing, seawater, malaria, typhus, epidemic jaundice, mustard gas, sulfanilamide, sterilization, bone, muscle and nerve regeneration and bone transplantation.

With his wife Anni, Brandt was part of Hitler's inner circle at Berchtesgaden, Hitler's Bavarian hideaway, and had a house near the Berghof. The *Führer* was furious when, in the last days of the war, Brandt sent his wife and son west towards the Americans' line, hoping to avoid capture by the Soviets. He was arrested by the Gestapo and condemned to death by a military court. Only the intervention of Himmler prevented the sentence being carried out. Admiral Karl Dönitz, Hitler's successor, ordered his release.

Brandt was captured by the British. He was found guilty and sentenced to death. On the gallows Brandt said: 'It is no shame to stand upon the scaffold. This is nothing but political revenge. I have served my Fatherland as others before me...' He was still talking when the hood was placed over his head and he was hanged.

Much of the organization of the killing in the *Aktion T4* programme was left to Brack, who oversaw the manning of the six killing centres. He and Adolf Eichmann began using gassing vans to murder Jews incapable of work. The first three were set up at the Chelmno extermination camp. However, with more men being committed to the Eastern Front there was a shortage of labour. So Brack wrote to Himmler saying:

Dear *Reichsführer*, among tens of millions of Jews in Europe, there are, I figure, at least two to three millions of men and women who are fit enough to work. Considering the extraordinary difficulties the labour problem presents us with, I hold the view that those two to three millions should be specially selected and preserved. This can, however, only be done if at the same time they are rendered incapable to propagate. About a year ago I reported to you that agents of mine have completed the experiments necessary for this purpose. I would like to recall these facts once more. Sterilization, as normally performed on persons with hereditary diseases is here out of the question, because it takes too long and is too expensive. Castration by X-ray however is not only relatively cheap, but can also be performed on many thousands in the shortest time. I think that at this time it is already irrelevant whether the people in question become aware of having been castrated after some weeks or months, once they feel the effects. Should you, *Reichsführer*, decide to choose this way in the interest of the preservation of labour, then *Reichsleiter* Bouhler would be prepared to place all physicians and other personnel needed for this work at your disposal. Likewise he requested me to inform you that then I would have to order the apparatus so urgently needed with the greatest speed.

Brack was transferred to the *Totenkopf* and the procedures were carried out at Auschwitz, where he aimed to sterilize 3–4,000 Jews a day without their knowledge. When this proved impractical, it was decided to exterminate the Jews by gassing them. The gas chambers Brack had used were dismantled and shipped eastwards to be installed at Majdanek, Auschwitz and Treblinka. On 20 May 1945, he was arrested by the American Counter Intelligence Corps while using a false name.

While denying that he had ever heard of the T4 programme he testified that euthanasia was a 'humane measure' for incurably sick people and denied all knowledge of the Holocaust. He also denied anti-Semitism or involvement with killing Jews and said that he had joined the *Waffen-SS* in 1942 to distance himself from the excesses of the regime. However, other defendants at the Doctors' Trial testified against him, while Brack himself gave evidence against Brandt. Evidence was given that sterilization using very high doses of X-rays during several minutes was conducted on other persecuted groups. They were also subjected to the excruciatingly painful procedure, and later castrated.

Brack was also implicated in the extermination of concentration camp inmates deemed unable to work. He was sentenced to death by hanging. On the gallows he said he 'wished for God to give peace to the world'. Bouhler and his wife committed suicide while in captivity.

Dr Fritz Fischer joined the SS in 1934 and the Nazi Party in 1937, graduating as a physician the following year. On 1 November 1939, he was assigned to the *Waffen-SS*'s Department of the Hohenlychen Sanatorium at Lychen, 80 km (50 miles) north of Berlin. In 1940, he became troop physician of the *Leibstandarte SS 'Adolf Hitler'*. After being wounded he was posted back to Hohenlychen and worked in the hospital of the Ravensbrück women's concentration camp nearby as a surgical assistant to Karl Gebhardt, carrying out experiments on inmates there. Their victims were known as 'The Rabbits'.

At the Doctors' Trial he testified in detail on the operations they had performed and showed remorse for having carried out experiments on healthy young women. In his testimony he described in detail how he removed a prisoner's arm, including the scapula, wrapped it in a clean sheet and drove with it back to Hohenlychen to surgically attach it to German man. He was convicted of war crimes and crimes against humanity and sentenced to life imprisonment. This was reduced to 15 years, but he served only nine. He died in 2003, aged over 90.

Gebhardt was Himmler's personal physician, a *Gruppenführer* in the SS and *SS-Obergruppenführer* in the *Waffen-SS*, Consulting Surgeon of the *Waffen-SS* and President of the German Red Cross. He had joined the Nazi Party in 1933. Two years later he joined the SS and was appointed Medical Superintendent of the Hohenlychen Sanatorium, becoming Himmler's personal physician in 1938.

Under his direction the Hohenlychen Sanatorium became a military hospital for the *Waffen-SS*. After the assassination attempt on Reinhard Heydrich he was sent to Prague to attend him, but he refused to administer the early antibiotic sulfonamide and Heydrich died of sepsis eight days after he had been attacked.

During the war, Gebhardt conducted medical and surgical experiments on prisoners in the concentration camps at Ravensbrück and Auschwitz. He tried to vindicate his decision not to administer sulfonamide on Heydrich by wounding and infecting women, and then splitting them into two groups. One group would be given the antibiotic, but received no nursing care; the other group, who were not administered with sulfonamide, were given proper nursing care, thus increasing their chances of survival against the sulfonamide group. In this way he was able to skew the results against the antibiotic, and so justify his decision not to use it on Heydrich.

A witness said: 'The ten Polish women were brought in, and behind closed doors they were examined.... The first day they operated on two. Two days later on three others. The screams never ceased from the chamber of torture. The Revier [hospital] was full of them. The girls were not given any pain killers, so that the course of the experiment would not be impaired in any way. Dogs that had undergone the same experiment received strong doses of morphine for five days. After a few days the first Pole, a girl of seventeen, died. Her leg was huge, swollen, monstrous, blue with red wounds, and the stench emanating from them was nauseating. The Poles from the Revier told us that Gebhardt cut the leg off and took it with him.'

Gangrene, tetanus and staphylococci bacteria were implanted or injected into artificially cut wounds of healthy extremities. This happened in the case of the first five women, who were desperately and hysterically screaming and who all died, one of tetanus, two of gangrene, one of blood poisoning, and one bled to death.

'The other operations were called by the "scientists" bone, muscle and nerve surgery. In such cases, for instance, parts as large as 2 inches were removed from the shin bone and replaced with metal supports or not replaced at all; in this case the doctors were waiting [to see] "how the organism will help itself",' a witness said. 'Muscles and nerves were removed and replaced by others taken from another healthy woman. The bone transplants were supposed to prove that without the periosteum bones could not grow; muscle and nerve operations served research on regeneration of tissue. Such operations took two or three hours. They repeatedly removed from some women's hips and calves larger and larger parts of muscles; naturally, this resulted in ever increasing weakening and deformation of the extremities. In order to carry out better and more detailed "research", they removed some women's entire hips, shoulder joints or the whole upper extremity along with the shoulder blade. Then the professor, or his assistants, also physicians from Hohenlychen, like Grawitz, Kogel and Schultz, wrapped these in sheets and carried them to their car. Naturally, the women thus operated on were immediately after the surgery killed by an injection.'

These experiments were repeated on the same 'Rabbit' twice, three times, even six times by both methods. If a wound caused by gangrene or some other suppurating infection healed, it was opened again and re-infected, or the limb opened at another, still healthy spot. New sections of bones were cut out, or other parts of nerves from the calf removed. As a result of the putrefaction and excised muscle tissues, the poor women's legs became several centimetres shorter and weaker. Healthy people were transformed into cripples, beautiful legs twisted limbs of skin and bone. It was all the more hideous because the majority of victims were young girls.

Gebhardt was convicted of war crimes and crimes against humanity, and hanged. Another of Gebhardt's assistants at Ravensbrück was Herta Oberheuser, the only female defendant at the Doctors' Trial. She was convicted of crimes against humanity and sentenced to 20 years, serving only seven.

Another *Gruppenführer* in the SS and *SS-Obergruppenführer* in the *Waffen-SS* was Karl Genzken. As Chief of the Medical Office of the *Waffen-SS*, he carried out typhus experiments at the concentration camps at Buchenwald and Natzweiler. He was found guilty of war crimes, crimes against humanity and membership in an illegal organization, and sentenced to life. This was reduced to 20 years. He served just nine and died three years after being released.

Waldemar Hoven was an *SS-Hauptsturmführer* in the *Waffen-SS* and Chief Doctor of the Buchenwald concentration camp. He was involved in the Nazi euthanasia programme. He also administered medical experiments regarding typhus and the tolerance of serum containing phenol, and which led to the deaths of many inmates.

In 1943, he was arrested, accused of giving a lethal injection of phenol to an SS officer who was a potential witness in an investigation against Ilse Koch, 'The Beast of Buchenwald' and wife of the commandant, *SS-Standartenführer* Otto Koch, who Hoven was rumoured to be having an affair with. He was convicted and sentenced to death, although he was released in March 1945 due to the shortage of doctors.

Otto Koch was convicted of murder and embezzlement by an SS court and shot by a firing squad a week before American troops arrived to liberate the camp. His wife was acquitted for lack of evidence. But she was arrested by the Americans and charged with 'participating in a criminal plan for aiding, abetting and participating in the murders at Buchenwald' where she was said to have had lampshades made out of tattooed skin. Seeking to avoid the death penalty she announced that she was eight months pregnant. She was sentenced to life imprisonment for 'violation of the laws and customs of war'. This was reduced to four years. In a German court, she was later convicted of incitement to murder and sentenced to life again. She committed suicide, hanging herself in jail in 1960, convinced that concentration camp survivors would abuse her in jail.

Hoven was arrested by the Allies and put on trial. He was found guilty of war crimes, crimes against humanity and membership in a criminal organization. Sentenced to death, he was hanged on 2 June 1948.

Joachim Mrugowsky was an *SS-Oberführer* in the *Waffen-SS*, Chief Hygienist of the Reich Physician SS and Police, and Chief of the Hygienic Institute of the *Waffen-SS*. In 1930, he joined the Nazi Party, joining the SS and the *Waffen-SS* the following year. In 1938, he was made a Colonel and promoted to the staff of the medical department of the SS Special Service Troops as well as the Medical Office of the *Waffen-SS*. In 1940, Mrugowsky took part in the conquest of Western Europe as the troop physician of a *Das Reich* hospital company.

He coordinated human experimentation at the Sachsenhausen concentration camp near Berlin. This involved testing typhus vaccines and biological warfare agents, including the use of poisoned bullets and lethal injections. He was convicted of crimes against humanity and sentenced to death.

The other defendants at the Doctors' Trial included members of the German Army, the *Luftwaffe* and the SS. Of the 23 defendants, seven were acquitted and seven received death sentences. The rest served relatively short periods in jail.

Epilogue

One of the anomalies about the Nuremberg Trials was that the Nazi prisoners were guarded by former *Waffen-SS* men. While the International Military Tribunal declared the SS, including the *Waffen-SS*, a criminal organization and barred all members from holding public office, or any government or local positions concerning law enforcement or state security, it specifically excluded 'those who were drafted into membership by the State in such a way as to give them no choice in the matter, and who had committed no such crimes'. This applied to the Latvian and Estonian *Waffen-SS* conscripts that had ended up in Western hands at the end of the war.

The ruling was strongly opposed by the Soviet Union, which saw these men as traitors. Largely nationalists who sought to free the Baltic States from Russian occupation, they had fought tenaciously on the Eastern Front. If they were returned to their homelands, now under the occupation of the Soviets again, they would have been executed or disappeared into the Gulags.

However, the Soviet view was overruled by the Western Allies. Captured Latvian and Estonian *Waffen-SS* conscripts were given identity papers and they were released from PoW holding camps in Germany and around Europe. While they were unable to return home, no other nation was prepared to take them. The question was: what to do with them?

With the end of the war in Europe and, a few months later, in the Far East, the Allied armies were keen to send their people home. However, personnel were needed for security not only at Nuremberg, but also at other installations in the zones of Germany under the occupation of Western forces.

It was decided that Latvian and Estonian former *Waffen-SS* soldiers would be formed into companies and placed in guard and security positions at the War Crimes Tribunal at Nuremberg. The first company was called *Viesturs*, after a medieval Livonian duke. These guards were particularly useful as, having been in the *Waffen-SS*, most spoke German and could communicate with the prisoners awaiting trials for war crimes.

During the trial of the Nazi leaders in 1946 the soldiers with white helmets were Americans. The following year, four companies of Baltic troops, around 1,000 men, took over the guard duties at the Nuremberg Palace of Justice and the associated prison. Their sleeves and later at their helmets were emblazoned with the red-white-red national colours of Latvia. They also took on garrison duties in several German cities.

In Nuremberg, they guarded not only at the perimeter of the Palace of Justice but also at the doors to the cells. Baltic guards were escorting inmates to the walking areas and to the interrogations. However, Americans still escorted inmates to the exercise yard and to their execution.

When the Soviets blockaded West Berlin in 1948 in an attempt to force the Western Allies out, the Baltic troops were transferred to the forests near the border to secure the most important field storage dumps of the US Army. After that, Latvian guards were transferred to Stuttgart to guard US Army Corps headquarters.

With the end of the Berlin Airlift, they were no longer needed, but they still could not return home. In 1950, the Allied High Commission said that the Baltic Legions 'were not to be seen as "movements", "volunteer", or "SS". In short, they had not been given the training, indoctrination, and induction normally given to SS members'. The US Displaced Persons Commission declared in September 1950 that: 'The Baltic *Waffen-SS* Units (Baltic Legions) are to be considered as separate and distinct in purpose, ideology, activities, and qualifications for membership from the German SS, and therefore the Commission holds them not to be a movement hostile to the government of the United States.'

The US then opened its doors to any who wanted to emigrate there. Some chose instead to relocate to other English-speaking countries such as Britain, Canada and Australia, while others decided to stay in Germany. But that was not the end of the matter.

KLOOGA CONCENTRATION CAMP

In 2001, after the fall of the Soviet Union, historian Ruth Bettina Birn was studying the records of the Estonian Security Police and SD held in the Estonian State Archives. She said that these two bodies were responsible for the murder of 2,000 prisoners in German camps in Estonia, including the notorious Klooga concentration camp, whose commandant *SS-Hauptsturmführer* Hans Aumeier, a veteran from Auschwitz, Dachau and Buchenwald, had been sentenced to death at Kraków in Poland for crimes against humanity in December 1947 and hanged the following month. Eleven members of 3. *Kompanie, Polizei-Bataillon 287* were convicted for the killings and they were sentenced to 25 years' imprisonment.

Inmates had been taken into a nearby forest where, according to Soviet sources, some 2,000 were shot. Their bodies were stacked onto wooden pyres and burned. By the time the Red Army arrived only 85 of the 2,400 inmates had survived, by hiding in the camp or escaping to the forest. Soviet soldiers found numerous pyres of stacked corpses left unburned by the camp's guards when they fled. *Polizei-Bataillon 287* was subsequently transferred to 20. *Waffen-Grenadier-Division der SS (estnische Nr 1)*.

The massacre had been ordered by *SS-Obergruppenführer* Walter Krüger, a holder of the Knight's Cross with Oak Leaves and Swords and former commander of the *Das Reich* SS division, then commander-in-chief of the *Waffen-SS* in Ostland. He committed suicide in the Courland Pocket in May 1945.

CONTROVERSY

In 2002, the Estonian government forced the removal of a monument to native soldiers erected in the Estonian city of Pärnu. Its inscription read: 'To Estonian men who fought in 1940–1945 against Bolshevism and for the restoration of Estonian independence.' In light of the atrocity at Klooga, the monument became a focus for controversy. The monument was rededicated in Lihula in 2004, but was soon removed because the Estonian government opposed its reopening. On 15 October 2005 the monument was finally moved to the grounds of the Museum of Fight for Estonia's Freedom in Lagedi near the Estonian capital, Tallinn.

On 28 July 2007, a gathering of some 300 veterans of 20. *Waffen-Grenadier-Division* and of other units of the *Wehrmacht*, including a few *Waffen-SS* veterans from Austria and Norway, took place in Sinimäe, in Estonia, where the battle between the German and Soviet armies had been particularly fierce. After that, a gathering took place there every year with veterans attending from Estonia, Norway, Denmark, Austria and Germany.

Similar controversy surrounded Latvian veterans. Despite allegations of atrocities, they sought to have a remembrance day on 16 March, commemorating a battle on the Velikaya River fought by both 15. *Waffen-Grenadier-Division der SS (lettische Nr 1)* and 19. *Waffen-Grenadier-Division der SS (lettische Nr 2)*. This became a bone of contention between Latvian nationalists and pro-Russian organizations.

In 2012, the Council of Europe's Commission against Racism and Intolerance recommended that 'the Latvian authorities condemn all attempts to commemorate persons who fought in the *Waffen-SS* and collaborated with the Nazis. ECRI further recommends that the authorities ban any gathering or march legitimizing in any way Nazism.'

In Germany, HIAG found that it could not achieve the legal rehabilitation of the *Waffen-SS* as public awareness of its atrocities grew in the 1970s and 1980s. It became a focus for right-wing extremists, neo-Nazis and Holocaust deniers. The press reported on the singing of forbidden Nazi songs and clashes between anti-Nazi demonstrators and *Waffen-SS* re-enactors (SS re-enacting was illegal in Germany). With public opinion turning against it, HIAG disbanded at federal level in 1992. Regional chapters struggled on into the twenty-first century alongside *Der Freiwillige*. However, as *Waffen-SS* veterans died out there was little reason to continue its publication, leaving only a lasting legacy of unspeakable brutality, slavish adherence to a repulsive ideology and unswerving loyalty to one of history's most terrible dictators.

Index

INDEX